EVENT TOURISM
AND
CROSS CULTURAL COMMUNICATION

EVENT TOURISM AND CROSS CULTURAL COMMUNICATION

By

Dr. ANNAMALAI MURUGAN

Assistant Professor,
Department of Tourism and Travel Management,
Tagore Arts College,
Puducherry

UNIVERSITY SCIENCE PRESS

(An Imprint of Laxmi Publications Pvt. Ltd.)

An ISO 9001:2008 Company

BENGALURU • CHENNAI • COCHIN • GUWAHATI • HYDERABAD
JALANDHAR • KOLKATA • LUCKNOW • MUMBAI • RANCHI • NEW DELHI
BOSTON (USA) • ACCRA (GHANA) • NAIROBI (KENYA)

EVENT TOURISM AND CROSS CULTURAL COMMUNICATION

Printed and bound in India
Typeset at Kalyani Computer Services, Delhi
First Edition: 2015
ISBN 978-93-5138-278-2

Branches

✆	Bengaluru	080-26 75 69 30	
✆	Chennai	044-24 34 47 26,	24 35 95 07
✆	Cochin	0484-237 70 04,	405 13 03
✆	Guwahati	0361-254 36 69,	251 38 81
✆	Hyderabad	040-27 55 53 83,	27 55 53 93
✆	Jalandhar	0181-222 12 72	
✆	Kolkata	033-22 27 43 84	
✆	Lucknow	0522-220 99 16	
✆	Mumbai	022-24 91 54 15,	24 92 78 69
✆	Ranchi	0651-220 44 64	

Published in India by

UNIVERSITY SCIENCE PRESS
(An Imprint of Laxmi Publications Pvt. Ltd.)
An ISO 9001:2008 Company
113, GOLDEN HOUSE, DARYAGANJ,
NEW DELHI - 110002, INDIA
Telephone : 91-11-4353 2500, 4353 2501
Fax : 91-11-2325 2572, 4353 2528
www.laxmipublications.com info@laxmipublications.com

C—
Printed at : Repro Knowledgecast Limited, Thane

CONTENTS

PREFACE

Modern practice in Tourism Management demands a complete knowledge in fundamentals of Event Management which is the foundation for an Event Organizer. The aim of the book is to insist about the knowledge on the fundamentals. This book is specifically intended to be a college and university level text. Compared to the majority of event-related books it places less emphasis on how to produce events, and more on the following:

- The value and specific contributions of research
- Integrative themes and methods
- Discussion of important issues
- The necessity and nature of ethics in professionalism
- Application of fundamental management theories and practices

In addition to the emphasis placed on establishing Event Studies as a legitimate field of inquiry, and Event Management as a profession, the contents of the book include:

- chapters beginning with learning objectives (which encompass pertinent management competencies)
- chapters ending with basic and advanced study questions (the advanced questions are more suitable for assignments and essays)
- internet addresses and sources which are provided throughout the text, especially with regard to organizations and events that are profiled.

The book has been planned for the students with necessary illustrative examples then and there... Event tourism is a field of inquiry drawing on many other sources of theory, knowledge and methods. Academic programs in event management is now well established in many institutions around the globe. Both the academic study of event management and the profession are maturing. It is important for students of tourism to understand how events are managed, and for event managers to know more about the important tourism market and the tourism-related roles and impacts of events.

—Author

ACKNOWLEDGEMENT

Many people provided information and ideas for this book. General thanks go to all the researchers and authors cited in this book, and the entire research community that continues to develop the event management field and event studies. The author acknowledges gratefully the excellent help and the involvement extended by the Publisher and also to everyone else involved in bringing out this book.

—Author

EVENT TOURISM

CHAPTER 1

EVENT TOURISM

Learning Objectives:

- Understand the relationship between events and tourism
- Define different types of events

Event tourism is the systematic planning, development and marketing of events as:

- Tourist attractions
- Catalysts for other developments
- Image builders

Event tourism strategies should also focus on a market segment consisting of those who travel to events, or who can be motivated to attend events while away from home.

1.1. WHAT ARE EVENTS?

Events are:

- Organized occasions such as meetings, conventions, exhibitions, special events, gala dinners etc.
- Often composed of several different-yet-related functions.
- A unique blend of management, programming, setting and people.

1.1.1. Types of Event

There are many different types of events. We can group them into three different categories, based on their form or content:

- Cultural events are activities that contribute to social and cultural life.
- Sporting events are tests of sporting skill through competition for the purpose of spectator entertainment and enjoyment.
- Business events are meetings, incentive travel, conferences and exhibitions.

Activity

Fill in the form with three India-specific examples. You also have to back up your answer by supplying detailed information on the content of each event.

Event	Examples:	Content
Cultural	1.	
	2.	
	3.	
Sports	1.	
	2	
	3.	
Business	1.	
	2.	
	3.	

CHAPTER 2

THE MICE BUSINESS

Learning Objectives:

- Understand the type of business MICE represents
- Understand the need for MICE
- Understand how MICE relates to the tourism and hospitality industry
- Find out about the players within the MICE sector

The term MICE (Meetings, Incentives, Conventions and Exhibitions) represents a sector of tourism which includes business events and activities.

Travellers attending MICE activities have a purpose beyond leisure tourism, and are in fact business travellers. These business travellers are connected to different sectors of the tourism and hospitality industry through their MICE activities. (See Figure 2.1.) Think of business travellers who travel to a city to attend an exhibition. They will need food, drinks, shopping, entertainment, transport, accommodation and more.

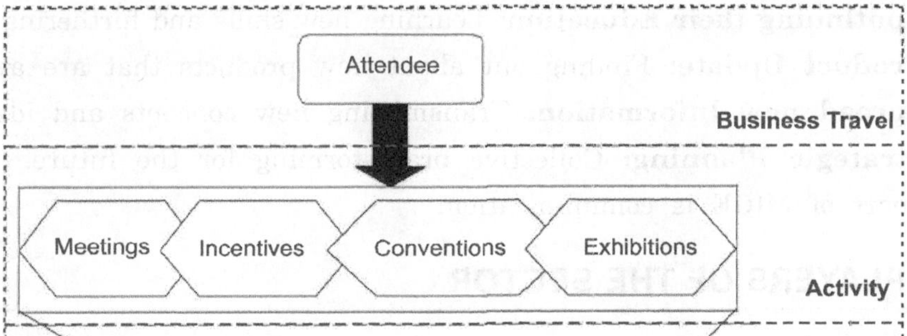

Figure 2.1: Nature of MICE.

Activity

Based on Figure 2.1, fill in the cells with what you would need if you were attending a MICE activity.

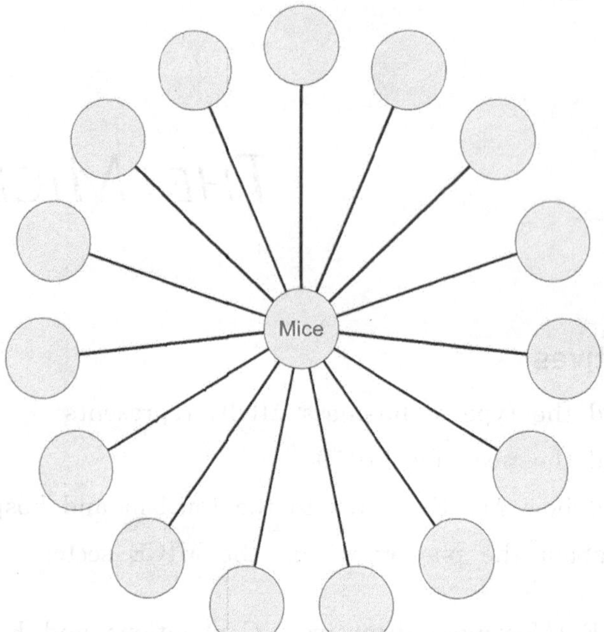

2.1. REASONS FOR MICE

People who attend MICE activities are mainly there for:

- **Stimulation:** Getting new ideas
- **Networking:** Meeting with others: colleagues, customers, buyers and people who share the same interests
- **Continuing their Education:** Learning new skills and furthering their education
- **Product Update:** Finding out about new products that are available
- **Spread new Information:** Transmitting new concepts and ideas
- **Strategic Planning:** Collective brainstorming for the future.

The heart of MICE is communication!

2.2. KEY PLAYERS OF THE SECTOR

2.2.1. Clients

These are the decision-makers who hold these activities. Clients are mainly:

- **Associations:** Non-profit professional, trade or industry organizations formed by their members.
- **Corporations:** Companies, entrepreneurial or business organizations.

- **Event planners:** Professional agents hired by organizations to plan their business activities.

2.2.2. Suppliers

These are the organizations and enterprises which provide services to MICE activities. Major suppliers include:

- **National Trade Organization:** The organization that promotes trade for the country. *e.g.*, Trade Development Council.
- **Convention and Visitors Bureau (CVB):** The organization or government department that promotes MICE activities to attendees and clients while regulating and supporting MICE clients and other suppliers. Some countries, such as the United States, not only have CVBs at a national level but on provincial and municipal (city) levels. Some states only have tourism boards to handle CVB responsibilities. India is one example.
- **Airlines:** Provides transportation services for attendees of MICE activities, such as Cathay Pacific.
- **Cruise Lines:** Provides transportation services, accommodation and venues for attendees of MICE activities.
- **Venues:** Provides spaces where MICE activities can be held, such as:
  - ➢ **Convention and Exhibition Centres**, built specifically for MICE activities
  - ➢ **Hotel Ballrooms, Conference Rooms or Meeting Rooms**
  - ➢ **Alternatives venues** include universities, castles and heritagehomes
- **Restaurants:** Provides food and beverage for MICE activities and at times can even be used as venues.
- **Accommodations:** Hotels, motels and hostels where housing is provided for attendees during MICE activities.
- **Professional Convention Organizers (PCO):** Also known as Professional Congress or Conference Organizers in some countries, help international conventions clients take care of the professional planning, organizing and management of conventions, including bank account set-up, delivery and site selection.
- **Destination Management Companies:** Takes care of MICE clients when they reach their destination cities.
- **Entertainment:** Includes performers, venues and performance, which can be part of the programme of MICE activities.
- **Technical Specialists:** Supports MICE activities by providing professional technology or equipment set-up and operating services, *e.g.*, audio/visual or lighting.
- **Intermediaries:** Agencies working as middlemen to book various services, *e.g.*, tour or travel agencies.

2.2.3. Other Players

- **Government Organizations:** Public organizations, agencies and departments at different levels that provide funding and ideas for various MICE activities:
  - ➢ Federal (national)
  - ➢ State (provincial)
  - ➢ Local (municipal)
- **Convention Industry Associations:** Organizations whose members are from the industry, including clients and suppliers, for example:
  - ➢ ICCA – International Convention and Congress Association
  - ➢ PCMA – Professional Conference Management Association
  - ➢ MPI – Meeting Professional Institute
- **Commercial Sponsors:** Companies who provide funding or resources for the MICE activities in return for promoting their brand and products.

Activity

Using the case of the New Delhi Book Fair List the key players in each sector.

Sectors	Who are they?	What are they doing?
Client	1. 2. 3. 4.	
Supplier	5. 6. 7. 8. 9. 10. 11.	
Other Player	12. 13. 14. 15. 16	

CHAPTER 3

HISTORICAL PERSPECTIVE

Learning Objectives:

- Understand the history of MICE
- Look at the development of MICE in different countries
- Take a preview of today's industry

Activity

Before the class, search dictionaries, encyclopaedias or the Internet with the keywords "conference," or "meeting," "incentive," exhibition" and "convention."

Find out about their backgrounds, stories, definitions and histories.

TIP: If you are using the Internet, besides the search engines Yahoo! or Google, you can also try Wikipedia.

3.1. HISTORY

Meetings in ancient times were discussions of communal interests. Cities acted as focal points. Rome, for example, had its Roman Forum and Comitium. In Latin, *conferentia* means "to bring together" while *auditorius* means "a place to listen."

3.1.1. Development over the Past Century

The industrialization of the late 19th to early 20th century increased the need for business meetings. There were also meetings on political, religious and recreational issues. *Associations* also began to include annual meetings.

In Europe, the history of conventions began with the Congress of Vienna in 1814–15. There was very little convention activity in the 20th century until the 1950s due to the influence of the two World Wars. The conventions industry began in the 1950s because of:

- An expansion in government organizations.
- A growth in multinational corporations and agencies.
- Developments in association interests, professional and pressure groups.
- Changes in sales techniques, including the use of product launches and sales promotion meetings.

- Need for in-company management training, continuing professional development and attendance at *ad hoc* or scheduled meetings.
- Development of subject specialization, with conferences enabling an expert to pass on information to a large number of peripherally involved colleagues.

In 1902, the first formal incentive travel programme was set up by the National Cash Register (NCR), a U.S. company. By the 1960s, long-distance incentive trips overseas came into view. Nowadays, incentives evolved into events, commonly held overseas, specially designed to attract people to achieve a specific goal. Sometimes, training activities would also be included. Because of the expense involved, incentive activity is tied to economic cycles. Companies who generate a lot of revenue during good times can organize longer trips at more expensive resort hotels with higher-priced meals.

3.1.2. The MICE Industry Today

Countries and cities (municipalities) emphasize heavy investment in infrastructure development to support industry development. National and local convention bureaus were set up to actively promote their countries and cities as travel destinations. There are also improved industry representation and co-ordination with the set-up of organizations such as the Professional Conference Management Association (PCMA), Meeting Professionals International (MPI) and more.

In the United States, Detroit established the first *convention bureau*, a government authority to promote and manage conventions, in 1896. This was followed by many other cities in the early 1900s after witnessing the benefits convention brought to the city. The International Association of Convention Bureau (IACB) was established in 1914. IACB was then reformed to become the International Association of Convention and Visitor Bureau (IACVB) in 1974. From 2004, the IACVB turned into the Destination Marketing Association International. The number of convention bureaus in 1920 was 28. Today, there are almost 600 convention and visitor bureaus in 25 countries.

3.1.3. Fast-Growing Segment

Europe and North America still play the leading role in the world convention and exhibition market in terms of number of events, but the convention and exhibition industry in Asia has shown stronger-than-average growth since the 1960s. The number of conventions in Asia-Pacific increased 124% from 1980 to 1996. The industry accounts for more than 39% of business trips and takes in 48% of business travellers.

CHAPTER 4

SECTOR OVERVIEW—MEETINGS

Learning Objectives:

- Understand the meaning of each sector of MICE
- Explain what meetings are
- Identify the types of meetings

In general, MICE events are events and activities that involve attendees who share a common interest and gather in a place. The place for the gathering needs to be a venue arranged before hand. The venue will provide space and facilities necessary to satisfy the needs of those who attend the gathering. We can further explain the gatherings by their different formats:

M = Meetings (Corporate)

I = Incentives

C = Conventions (Association)

E = Exhibitions

4.1. MEETINGS

Meetings bring people together in one place for the purposes of sharing information and discussing and solving problems. Meeting attendance can range from ten to thousands of people. During a meeting, there will usually be food and beverage served. Meeting times vary depending on the meeting type.

Most of the time, meetings refer to corporate meetings which are held by companies in the following ways:

- **Board Meetings:** Meetings of the board of the directors of a corporation, usually held annually.
- **Management Meetings:** The managers from different regions of a corporation meet when necessary to make decisions for the corporation.

- **Shareholder Meetings:** Investors who own a share in a company meet quarterly.
- **Training Seminars:** A company conducts these to train employees when needed.
- **Meetings with Partners, Suppliers and Clients:** A gathering to discuss business deals, usually held with little prior notice.
- **Product Launches:** Usually a meeting with clients, the public, and journalists and reporters when new products are announced on the market
- **Strategic Planning:** Managers meeting with employees to discuss the future of the company
- **Retreats:** The entire company staff spends a day or two together to participate in team-building activities, training seminars and strategic planning sessions

Activity

Visit Ministry of Tourism, Government of India website and find out from the MICE event calendar about what meetings have been scheduled to be held in INDIA for the coming year.

CHAPTER 5

SECTOR OVERVIEW—INCENTIVES

Learning Objectives:

- Explain what incentives are
- Get an overview of incentives development
- Understand the factors behind incentive travel decisions

Incentive travel is a management tool for rewarding and motivating sales representatives, dealers, distributors, production workers, support staff, and in some cases, customers. The company rewards sales representatives who reach sales targets by sending them on trips. Usually, the incentive trip will last three days, with hotel stays, tour packages and planned activities such as dinners, parties and games. The incentive travel market is mature in the U.S. and Europe, and is developing in Asia; especially in Singapore and Japan.

5.1. FACTORS BEHIND INCENTIVE TRAVEL DECISIONS

- **Incentive budget economy:** How strong is the economy in the country in which the sponsoring group is headquartered?
- **Buying power:** Strength of the exchange rate in the countries being considered as the destination for the trip.
- **Political climate:** Terrorist alert levels after the 911 incident.
- **Value:** How do facilities and services compare with other choices of destination?
- **Uniqueness of experience:** Takes into consideration whether these participants have experienced this type of trip before.

Activity

Check out the Ministry of Tourism, Government of India, website to find out what activities can be included in an incentive trip to India.

TIP 1: Click on the **Incentive – Inspired Team-Building Activities** to look for different activities and services in Hong Kong.

TIP 2: Click on the **Unique Theme Parties** page to see some sample activities.

CHAPTER 6

SECTOR OVERVIEW—CONVENTIONS

Learning Objectives:

- Explain what conventions are
- Observe an example of a convention
- Understand the difference between meetings and conventions

Similar to meetings, conventions are gatherings of people with common objectives, organized to exchange ideas, views and information of common interest to the group. An organization, usually an association, will organize a convention each year with a theme related to the organization's topic. Those interested in registering for the convention can pay the association a fee for all the sessions, discussions, food and beverage, dinners, and site visits.

The major differences between a meetings and conventions is that a convention:

- Is a large event often lasting for several days and involving a social programme
- Is organized by **associations:**
  - ➢ Professional and trade associations, *e.g.*, the Dentist Association
  - ➢ Voluntary associations and societies
  - ➢ Charities
  - ➢ Political parties
- Usually conducted once a year
- Generates income for the association
- A long time is spent on selecting the site of the convention

Conventions are also known as conferences or congresses. Because conventions are usually held by an association, they can be organized into different levels: international, national, regional, etc. See Table 6.1 for an example of a programme.

Activity

Fill in the following Table to compare the difference between meetings and conventions:

Table 6.1

	Conventions	Meetings
1. Can you find out the background information or history about the event?		
2. Who will be the contact person?		
3. How long does it take to plan this event?		
4. How often does this event occur?		
5. Who decides where to have this event?		
6. Do attendees choose to attend this event?		
7. Who is paying the fee for the event?		
8. Are there any restrictions on site location?		
9. How many people attend this event usually?		
10. How many of this event will a city hold in a year?		
11. How long does this event usually last for?		
12. What kind of hotels do the attendees tend to stay in?		
13. What kind of venues or facilities does this event need?		

CHAPTER 7

SECTOR OVERVIEW—EXHIBITIONS

Learning Objectives:

- Explain what exhibitions are
- Identify the purpose of exhibitions

Exhibitions are activities organized to show new products, services and information to people who have an interest in them, such as potential customers or buyers. The company showing their new products, the **exhibitor**, typically rents an area from the organizer and sets up a **booth** to meet with potential buyers. The **buyers** or the public need an invitation or a ticket to be allowed into the exhibition.

- Purpose:
  - ➢ Get sales leads
  - ➢ Build a network for influential contacts
  - ➢ Gather new information on the competition
  - ➢ Build the company's image
- Industry Associations:
  - ➢ International Association for Exhibition Management (IAEM)
  - ➢ Centre for Exhibition Industry Research (CEIR)
  - ➢ Indian Exhibitions organisations - (www.exhibitions.org.in)

Depending on the size and type, exhibitions may also be called:

- For the public:
  - ➢ Show – *e.g.*, Aerospace Show 2013
  - ➢ Fair – *e.g.*, Comic Fair
  - ➢ Exposition or expo – *e.g.*, Food Expo, Industries Expo 2012 at New Delhi.
- Open only to business buyers:
  - ➢ Trade show
  - ➢ Trade fair
  - ➢ Trade expo

Activity

Recount the experience a show or fair you attended recently by answering the following questions.

1. What was the show?
2. When was it?
3. Where was it?
4. How much was the ticket?
5. How many days did the show last for?
6. How many people did the show attract?
7. How many exhibitors were there?
8. Why were you participating?
9. Did you buy anything?
10. Will you join the same show next year?
11. Were there any activities besides booths?

CHAPTER 8

INDUSTRY BENEFITS

Learning Objectives:

- Explain why meetings, incentives, conventions and exhibitions are an important part of the tourism and hospitality industry
- Understand what impacts MICE can bring to a destination
- Look at the importance of MICE to India.

8.1. VALUE OF MICE

Many cities would like to develop MICE because of the benefits MICE bring to a city.

- **Higher expenditures:** A business traveller usually spends on more than the average tourist, as they stay in better hotels and dine at fine restaurants since they are meeting with business clients.
- **Demand period occurs on low seasons:** Many destinations have different travel seasons. Because the business traveller travels to a destination with the main purpose of attending a MICE event, the MICE event does not have to be scheduled during the peak season when most tourists tend to travel. The business traveller can help the city by taking up some of the empty hotel rooms available during off seasons.
- **Stable arrangement well in advance:** Usually the planning of a MICE event takes one to two years in advance, and even three to five years for international events due to the number of participants at the event. The event planners also need to book well before the event in order to select their preferred rooms and venues. Repeat events also require a stable method of booking. If the book fair goes well this year, the planner will book similar halls and rooms the year after.
- **Large scale:** Most MICE events may have a large number of attendees. An international convention usually requires 500 hotel rooms per night and big conference rooms in the day. An exhibition, either local or international, expects to have over thousands of attendees and requires several large exhibition halls.

- **Standardized services:** All attendees for the same MICE event will have very similar requirements as to service standards while similar MICE events would usually have similar programmes and thus standardized services are required.
- **Enhance secondary businesses:** Many suppliers are needed for MICE events. Booth set-up companies and decoration experts are necessary for the exhibition. Entertainment agencies are needed for incentive travel parties.
- **Improve host city image:** The city which holds the international MICE event can give travellers a professional image.
- **Indifference to lack of tourism attractions:** Business travellers travel primarily for the purpose of attending a MICE event, not for the attractions of a destination. Even if a city does not have unique attractions, it can still be chosen to hold an event due to other reasons, such as ease of access.
- **With no particular fixed destination, there is a free field for competition:** Many MICE events are not fixed on a host city or country. As long as a city has adequate MICE venues and facilities, it is possible for the city to be selected to hold the event.
- **Using facilities for other purposes:** Other than traditional venues such as exhibition centres or conference halls, MICE events can make use of existing facilities that may originally have other purposes, *e.g.*, universities.

Importance of MICE to INDIA

- From 1999 to 2012, the number of convention and exhibition attendees jumped by 211%
- Business/Meetings as the major purpose of visit - 25% in 2012
- Number of Overseas visitors
  - ➢ Conventions & Exhibitions 779,000
  - ➢ Corporate Meetings & Incentives 829,000
- Number of Events in 2012
  - ➢ Conventions - 218
  - ➢ Exhibitions - 78
- Intended Per Capita Spending - $10,349
- Average Length of Stay - 4.7 days

Economic Impact

1. Expenditure: $26.4 billion to India's economy in 2012

- Direct expenditure (expenditure specifically by exhibition organizers, exhibitors and visitors)
  - ➢ $13.2 billion

62% from visitor spending

38% from spending by event organizers and exhibitors

- International visitors were responsible for $8.2 billion
- Most visitor spent cash on food, accommodation and shopping ($7 billion).
- Indirect expenditures (when exhibition suppliers purchase goods and services from elsewhere)
  - $7.9 billion
- Induced expenditures (spending in the local economy by those employed in and supplying the industry)
  - $5.3 billion

2. Fiscal impact: $970 million Tax

- This tax estimate is based on $26.4 billion
- Profits tax of $510 million
- Salaries tax of $280 million
- Hotel tax of $130 million
- Airport tax of $50 million
- The industry accounts for 1.8% of India's GDP

3. Employment: Equivalent to 58,500 full-time jobs across related industries

- Only 2,100 full-time jobs were directly provided by event organizers and venue providers
- 56,400 full-time jobs in support sectors
- Services provided to events and visitors, included retail, transport, food and beverage, hotel, exhibition stand design and construction, freight forwarding, and advertising
- The sectors benefiting most were food and beverage, hotel and retail (76% of the jobs).
- 24% were spread across other sectors: Stand construction, advertising and logistics/freight services

Activity 1

Visit the Ministry of Tourism, Government of India, to find information on the average spending and length of stay of leisure tourists to India, compare the statistics with the Quick Facts above to discuss the value of MICE to India.

Activity 2

Brainstorm the possible benefits that MICE can bring to India. Then draw a mind map to link them together. The mind map may start with the arrival of the tourist. Add to it and keep expanding to further levels. You may end up with a map with many levels, allowing you to see the complex effects and interrelationships.

CHAPTER 9

INDUSTRY SECTORS INVOLVED—HOTEL

Learning Objectives:

- Describe how the different sectors of the tourism industry are involved in hosting MICE
- Identify the roles of different types of hotels
- Look at the contribution of MICE to hotels

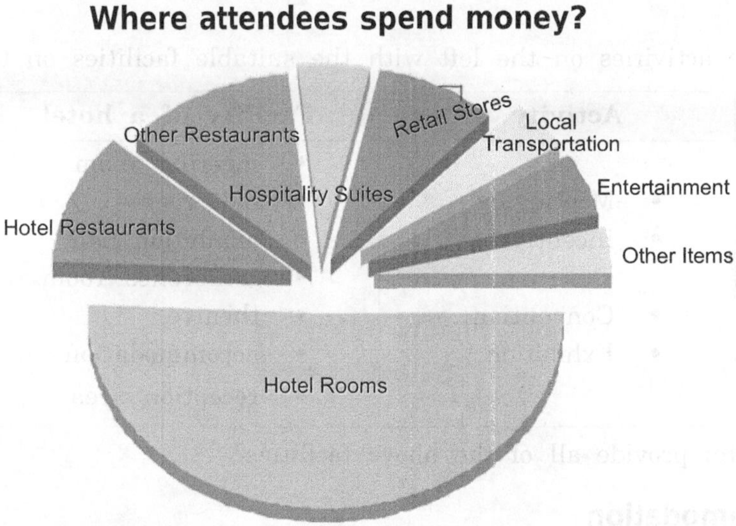

Figure 9.1: Where attendees spend money?

Hotels are the main suppliers of MICE and are the main beneficiaries as well. Business travellers who attend MICE events spend over 65% of their money on hotels for rooms and hotel dining while 15% is spent on other restaurants outside the hotel. Around 10% is spent on shopping and another 10% on local transportation.

9.1. ROLES OF HOTELS

One of the most common sites for a MICE event is a hotel. Hotels can provide **facilities,** space and function rooms for MICE activities; **accommodations**, the housing of the business travellers who attend the MICE event; and **food and beverage** services at the event, as well as meals for travellers who stay in the hotel. Typical hotels have accommodation rooms, restaurants, ball rooms, meeting rooms, swimming pools, a business centre and more. In relation to MICE activities, a hotel plays different roles depending on its facilities and the size of the MICE event:

1. Accommodation and meals
    - When all the activities of the convention are held elsewhere
2. Accommodation, meals, seminar rooms for supplementary sessions
    - When the major convention is held elsewhere
3. Facilities for associated receptions, banquets and support events
    - When some of the convention activities are held elsewhere and delegates stay in other hotels
4. Inclusive residential conferences and meetings
    - All the activities related to the convention are held and delegates stay at the same hotel

9.1.1. Facilities

The facilities in a hotel vary in size and set-up, ranging from a small meeting room for 10 people to a large theatre for thousands. Different types of facilities can be suitable for the different functions of a MICE event.

Activity

Match the activities on the left with the suitable facilities on the right.

Activity	Facility of a hotel
	• meeting room
• Meeting	• ball room
• Incentive	• exhibition hall
	• conference room
• Convention	• theatre
• Exhibition	• accommodation
	• reception area

Can a hotel provide all of the above facilities?

9.1.2. Accommodation

When providing housing for business travellers to stay during the MICE event, the hotel will have the following services for the **delegates**, the business travellers who attend the MICE event; and **entourage**, persons who travel with the delegates, usually the spouse, children, personal assistants, secretaries etc.

1. When delegates and their entourages stay in the same hotel where the convention activities are held:
    - Large hotels can take advantage by housing all related activities (in the case of a convention), including all accommodation and food and beverage services.

2. When delegates and their entourages stay in other hotels where the convention activities are held, the hotel which holds the main activity should:
    - Provide a range of choices
    - Keep in close contact with other hotels and the main convention venue.
3. When delegates and their entourages stay in the hotel while all the convention-related activities are held in other venues such as a convention and exhibition centre:
    - The hotel and main event venue must keep in close contact.

9.1.3. Types of Hotel

Certainly, different types of hotel are suitable for different types of MICE activities. In general, hotels can be grouped into five types, based on the hotel facilities:

Types of hotel	Location	Distinctive features	Example
Large city business hotels (250–600 rooms)	• Central location • Commercial business/districts nearby • Good access with public transport • Parking	• High standard of business • services • Large ball room • Spacious lobby • Room service • Leisure/fitness centre	The Grand Hyatt Hotels
Medium-sized suburban/ motor hotels (150–250 rooms)	• Near major junctions • Access to highway routes and downtown	• Meeting rooms for 25–100 max • Work stations in guest rooms • Easy access and parking • Small gym	The Royal Park Hotels
Large resort hotels and integrated resorts (300–1,200 rooms)	• Nearby attractions • Spacious	• Large ball room(s) • Extensive meeting and function rooms • Pools and recreation facilities • Golf course	The Taj Resorts Hotels
Airport hotel (250–400 rooms)	• Linked to or near an airport terminal • Easy access to city and regional transport and highways • Signposted	• May have purpose-built theatre • Usually provides a range of medium-sized and small function rooms • Health and fitness suite • Extensive glazing and soundproofing	The Airport Hotels
Country hotels, Boutique resorts (80–120 rooms)	• Remote locations • Spacious grounds	• Small meeting rooms and suites • High-quality service • Health and fitness suite • Golf course	ITC Hotels

9.1.4. Large Properties vs. Small Properties

Hotels of different sizes are suitable for different types of MICE activities.

- Large properties
  - ➢ can cater to a wider range of MICE activities, from small corporate meetings of 30 to international association conventions of 1,000
  - ➢ tend to host international MICE activities.
- Smaller properties
  - ➢ can take advantage of nearby convention and exhibition centres by hosting all food and beverage functions such as banquets and housing supplementary sessions such as small talks
  - ➢ tend to hold local MICE activities such as local corporate meetings and small local shows.

Activity

Complete the Table below to specify which types of hotel is suitable for what kind of MICE events.

Types of hotel	Suitable for this MICE activity because:
Large city business hotels	M I C E
Medium-sized suburban/ motor hotels	M I C E
Large resort hotels and integrated resorts	M I C E
Airport hotels	M I C E
Country hotels, Boutique resorts	M I C E

9.1.5. Food and Beverage

Other than supplying meals such as breakfasts, lunches, afternoon teas and dinner banquets for different sessions included in a MICE event programme, a hotel can also provide delegates and entourages with food and beverages through its restaurants, cafes and coffee shops, as well as through room service.

9.2. HOTEL CONTRIBUTION

MICE activities contribute the following to the hotel sector:

- MICE accounts for up to 65% of total sales in major hotels
- MICE attendees tend to use other hotels services, such as restaurants etc.,
- Spouses and entourages bring in additional business
- MICE events allow a hotel to forecast advance bookings and can help fill gaps during low seasons
- MICE customers have an excellent chance of becoming repeat guests

The cost of the hotel will in turn affect the attendance of a MICE event. Particularly for incentive trips, many activities take place in a Hotel's or resorts and the company is responsible for the cost of a few nights' accommodation. For international conventions and exhibitions, the cost of staying a few nights is part of the total travel cost.

CHAPTER 10

INDUSTRY SECTOR INVOLVED—TRANSPORTATION

Learning Objectives:

- Describe transportation management in relation to MICE
- Outline the roles of different types of transportation

Transportation management covers routing, vehicle use, staff requirements, maps, signage and preparation. The cost of transportation will also have an impact on the number of attendees. For incentive trips, transportation management is crucial, as most trips will involve large group travel. Group air tickets and ground coach bus tickets are also frequently used.

10.1. INTERNATIONAL

Major international transportation methods include flights, cruise ships and trains.

For MICE events that involve international attendees, transportation plays a major role in determining the success of an event. Cities located near major air or land transport hubs have the advantage of being able to draw in more attendees. While travellers can fly directly from New York to Mumbai on a direct flight using Cathay Pacific, they will need to tack on a road trip to reach Goa. In such cases, India is more convenient due to its sophisticated and well-developed transportation network.

Quick Fact:

India is

- **Easily accessible worldwide with almost 500 and more flights a week connecting with the rest of the world.**
- **Allows visa-free entry from citizens of over 10 nations**
- **The gateway to Asia**

10.2. LOCAL

Once the travellers arrive at the airport, they can be connected via the local transport system. This includes transportation:

- from the airport to the hotel
- from the hotel to MICE event venues
- from venues to various site visit spots
- from the hotel to the different attractions
- from the hotel to the client's office
- from the hotel to the central business district
- from the hotel to the airport.

Cities offering different vehicles of public transportation enhance the travel experience and increase traveller expense. Local public transports include:

- Water—cruise ships, ferries, etc.
- Land—limousines, taxis, buses, shuttle buses, trains, trams, cable cars, etc.

CHAPTER 11

INDUSTRY SECTOR INVOLVED—ATTRACTIONS AND SUPPORTING INFRASTRUCTURE

Learning Objectives:

- Illustrate how attractions can be linked to MICE events
- Obtain an overview of the various attractions in India
- Explain the importance of supporting infrastructure to planners and attendees

11.1. ATTRACTIONS

Although the main purpose for business travellers is to attend a MICE event, they would usually prefer to visit some of the local attractions. Most of the time, a *post-conference tour* is organized after the convention for international attendees to visit the attractions in and near the host city. For incentive travels, visiting local attractions might even be the objective of the trip. The MICE attendees are also good potential future visitors to these attractions. Therefore, when deciding whether or not to attend the MICE event, business travellers may also keep local attractions in mind.

An official travel agent will usually be contracted to organize the post-event tour. This travel agent also takes care of the travel arrangements of the attendees, if necessary, by providing a local guide.

Activity

Based on the map of attractions above, plan a one-day post-conference tour for the attendees to experience India You can:

1. Draw the route on the map by linking different attractions
2. List out the number that represents the different attractions
3. Plan out the time required for each point of interest.

11.2. SUPPORTING INFRASTRUCTURE

Advances in technology have made trade show and exhibition management easier and more productive. Providing infrastructure for information and communication technologies (ICTs) depends on the development and planning of the city.

11.3. TECHNOLOGY INFRASTRUCTURE

Bandwidth is the amount of information that can pass through a communications line. As it relates to the Web, bandwidth typically comes in two options: *dial-up* and *broadband*. Dial-up is insufficient for handling on-line needs at MICE events. High-speed broadband is therefore required to meet the on-site needs of:

- registration networking – to support the on-line registration system
- attendee e-mail kiosks – a centre for attendees to access their e-mail
- attendee messaging centre
- office and press room communications centres
- speaker Internet access for presentations
- live Web conferencing for sessions – streaming audio and video via the Web.

CHAPTER 12

ROLES OF THE PUBLIC SECTOR—MICE INFRASTRUCTURE

Learning Objectives:

- Outline the role of the public sector in developing MICE infrastructure
- Look at how and why the public sector invests in and develops infrastructure
- Observe a India sample case

Usually, venues for MICE events can be grouped into three types:

1. Purpose built
   - Built specifically for the purpose of holding MICE events
   - Convention centres, conference hotels and exhibition halls
2. Multi-purpose premises
   - Hotels, motels, lodges, function centres and resorts
3. Others
   - Function halls in stadiums, arenas, show grounds or even museums

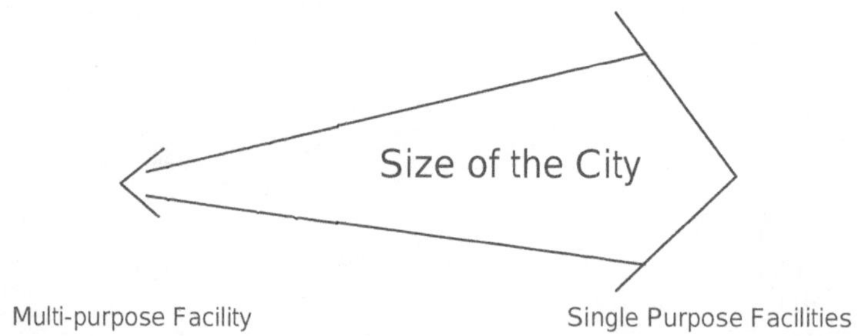

Figure 12.1: Relationship between the size of a city and the types of venues.

The larger the city, the greater the need for purpose-built facilities. Smaller cities often have multi-purpose facilities to cater to different types of MICE events.

Because of the economic impact of MICE meetings, the public sector plays an important role, investing significant public funding in the set-up and development of facilities and infrastructure. Countries in Asia, including Singapore, Indonesia, Thailand, Philippines and Japan have recently developed venues with public funds.

12.1. PUBLIC INVESTMENT IN VENUES

Various positive impacts are considered when investing public money on building new venues, which can:

- Provide a catalyst for the regeneration of a run-down city
- Revitalize traditional resorts
- Support the area's role as a focus for business, trade, technology and research
- Allow the city to emphasize its independence and maturity as a MICE destination

12.1.1. Nature of Public Funded Premises

- Vast amounts of capital required – World-class convention and exhibition centres involve high design fees, high-quality construction materials and high-tech specifications for the set-up of a large building
- Long process required – It may take over 10 years of public and private consultation, planning and construction
- Funded by local, provincial or even national governments
- Considered as drivers of economic growth and development
- "Not a must"; a non-traditional government enterprise
- Controversial – Arguments can be made for funding other programs due to the large capital investment involved
- Political liabilities – The political party who supports the development of this venue must take responsibility in the event of public opposition to the idea or construction delays
- Lose money – In most cases, these venues do not generate a profit
- Direct revenues may not meet operating costs
- Supporters are usually concert and large event promoters and hotel managers

Exercise

India case study: How the government supported the development of a convention venue to enhance MICE development, in line with its goal of turning the city into the "Event Capital of India" and the "Trade-Fair Capital"?

Activity

- Find an example of a MICE venue
- Tell the class:
  - ➢ What functions/MICE activities can be held at this venue?
  - ➢ Why did you choose this venue?
- Find some background material about this venue and show it to the class.

CHAPTER 13

ROLES OF PUBLIC SECTOR

Learning Objectives:

- Outline the role of the public sector in developing the MICE industry
- Identify the roles of different levels of public agencies in promoting, co-ordinating and managing different MICE events
- Understand the difference between them

13.1. EVENT STRATEGIES

Sometimes, the government requires the tourism board or tourism commission to develop event tourism and MICE tourism.

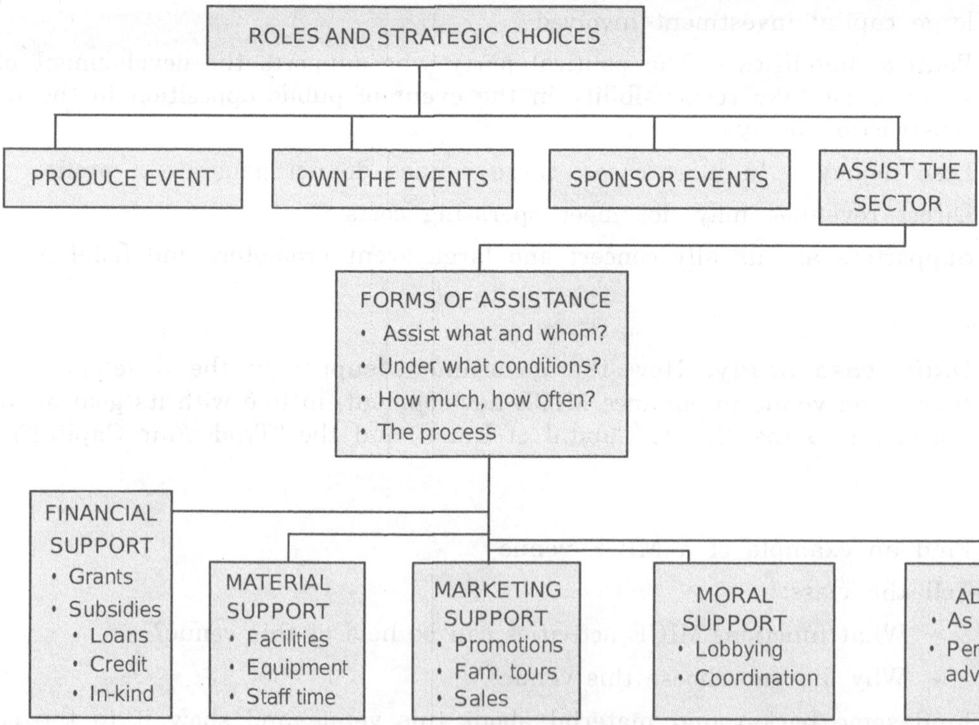

Figure 13.1: Roles and strategic choices of the public sector for event and MICE tourism.

Government support at all levels has been vital to the expansion of event tourism. Sometimes, governments not only invest in forming specialist bodies to manage event tourism development, but also fund, subsidize or support the building of infrastructure, such as convention and exhibition centres. Many governments also support event tourism through policy and legislation, such as by setting up a special counter at the immigration port to process MICE attendees.

Event tourism promotional efforts depend on the size of the destination. Administrative involvement at smaller destinations (towns and regions) may be limited to tourism promotional bodies, local government and local chambers of commerce. Larger destinations (cities, regions, countries) may have an expanded range of organizations, such as:

- convention and visitor bureaus
- tourism commissions/agencies
- government departments involved in event-organizing companies

13.2. THE CREATION OF EVENT TOURISM ORGANIZATIONAL STRUCTURE

Figure 13.2: Event tourism organizational structure.

Usually, the government has three different levels of organizations to take care of the various duties.

13.2.1. Major Event Agencies

- Are typically regionally or nationally based
- Have roles that vary depending on charter
- Seek to attract large-scale events through the **bidding** process (for example, the WTO conference in 2005 or the ITU in 2006)
- Are responsible for creating new events and developing existing events
- Facilitate development of event tourism at the target destination.

Event Bidding

Event bidding is the process of attracting *mobile events*, which move regularly between different destinations. Some sporting events and many business events (for example, association/corporate conferences) fall into this category. Event tourism organizations (national or region-based major event agencies and MoT) were specifically established for the purpose of attracting new events to a travel destination via the bidding process. Bodies of this nature need to be able to identify events of this type—a task CVB undertakes by sending representatives to other regions and overseas, and by directly communicating with MICE planners.

Organizers of these mobile events will set up a formal invitation for bids. Cities interested in hosting the mobile event will submit a *formal bid* through the event organization. A formal bid is a persuasive case for why an event should be conducted at the candidate destination. The following are two recent events that were successfully moved to India through the bidding process:

- The World Trade Organization (WTO) 6th Ministerial Conference in December 2005.
- The Asian Aerospace International Expo and Congress in September 2007

Activity

Browse the India Trade Development Council Website then research the role that as an event tourism organization, played in helping India successfully bid for four recent events.

Roles	Events

13.2.2. Government Tourism Organizations

- exist at the local, regional and national level
- are responsible for developing and implementing a comprehensive destination event tourism strategy
- provide a range of services designed to support and develop the sector, such as promotional assistance, grants, the maintenance of event calendars, and advice and assistance in a variety of areas.

13.2.3. Specialist Event Agencies

- government-sponsored bodies acting to develop and support specific events within a destination
- for example, the Convention and Visitor Bureau acts to promote the development of destinations as locations for meetings, incentives, exhibitions, conventions and special events.

13.3. DMO (DESTINATION MARKETING ORGANIZATION)

13.3.1. CVB or NTO = DMO

Definition: Convention and visitor bureaus are not-for-profit organizations charged with representing a specific destination and helping the long-term development of communities through a travel and tourism strategy.

Convention and visitor bureaus are usually member organizations that bring together businesses relying on tourism and business meetings for revenue.

13.3.2. Role and Services

- Provide unbiased representation of destination facilities
- Are government or quasi-government organizations
  - ➢ Funded by governments, taxes and membership dues
- Have sales and marketing representatives for
  - ➢ Hotels
  - ➢ Attractions
  - ➢ Convention centres
- Offer unbiased information about a destination's services and facilities
- Save visitors time and energy, as they are one-stop shops for local tourism interests
- Can provide the full range of information about a destination

Most services provided by CVBs are free.

13.3.3. Advantages of Meeting Professionals/Trade Show Managers

- Assist planners in all areas of meeting preparation
- Provide planners with detailed reference material
- Arrange block bookings at local hotels
- Market the destination to potential attendees via promotional material; thereby encouraging attendance
- Act as a liaison between the planner and community officials, thus clearing the way for special permits, street closures etc.
- Secure special letters of welcome from high-ranking government officials, and in some cases, can bring officials to speak at a meeting
- Offer suggestions about ways meeting participants can maximize their free time and help develop activity programs for spouses, pre- and post-convention tours

Activity

True of False. Decide which of the following services are true of a CVB. Tick ( ) the correct answer.

Services	True	False
They can assist in the creation of collateral material		
They can assist with on-site logistics and registration		
They can provide housing bureau services		
They can develop pre- and post-conference activities, spouse tours, and special events		
They can assist with site inspection and familiarization tours, as well as site selection		
They can provide speakers and local educational opportunities		
They can help secure special venues		
They can assist in the co-ordination of local transportation		

CHAPTER 14

CLIENTS

Learning Objectives:

- Outline the characteristics of different markets
- Understand the difference between the various professional planners and clients

14.1. CHARACTERISTICS OF DIFFERENT MARKETS

Clients who organize different MICE activities have differing characteristics. The four major types of clients can be grouped into the Corporate, Association, Government and SMERF categories.

14.1.1. Corporate

- The process of deciding where to hold events is relatively straight-forward
- The actual corporate meeting buyers within the organization may be difficult to identify:
  - ➢ Secretaries, personal assistants, marketing executives, directors of training and many others may book corporate meetings
- Company employees are usually required to attend the MICE activity
- Lead times and decision-making times can be very short
- Events typically last one to two days
- A higher budget per delegate is common
- Venues used include hotels, management training centres and unusual venues
- Spouses are rarely invited, except in the case of incentive trips

14.1.2. Association

- The process of choosing a destination can be long and drawn out
- A committee is usually involved in the selection of the destination; and the organizers may be volunteers from within the association's membership
- Attendance is voluntary

- The annual convention may be booked many years in advance
- Events typically last two to four days
- A lower budget per delegate; some attendees may be paying their own way, and price can be a sensitive issue
- Venues used include conference centres, civic and academic venues
- Spouses frequently attend

14.1.3. Government

- A large variety of events and budgets are available
- Budgets are usually examined very carefully, since public money is being used
- High security measures are necessary: these meetings are frequently accompanied by demonstrations and disruption

14.1.4. Social, Military, Educational, Religious and Fraternal (Others)

- Price sensitive in regard to accommodation rates and venue rates
- Held by volunteer-run organizations; therefore, the task of identifying them can be challenging
- Frequently held over weekends and during off-peak periods
- Often held in second-tier cities with simple accommodation and modest facilities
- Attended by delegates who bring their spouses and families and are likely to extend their trips for leisure purposes

Activity

Outline the differences between the various types of clients.

	Corporate	Association	Government	Others
Frequency				
Length				
Budget				
Decision				
Process				
Attendees				
Site Selection				

14.2. PROFESSIONALS

The clients can either organize their own MICE activities or hire a professional team to help them. Typical professionals include event planners, PCOs and DMCs.

14.2.1. Event Planners – Professional Conference Organizer (PCO)

PCOs are the equivalent of meeting planners or managers in the United States. Meeting co-ordinators, conference managers or event managers are other frequently used terms. Types of meeting planners include corporate meeting planners, association meeting planners and independent meeting planners. They will be in charge of organizing the details of a meeting or convention.

Their services include:

- basic logistics such as site selection, negotiations and contract interpretation
- can explain and speed up international paperwork such as freight forwarding, banking and customs
- provide valued guidance on finding reputable suppliers.

Compensation:

- PCOs normally receive a service fee from the client
- They may also charge a commission to the venue (usually 8–10% of the value of the conference to the venue).

14.2.2. Destination Management Companies (DMCs)

Primarily found in North America, DMCs are similar to PCOs in that they provide services to in-bound MICE professionals. They differ in their types of services by their more social-oriented services — they enable meeting attendees to "experience" the unique attributes of a particular city or region. Most MICE events require the help of DMCs, particularly for incentive trips. One India-specifc example of a DMC is Kuoni Ltd.

14.2.3. General Service Contractor (GSC)

GSCs, also called official show contractors or exposition services contractors, are hired by the show manager to handle the general duties necessary to produce a show on site. They are organizations that provide event management and exhibitors with a wide range of services, including:

- installing and dismantling
- creating and hanging signage and banners
- laying carpet
- providing booth equipment and furniture
- setting up and tearing down displays and booths.

CHAPTER 15

MICE PLANNING

Learning Objectives:

- Understand the planning process components
- Introduce the aims and objectives of a MICE event
- Explore the basic tasks involved in planning

The planning process component:

1. What to achieve?	***Mission and objectives***
2. What works?	***Feasibility study***
3. Who to ask?	***Stakeholders/organizational structure***
4. Deciding factors?	***External/internal analysis***
5. Risk/challenges?	***Opportunities and threats***
6. Moving forward?	***Select strategy and operational plan***
7. Who is in charge?	***Roles and responsibilities***
8. Doing the right thing?	***Control system***
9. How to do it better next time	***Evaluation and feedback***

The planning starts with setting objectives. Objectives must be SMART:

- **S**pecific–focused on goal and purposes
- **M**easurable–expressed in a way that is quantifiable
- **A**greeable–agreed to by all stakeholders
- **R**ealistic–the needed resources must be available to achieve them (human, financial and other...)
- **T**ime specific–can be completed within a particular time frame

15.1. ORGANIZATIONS GOALS

Different types of organization have different goals when producing events.

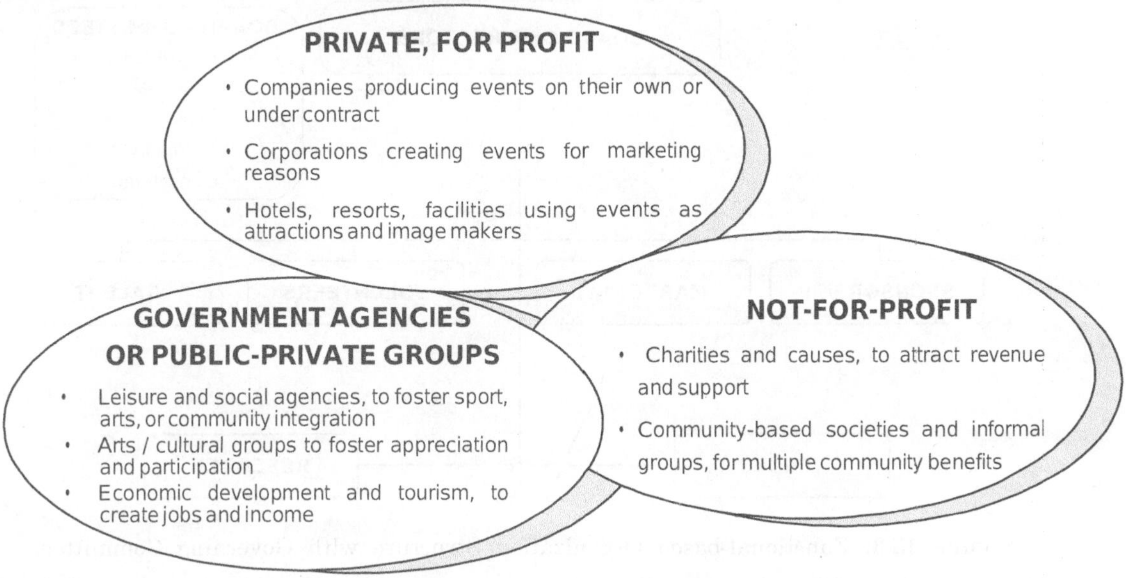

Figure 15.1: Organizational goals for producing events.

15.2. ORGANIZATION STRUCTURE

Planning a MICE event or any event involves different teams working on different functions. Depending on the type of organization, these teams can be entire departments or committees. Regardless of organizational background, each team must perform its specific function.

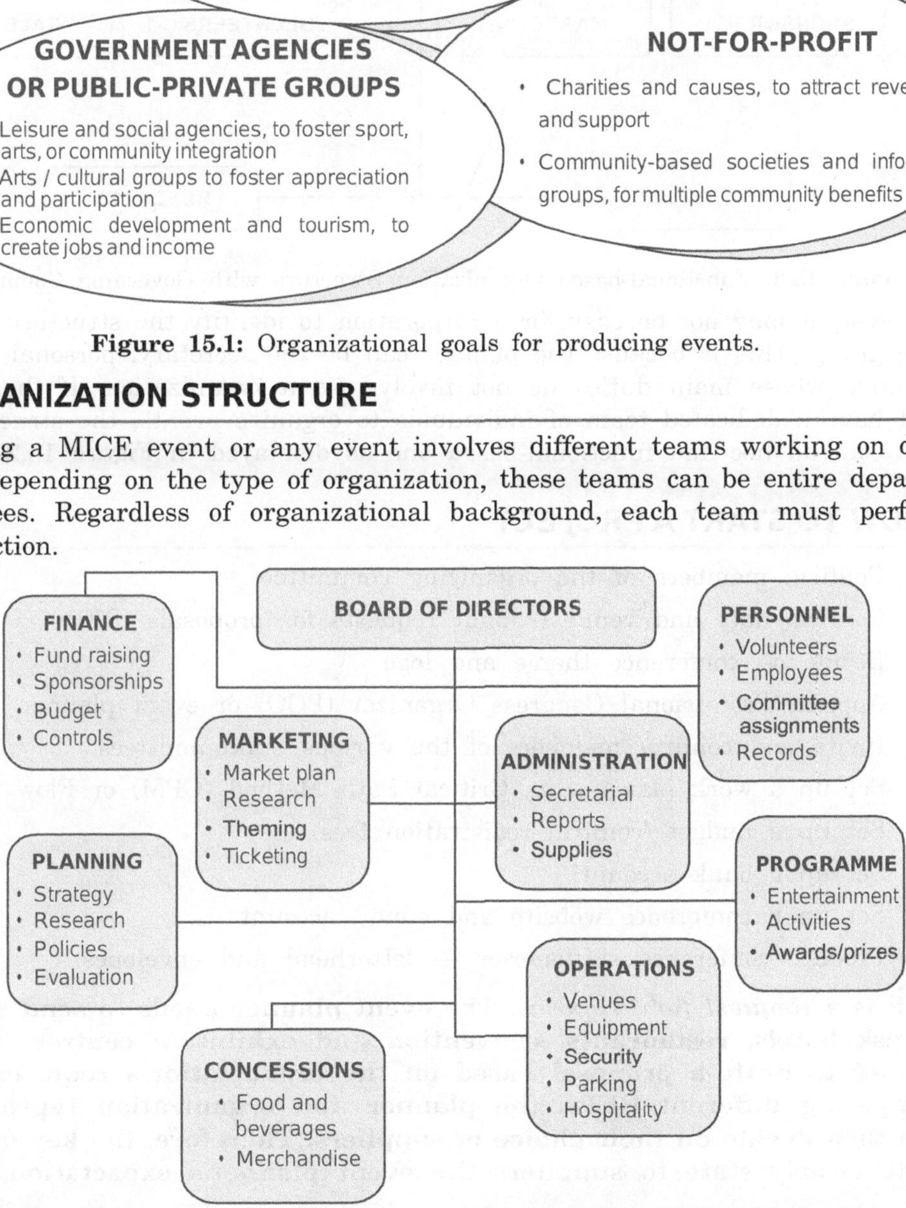

Figure 15.2: Organizational structure – Functional-Based (Not for Profit).

Sometimes, the organizational structure can be monitored by a governing committee; especially when the event is organized by a membership association.

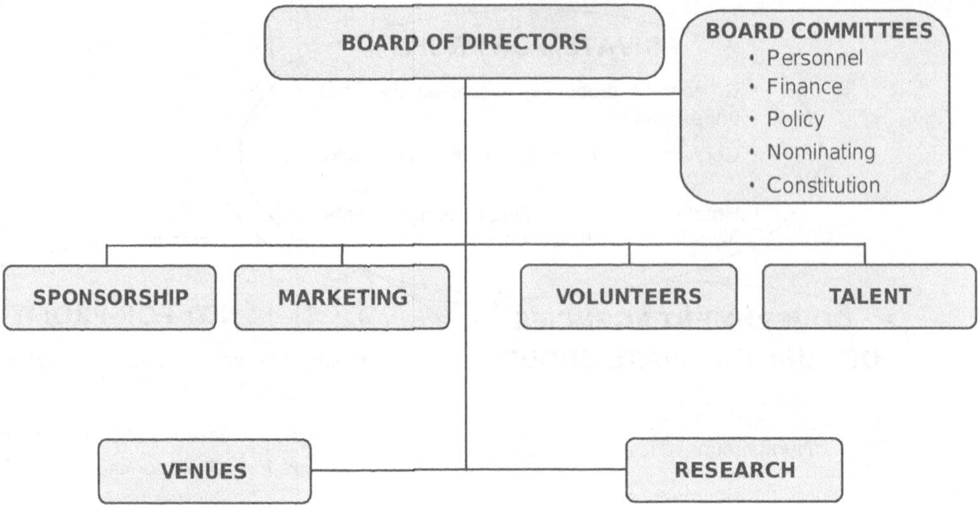

Figure 15.3: Functional-based Organization Structure with Governing Committee.

However, it may not be easy for a corporation to identify the structure of an event planning group. This is because the planner can be the secretary, personal assistant or an executive whose main duties do not involve event organization. If the corporation does not have a dedicated team of individuals to organize events, the structure will be similar to an ad hoc and functional-based one as displayed in Figure 15.2.

15.3. HOW TO START A PROJECT

- Confirm members of the organizing committee
- Confirm date and venue (submit requests for proposals (RFP))
- Decide on conference theme and logo
- Appoint Professional Congress Organizer (PCO) or event planner
- Invite and confirm members of the various subcommittees
- Set up a work plan – *e.g.*, Critical Path Method (CPM) or Flow Chart
- Set up a budget (confirm registration fees)
- Set up a bank account
- Set up a conference website and e-mail account
- Produce conference stationeries — letterhead and envelopes

RFP is a *Request for Proposal.* The event planner needs to send out a RFP to ask hotels, restaurants, convention and exhibition centres, and other venues to draft a proposal based on the organization's requirements. By comparing different RFPs, the planner and organization representatives can then decide on their choice of suppliers. Therefore, the key of the RFP is to clearly state to suppliers the event planner's expectations.

15.4. PREPARATION STAGE

A typical MICE event will have the following subcommittees to perform different functions:

1. Program subcommittee
2. Social subcommittee
3. Registration and hotel and tour bookings
4. Publicity subcommittee
5. Sponsorship subcommittee
6. Printing and production

15.4.1. Program Subcommittee

- An Example of a Set up Programme Structure:
- Opening ceremony
- Keynote presentation
- Plenary session
- Committee programs
- Breakout sessions
- Closing ceremony, if any
- Nominate guest of honour and speakers/call for paper
- Follow-up speakers with bios, photos and/or abstracts
- Fix the program rundown
- Protocol
- Security
- Invitation to VIPs
- Confirm venue set up, decoration and A/V requirements **(on stage/off stage)**

Usually, it takes around 12 months or more to plan for a MICE event. (For large international events, the planning time can be up to 24 months or even up to 36 months.)

Activity

Plan the above tasks. Think about which task should be done first and the best time to complete the tasks that are not as important.

12 Months		
11 Months		
10 Months		
9 Months		
8 Months		
7 Months		
6 Months		
5 Months		
4 Months		
3 Months		
2 Months		
1 Month		

15.4.2. Social Subcommittee

- Set up the type/nature/quantity of social programs
- Confirm date/time/venue
- Decide on the program rundown
- Guest of honour
    - ➢ protocol
    - ➢ entertainment
    - ➢ transportation
    - ➢ security
- Confirm venue set-up, decoration and A/V requirements (on stage/off stage)
- Confirm food and beverage plan
- Menu (Chinese or Western)
- Drink package (wine, beer, juice, soft drinks)
    - ➢ Special meal requirements (no beef/pork, vegetarian etc.)

Activity

Plan the above tasks. Think about which tasks should be completed first and the best time to complete the tasks that are not as important.

12 Months		
11 Months		
10 Months		
9 Months		
8 Months		
7 Months		
6 Months		
5 Months		
4 Months		
3 Months		
2 Months		
1 Month		

15.4.3. Registration and Hotel and Tour Booking

- Prepare registration forms (on-line/hard copy)
- Set up registration database
- Identify and reserve hotels
- Set up optional tour program for:
    - ➢ Accompanying persons during the conference
    - ➢ Pre/post-congress tour
- Send confirmations to delegates as registrations arrive

Activity

Plan the above tasks. Think about which tasks should be completed first and the best time to complete the tasks that are not as important.

12 Months		
11 Months		
10 Months		
9 Months		
8 Months		
7 Months		
6 Months		
5 Months		
4 Months		
3 Months		
2 Months		
1 Month		

15.4.4. Publicity Subcommittee

- Individual connections and past conference delegates
  - ➢ Direct mail - send registration brochures by mail
  - ➢ Group e-mails - organize regular e-newsletters
- Professional associations
  - ➢ Regular publications
  - ➢ Event calendars
  - ➢ Group e-mails
- Event Marketing
  - ➢ Attend similar events to promote own event
- Media
  - ➢ Ad/Inserts in publications
  - ➢ Press releases
- Sales Promotions
  - ➢ Complimentary/discounted registrations

Activity

Plan the above tasks. Think about which tasks should be completed first and the best time to complete the tasks that are not as important.

Months		
12 Months		
11 Months		
10 Months		
9 Months		
8 Months		
7 Months		
6 Months		
5 Months		
4 Months		
3 Months		
2 Months		
1 Month		

15.4.5. Sponsorship Subcommittee

- Prepare a sponsorship and exhibition prospectus
- Appoint official contractors for exhibition floor plan and booth set-up
- Identify and recruit potential sponsors and exhibitors
- Send technical and instruction manuals to confirmed exhibitors
- Monitor all terms and conditions stated in the sponsorship contract

Activity

Plan the above tasks. Think about which tasks should be completed first and the best time to complete the tasks that are not as important.

12 Months		
11 Months		
10 Months		
9 Months		
8 Months		
7 Months		
6 Months		
5 Months		
4 Months		
3 Months		
2 Months		
1 Month		

15.4.6. Printing and Production

- Registration brochures
- Invitation cards
- Conference proceedings–a book or CD that contains all written articles for presentation
- Conference program
- Delegates' list
- Badge
- Name plates
- Conference satchels
- Pens and pads
- Souvenirs–guests of honour, speakers, delegates
- Tickets

Activity

Plan the above tasks. Think about which tasks should be completed first and the best time to complete the tasks that are not as important.

12 Months		
11 Months		
10 Months		
9 Months		
8 Months		
7 Months		
6 Months		
5 Months		
4 Months		
3 Months		
2 Months		
1 Month		

15.5. ON-SITE PREPARATION

- Set up an on-site work and manpower plan
- Prepare the venue operation order and food and beverage plan
- Buy insurance
- Arrange photographer/videographer
- Arrange transportation for on-site equipment
- On-site staff briefing

Timeline: Six to eight weeks before conference start.

15.6. WRAP UP

- Send relevant thank you letters with photos
- Settle all payments
- Prepare an income and expenditure report
- Prepare a final report with statistics and recommendations
- Finalize all matters

Timeline: Within two months after conference end.

CHAPTER 16

SITE SELECTION

Learning Objectives:

- Describe the site selection process
- Identify site selection criteria
- Understand the importance of site selection

Selecting a site is the most important step in planning a MICE event. This process usually takes place several years prior to the event because it plays a deciding factor in whether the MICE event is successful. The process also takes a few months or even up to a year because it involves travelling to the candidate cities, sites, venues and hotels before a final choice is made.

Before selecting the site, the planner needs to understand the target market. Let's take a look at the three major markets:

Table 16.1: Differences between the Three Major Markets

Association	Corporate	Government
• Flexible site selection • Committee decision • Participants pay • Voluntary attendance	• Restricted site selection • Individual decision • Employers pay • Compulsory attendance	• Sites with high-security priorities • Tendering process • Costs shared between departments • Attendance depends on need

16.1. THE SITE SELECTION PROCESS

1. Identify objectives
2. Gather historical data
3. Determine the physical requirements for the meeting

4. Consider attendee interests and expectations
5. Select a destination and type of facility
6. Prepare meeting specifications and a request for proposal (RFP)
7. Review and evaluate sites
8. Select the site

16.1.1. Identify Objectives

- The purpose or expected outcome of the meeting must be clearly understood before the RFP is prepared
- A few events, however, serve a single purpose:
  - ➢ to educate
  - ➢ to discuss business
  - ➢ to attend a trade show
  - ➢ to provide a social setting for personal relaxation or professional growth
- The needs assessment or organization's culture may determine:
  - ➢ What is to be accomplished as a result of this meeting
  - ➢ The meeting objectives, which will indicate the appropriate setting

16.1.2. Gather Historical Data

- Hotels and facilities typically require three years of history (documented within the RFP)
- When preparing an RFP, provide as much historical background as possible
- For a first-time event, gather historical data from previous similar events conducted by the group. The current demographics can provide a profile of the potential audience, including:
  - ➢ the location of most of the attendees,
  - ➢ their purchasing habits
  - ➢ an educational needs assessment and related remarks.

16.1.3. Determine Physical Requirements

- Preferred Dates
- Attendance
- Sleeping Rooms
- Meeting Space
- Food and Beverage Events
- Exhibits
- Registration
- Ancillary Space Needs
- Other Logistical Considerations
- Site Inspection Requirements
- External Factors

16.1.4. Consideration of Attendee Interests and Expectations

Usually the following questions will be considered at this stage:

- What is the average age of the meeting participants and how do their ages affect on-site expectations?
- What is the male/female ratio of the participants?
- Would attendees be bringing family members?
- Are programmes for spouses, guests or children needed?
- How relevant are local attractions and cultural events to the attendees?
- Are recreational activities such as golf, tennis or skiing important?
- Should a golf tournament be included as part of the conference?
- Are spa services and fitness facilities expected?
- Should the site have easy access to shopping and dining options?
- Do the international attendees have special needs?

16.1.5. Select Destination and Facility Types

- Metropolitan Area
- Suburban Area
- Airport Area
- Resorts
- Conference Centres
- Convention Centres

16.1.6. Prepare Specifications and RFP

- the event specifications document prepared for facilities assists them in evaluating their suitability for the potential client
- presents the event objectives, historical data, physical requirements, and attendee interests and expectations, and identifies the general area and type of facility needed
- preparing the RFP requires careful deliberation and communication of the group's needs
- professionally prepared documents facilitate consistent communication with suppliers

16.1.7. Review and Evaluate Sites

- Local CVB/DMO assist in obtaining information
- Initial contact with the facility representative
- Assess adequacy of space
- Site inspection
- Site inspection checklist

16.1.8. Site Selection Criteria

Upon understanding the process for selecting a site, the site suitability for the MICE event may be measured using certain criteria. Usually, criteria from the following eight categories are considered:

Category		Dimensions
Accessibility	**Cost**	What is the transportation cost? How long is the travel time to this city?
	Time	
	Frequency	How many flights a day are there to this city?
	Convenience	How convenient is scheduling for the different connecting flights and other transportation?
	Barriers	Do travellers need a visa to travel to this city?
Local support	**Local chapter**	Does the association have a local chapter to offer support and resources?
	CVB/convention centre	Will the tourism board or the convention centre offer help?
	Subsidies	Is there any funding from the local government for this type of activity?
Extra-conference opportunities	**Entertainment**	Are there a lot of restaurants, bars, theatres and night clubs in the city?
	Shopping	Are there a lot of malls, department stores and markets to shop at?
	Sightseeing	Are there many architectural landmarks, museums, monuments, attractions, parks, historical sites and local tours?
	Recreation	Are there sports competitions, games and activities?
	Professional opportunities	Are there opportunities to get in touch with clients or local agents for talks, visits and business transactions?
Accommodation facilities	**Capacity**	How many rooms are there in a single hotel? Are more than one hotel needed to accommodate all the guests?
	Cost	What is the rate per room?
	Service	What is the standard of service?
	Security	Can the hotel provide a safe environment?
	Availability	Will the hotel be available at the time of the event?
	Capacity	Does the convention and exhibition centre have enough space for this event?
	Layout	Is the floor plan flexible and suitable for the event?

Meeting and exhibition facilities	**Cost**	How much is rent?
	Ambiance	Is the lighting suitable for this event?
	Service	What is the standard of the service?
	Security	Will the convention and exhibition centre provide a safe environment?
	Availability	Will the convention and exhibition centre be available?
	Experience	Has the convention and exhibition centre held a similar event before? Did they perform satisfactorily?
Information	**Reputation**	What do other event planners think about the city?
	Marketing	Is the promotion activity by the tourism board effective?
	Climate	Is the climate of the city severe?
	Setting	Is the surrounding environment attractive?
Site environment	**Infrastructure**	Does the city have enough infrastructures to support the event?
	Hospitality	Does the local community welcome tourists and/or this event?
Other criteria	**Risks**	What is the possibility of the city being affected by labour strikes, natural disasters, boycotts or terrorist attacks etc.?
	Profitability	Will the city help the event make money?
	Association promotion	Will the city add status to the association or organization?
	Novelty	Is the city unique?

Activity 1

- If you are planning an international convention for 500 people next October, is India a suitable site for this event? First, pick a hotel and/or a convention venue. Based on the above criteria, answer all the questions.

Activity 2

- Based on Activity 1, choose another nearby city such as Goa or Bangalore, and repeat the process. Find out if the city can also be a suitable site for this convention.

Activity 3

- If we are planning an exhibition with 500 exhibitors, will this make a difference? TIP: Consider only the applicable criteria.

CHAPTER 17

BUDGETING

Learning Objectives:

- Explain the budget process
- Understand the reasons for budgeting
- Know how to set budgetary goals
- Identify different budgetary viewpoints

17.1. WHAT IS A BUDGET?

- A quantified statement of plan
  - ➢ The plan is expressed in numerical terms
- The process includes
  - ➢ Costing
  - ➢ Estimating income
- Allocation of financial resources
  - ➢ To be used to compare costs and revenues with projected costs and revenues
  - ➢ Maximum possible expenditure for each area of the event is estimated
- Can take many forms.

17.2. CONSTRUCTING THE BUDGET

17.2.1. Budgeting Process

- **Instructive phase:** Committee will instruct the event planner on the content of the budget
- **Consultative phase:** Event planner would ask the advice of other event specialist and the subcontractors.

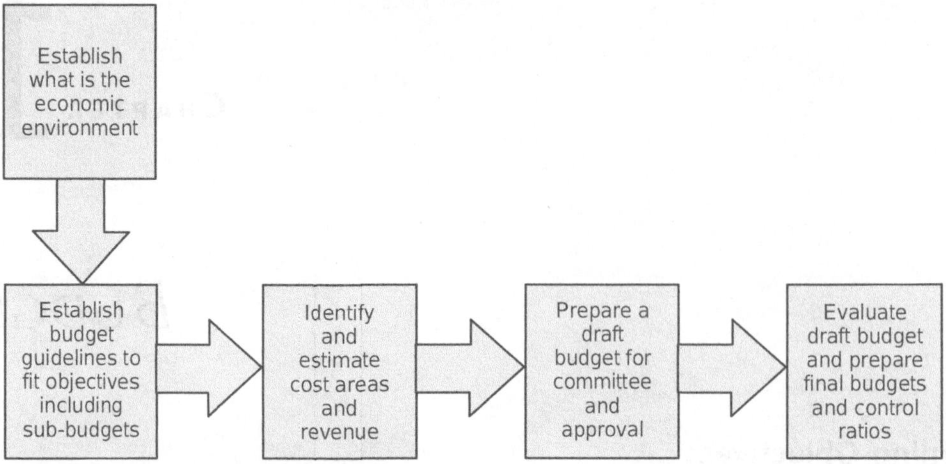

17.3. REASONS FOR BUDGETING

- To monitor the financial situation as it relates to the goals and objectives of the meeting
- To understand where the income is coming from and where it is going
- To identify the percentage of income and expenses from individual areas
- To analyze and control expenditures
- To determine areas that allow for an increase (↑) in revenues and a decrease (↓) in expenses to avoid losses and determine program options.

17.4. BUDGETARY GOALS

There are three types of goals when setting a budget:

- To **break even**: when income = expense
- To generate **profit**: when income > expense
- To minimize **loss** and subsidize if necessary: when income < expense.

17.4.1. Budgeting at a Loss

While it may sound strange, many meetings are budgeted, technically, to lose money. This loss may be the result of meetings that have no income (registration fees, exhibitors, sponsorship) to cover expenses. Typical meetings that are budgeted at a loss include:

- board meetings
- committee meetings
- training meetings
- product launches

Typically, these situations are viewed as investments and subsidizing the event is acceptable because of its benefit to attendees.

17.4.2. Use of Information

When setting the budget, the first questions involve how much is to be spent.

The planner often examines the history of previous event budgets. Prices may increase because of the date and location of the event. Differences in programming, attendance and other aspects of the event will also dictate an increase or decrease in income and expenses. Demographics of the participants will also impact on budgeting as the financial status of the attendees may affect the amount they are willing to pay for registration. For first-time events, usually zero-based budgeting will be used. Planners can also research other MICE events of similar size and scope and identify all possible expenses to determine a realistic budget.

Activity

Discuss the potential budgetary goals for:

- an incentive trip
- a shareholders meeting
- a retreat

What do they have in common?

17.5. INCOME

Income is the money gained as revenue from the MICE event. Sources of funding include:

- Allocation of funds from an organization's budget
- Revenue generated from:
  - Registration fees
  - Exhibition fees
  - Advertising fees
- Sponsorships
- In-kind donations (goods, services and function space)

17.6. EXPENSE

Expenses are moneys that need to be spent in order to hold the MICE event. Typical expenses originate from fixed, variable and indirect costs.

Fixed Costs are costs that have to be met. These expenses remain the same regardless of the number of delegates.

- Venue/room rent
- Speakers
- Marketing
- Office supplies and expenses
- Multimedia

Variable Costs are costs that vary with the number of delegates. These expenses are based on a per-person basis.

- Food and beverage (F&B)
- On-site materials
- Ground transportation
- Entertainment

Indirect Costs are listed as overhead or administrative items on a programme budget and are organizational expenses not directly related to the event.

- Staff salaries
- Overhead
- Equipment repair.

Activity

Below is a list of expense items. Discuss what categories these costs fall into. ✔ the appropriate column.

Tip: Think of which group of examples discussed above that these costs belong to.

Expenses	Fixed?	Variable?	Indirect?
Administrative overhead			
Car rental			
Complimentary registration			
Decoration			
Flowers			
Food and Beverage functions			
Gratuities and gifts			
Insurance			
Labour charges			
Multimedia equipment			
Office furniture and equipment			
Photography and video taping			
Postage and delivery costs			
Printing and photocopying			
Promotion			
Registration materials			
Room rental			
Security guards			
Shipping and freights			
Signs, posters, banners			
Shuttle bus services			
Speakers			
Staff travel expenses			
Stationeries			
Taxes			
Telecommunications			
Temporary Staffing			
Translators and interpreters			
Website design and maintenance			

17.7. BUDGET VIEWPOINT

Different organizations will have different views on whether or not their MICE events should make money. There are two ways to achieve their budgetary goals—increase income or cut costs.

17.7.1. Associations

Budget Viewpoint	• For "non-profit" organizations, profits cannot be excessive and must be used to operate or grow the association • Charitable organizations must distribute all excess income over expenses
↑ Income	• Increase the level of advertising on on-site programming and on the website; • Consider marketing to related groups, competing organizations and/or students; • Creatively packaged sponsorship opportunities.
↓ Cost	• Create guidelines for staff and speaker travel and expenses; • Use member speakers at no fees where possible; • Review banquet and event orders and audio-visual equipment orders to make sure there are no hidden costs; • Print programme materials at a discount printer at the meeting destination; • Use volunteers, host committees, students in place of CVB or temp company staff for registration staffing.

17.7.2. Government

Budget Viewpoint	• Breaking even is the main objective • Registration fees must be kept within reasonable ranges and expenses must be tightly controlled. • Attendees must stay within per diem guidelines.
↓ Income	• Increasing registration fees is rarely an option and sponsorships are not typically allowed; • Increasing attendance by including other departments or entities; • Some vendor exhibits may be allowed, but strict guidelines must be followed.
↓ Cost	• Shorten the schedule by a day; • Use "non-traditional" venues such as university campuses • Reduce portion sizes for food or "gang" up menus with another larger group; • Negotiate food outlet pricing to allow purchases within individual meal per diems; • Use students in place of additional staff for registration and other duties.

17.7.3. Corporation

Budget Viewpoint	• Meetings typically do not generate "income" • Companies are under pressure to limit expenditures in all areas, including meetings • Budgeted "loss" or subsidies must be kept within reasonable limits
↑ **Income**	• Not applicable.
↓ **Cost**	• Consider shortening the meeting by a day; • Hold meetings in smaller cities and/or during "shoulder" or "off-peak" period in order to negotiate better rates and other items at the facility; • Control travel costs by dictating preferred vendors for airline and ground transportation; • Negotiate multi-meeting contracts with vendors to secure better prices; • Hold creative and fun activities during receptions to allow for the reduction in high-end food offerings and quantity of food needed.

CHAPTER 18

SPONSORSHIP AND FINANCIAL ANALYSIS

Learning Objectives:

- Understand the importance of sponsorships
- Identify different sponsorship frameworks
- Explain the function of continual and post-event analyses

One of the common ways to increase income is to seek sponsorship. Sponsorship can be in cash or **in-kind** (goods or services donated). The **sponsor**, a company who would offer cash or in-kind fees at an event, will gain in return commercial potential by associating with the event. Most of the time, such "affiliation" or "association" between the event and company are mutually beneficial. For a convention to be a financial success, it is critical to secure adequate sponsorship. The key is to provide sponsorship packages that detail the required contribution and list the benefits to the sponsor. Organizers must also fulfil all the sponsor benefits as set out in the package in order to attract repeat sponsorship.

18.1. SPONSORSHIP FRAMEWORK

Two typical approaches are commonly used:

1. **A simple-to-develop hierarchical approach** – based on a differentiation of fees and benefits. For example:

- Title sponsor (one only) – There may not be a title sponsor for some conventions, due to the topic and nature of the event. A *title sponsor* refers to a sponsor who can name the event. They:
  - ➢ receive free tickets
  - ➢ receive prominent signage at all venues
  - ➢ are allowed a hospitality tent;
  - ➢ cost ₹ 100,000
- Gold sponsor (₹ 50,000) (no limit on numbers). Receives fewer benefits than the title sponsor

- Silver (₹ 25,000)
- Bronze (₹ 5,000 to ₹ 10,000)

2. **Tangible approach** – based on the goods and services needed. For example:
   - Title sponsor (one only; sum to be negotiated)
   - 7 "presenting" sponsors
   - 5 product-exclusivity sponsors
   - 3 exclusive media sponsors
   - Donor: any number

There is no universal framework for a sponsorship hierarchy. In other words, there is no set contribution amount required for each level of sponsorship, as long as the higher-level sponsors are contributing more than the lower-level sponsors and receive more benefits. You can also name the sponsorship levels in any way you see fit.

Activity

Look at some poster of international congress as you like. Identify the sponsors listed in the poster for this international congress. Fit these sponsors into the above sponsorship framework and discuss how these sponsors are helping the congress.

Sponsor	Level	How can they help?

18.1.1. Continual Financial Analysis

On-going financial analysis during planning and implementation of the event can help the organization:

- identify potential problems;
- make required changes or corrections; and
- better inform facilities and vendors on the status of the event well in advance.

18.1.2. Post-Event Financial Analysis

After the event, it is important to review and analyze financial performance. By comparing actual income and expenses with the budget once the event is over and after income and expenses have been reconciled, organizers can analyze budget item variances and determine the reasons behind them. The post-event financial analysis also allows improved understanding as to why actual financial performance differed from anticipated performance. As a result, the organization may formulate new policies, from site selection and contract negotiation to speaker guidelines and future pricing. The emphasis here is an analysis of the overall financial records to confirm or change the financial viewpoint, based on actual performance.

CHAPTER 19

NEGOTIATION

Learning Objectives:

- Identify negotiable items
- Understand how negotiation relates to cost

One key responsibility that affects planning and budgeting is negotiation. This process helps to control costs and communicate needs to the suppliers. The major negotiation items at MICE events include hotel guestrooms, meeting spaces and other services.

19.1. GUESTROOMS – ITEMS TO NEGOTIATE

- Rates (discount off published prices)
- Increased complimentary room ratio (ensure a cumulative rather than a per-night basis)
- Complimentary guestrooms for move-in
- Complimentary presidential or executive suites during the event for the host
- Complimentary rooms for event professionals during the scheduled event
- VIP room upgrades at the group rate
- Speaker and staff rooms discounted during the event
- Room blocks – a guaranteed minimum number of rooms to be paid by the client. Reservation cut-off closer to the meeting date than the typical 30 days and rooms sold after cut-off date sold at the group rate
- Ability to reduce room blocks without penalty
- Optional or reduced service charges for bell service and housekeeping
- VIP amenities
- Satellite check-in with extra bell staff available
- Free or reduced parking fees or valet service
- Complimentary rundown service
- Complementary daily newspapers
- Pre- and post-conference guestroom rates at the conference rate
- Toll-free access, free local calls

19.2. MEETING SPACE – ITEMS TO NEGOTIATE

- A waiver or reduction in meeting rentals in return for guaranteed food and beverage expenses
- A waiver or reduction in exhibit space rental fees in return for an adequate guest room block
- House telephone at registration within a secured meeting office
- Pads, pencils, candies, easels, corkboards, chalkboards, whiteboards
- Complimentary or discounted on-site services
- 24-hour meeting space rates
- Additional utility charges (electrical, cleaning)

19.3. OTHER SERVICES – ITEMS TO NEGOTIATE

- Children's programming and child care services
- House limousine or shuttle service to nearby attractions
- Guaranteed service levels for all food outlets and functions
- Free self-mail registration and pre-printed promotional brochures
- Reduced or complimentary corkage charges
- Clear access to fire exits, fire hose cabinets, fire extinguishers and pull stations
- Exit pathways from large sessions and activities
- Informational displays and registration equipment in lobbies
- What is considered exit pathways and *not* function space
- Types and concentration of exhibits in the exhibit hall
- Potential obstructions caused by A/V requirements
- Drapery or cabling across entrance or exit doorways, pyrotechnics, mobile microphone and camera cables
- What is not negotiable?

19.4. WHAT IS NOT NEGOTIABLE? – ITEMS TO NEGOTIATE

- Not all items are negotiable, including:
  - ➢ Items that are related to safety
  - ➢ Items that are illegal
  - ➢ Items that may cause harm to the host and attendees

Activity

Discuss what is not negotiable. Brainstorm all non-negotiable items and list them out.

TIP: Think of items related to safety that may cause harm and are against the law.

CHAPTER 20

PROGRAMMING PLANNING AND DESIGN

Learning Objectives:

- Explain programme planning and design
- Understand the programme outline
- Identify different formats and timing of the programme elements

20.1. WHAT IS A PROGRAMME?

Programme:

- Includes the flow of the performers, speakers, catering and the other elements of the event
- Includes the schedule for all the elements.
- Depends on:
  - ➢ The expectations of the audience
  - ➢ The constraints of the venue and infrastructure
  - ➢ The culture of the client and main sponsors
  - ➢ The availability of elements for staging, and their mutual relationships
  - ➢ Logistics

20.2. PROGRAMME PLANNING AND DESIGN

Programming for events is both a technical and creative process. Programme planning starts with the concept and leads to considerations on how to manage and market it. Ideally, programming ideas and decisions form part of the ongoing planning strategy.

Programme design involves planning and co-ordinating every aspect of a MICE event. The planning starts with the set-up of the programme committee. The key issues are programme schedule and inclusion. The design and planning process also concern the speakers and *accompanying persons*' (AP) programme, for those who travel with the MICE event attendees.

20.2.1. Factors Affecting Programme Design

- The type of MICE event
  - To instruct
  - To share information or knowledge
  - To market a particular product
- Objectives
  - To earn money
  - To enhance the organizer's image
  - To serve its membership
- Implications for
  - Attendee profile
  - Length of the convention
  - Convention location/venue

20.2.2. Session Structure

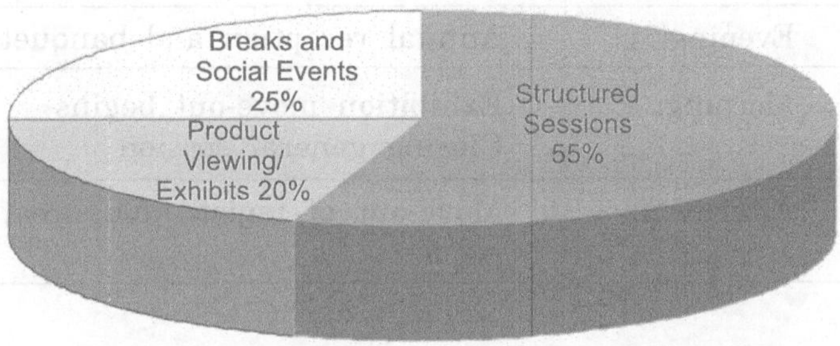

Figure 20.1: Percentage of different programme items.

20.2.3. General Programme Outline

- Categorizes the meeting into its various activities
- Combines the appropriate number of professional development hours with social and recreational activities
- Should include the time for registration, opening ceremonies or general session, exhibition hours, meal and social functions, breaks, and a formal closing session, if appropriate for the type of MICE event.

To start with, always have an outline in mind. (See Table 20.1 for an example) The planner can then fill in the different elements to the programme. All other details can then fit into the schedule.

Table 20.1: An Example of a General Programme Outline for a Combined Conference and Exhibition

Day 1	Morning:	Office and press room set-up begins Registration set-up begins Exhibition set-up begins
	Afternoon:	Meeting room set-up begins
Day 2	Morning:	Governance and/or committee meetings Registration opens Office and press room open Exhibition and meeting room set-up continue
	Afternoon:	Pre-meeting workshops
	Evening:	Opening reception
Days 3–5	Morning:	General session Exhibition opens Registration, office, press room open
	Afternoon:	Concurrent sessions Annual business meeting (Day 4 only)
	Evening:	Annual reception and banquet (Day 4 only)
Day 6	Morning:	Exhibition move-out begins Closing general session
	Afternoon:	Move-out of registration area, office, press room

Activity

Draft a programme outline for a three-day combined conference and exhibition programme. Reminder: Pay attention to items that have to be kept.

20.3. GOOD PROGRAMME DESIGN

You can achieve structure, balance and pacing for the programme by combining major topics and sub-topics, passive and active sessions, formal and informal times to provide professional and personal growth and networking among practitioners. (Price, 1989)

20.3.1. Session Format

Breakout	Small group sessions within a meeting, organized to discuss specific subjects
Concurrent sessions	Multiple simultaneous topics covering a wide range of interests
Exhibit/trade show	Event at which products and services are displayed

General/Plenary	General assembly for all persons actively involved in a meeting
Labs	A replicated working environment with equipment to practice or to learn new skills
Tour/Site visit	Trips to related sites or industry venues
Workshops	Seminars emphasizing free discussion, exchange of ideas, demonstration of methods and practical application of skills and principles. They also involve meeting in small groups for intensive discussions
Symposium	A meeting of a number of experts in a particular field, at which papers are presented and discussed by specialists on particular subjects with a view to making recommendations concerning the topic under discussion.
Keynote	Opening remarks or presentation at a meeting that sets the tone or theme of the event and motivates the attendees
Keynote address	A session that opens or highlights the show, meeting or event

20.3.2. Instructional Style

Case study	An intensive analysis of an individual unit or situation
Lecture/Paper	An informative and instructional speech
Panel	Several speakers (e.g. four is a manageable number) with different perspectives on the same topic; may include a moderator
Poster session	Display boards placed around the room with visual informational presentations; often scientific and accompanied by an author
Demonstration	One or more persons showing how a particular product functions
Roundtable discussion	Approximately eight to 10 attendees with a group leader; involving an informal discussion of issues or an exchange of ideas
Talk show	Moderator interview with two to three experts, often with varying perspectives

Table 20.2: A Sample Conference Programme with Different Session Format and Instructional Style

Time	May 21(WED)	May 22(THU)	May23(FRI)
09:00 – 10:30		**Paper Session II**	
10:30 – 11:00		Refreshment Break and Poster Session II	
11:00 – 12:30	Registration	**Paper Session III** (Breakout Session including Panel Session)	
12:30 – 14:00		Luncheon (with keynote speaker)	
14:00 – 15:30	**Inaugural Plenary Session**	**Paper Session IV** (Breakout Session including Panel Session)	Optional Technical Visit (Tours)
15:30 – 16:00	Refreshment Break and Poster Session I	Refreshment Break and Poster Session III	
16:00 – 17:30	**Paper Session I** (Breakout Session)	**Paper Session V** (Breakout Session)	
17:30 – 18:00		Concluding Plenary Session	
18:00 – 19:30	Welcome Reception	Cultural Night with Dinner (19:00 ~ 21:30)	

20.3.3. Room Set-up

Roundtable Banquet

Classroom

U-shape

Boardroom

Hollow / Open square

Theatre

Banquet

Modified-Chevron/

Herringbone Cocktail

Activity

Label each of the items below with **A** and **B**.

A: Match the diagrams below with the different room set-up

B: Match the setting with the session format or instruction style

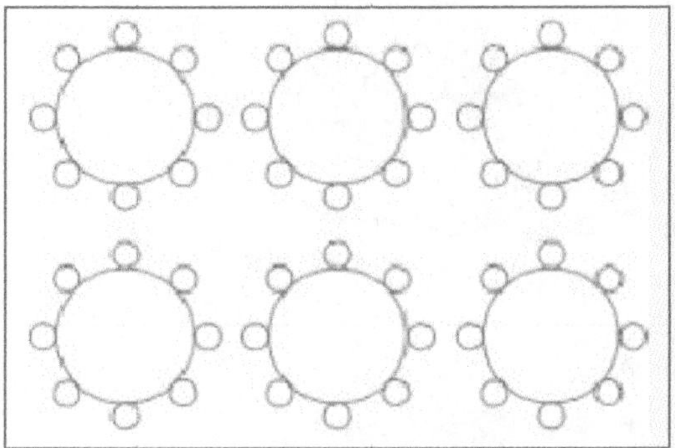

A:

B:

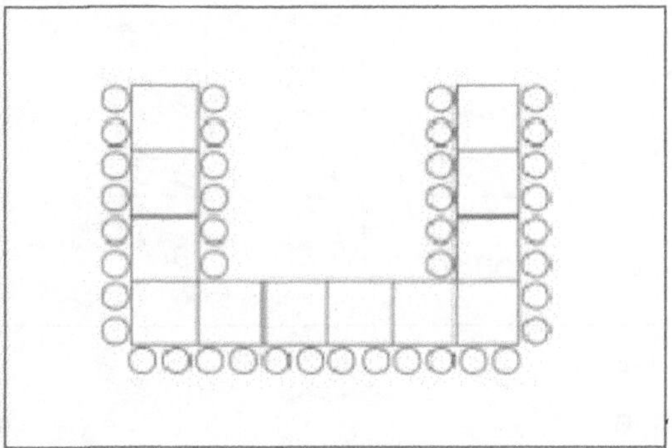

A:

B:

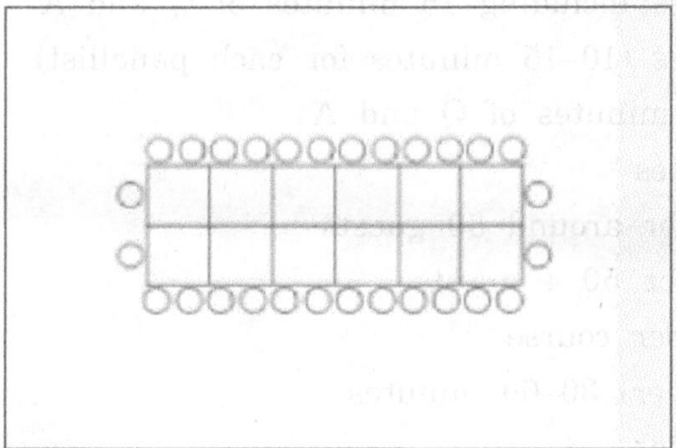

A:

B:

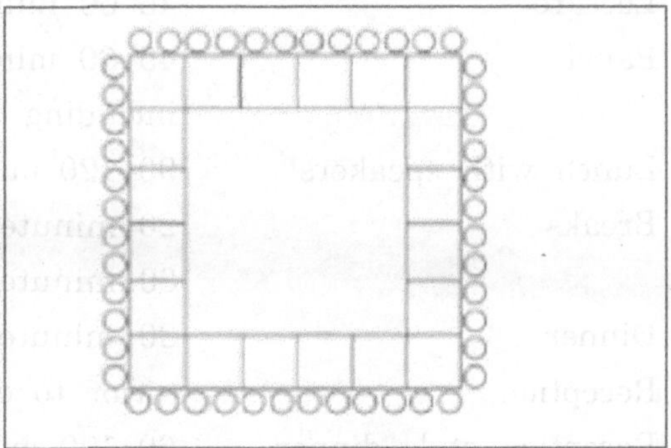

A:

B:

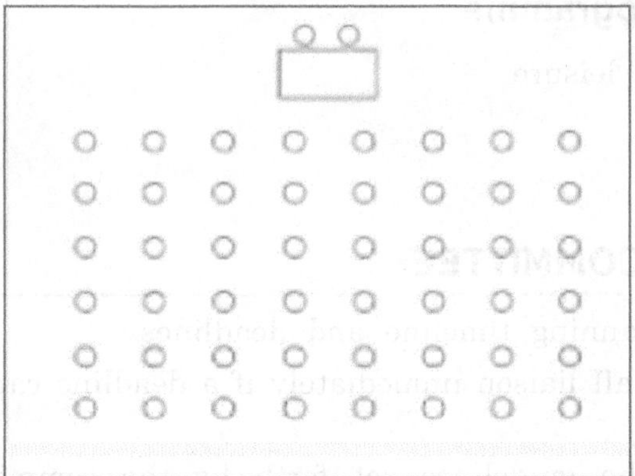

A:

B:

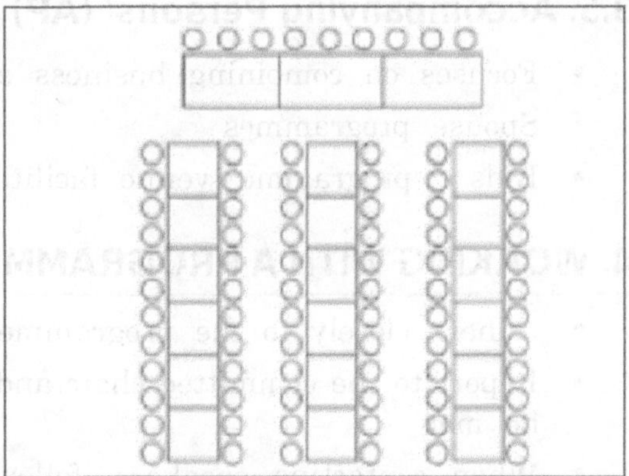

A:

B:

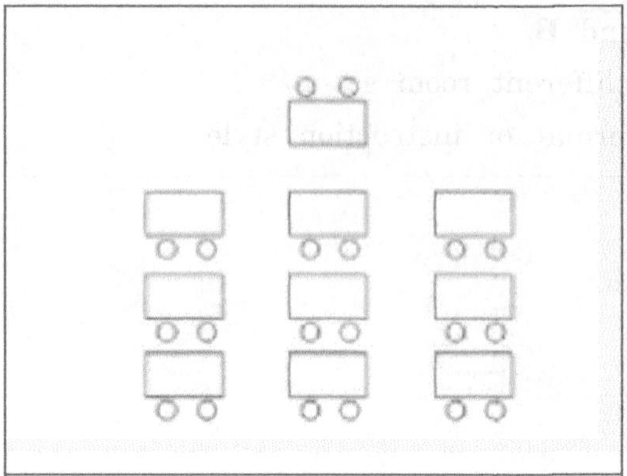

A:

B:

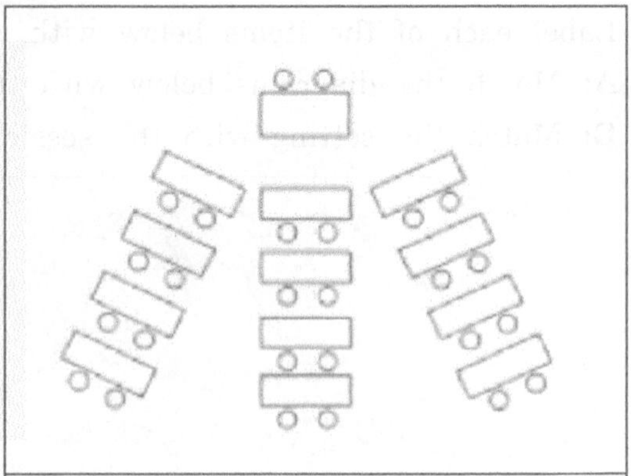

A:

B:

20.3.4. Session Timing

Lecture	45–60 minutes including 15 minutes of Q and A
Panel	45–60 minutes (10–15 minutes for each panellist) including 15 minutes of Q and A
Lunch with speakers	90–120 minutes
Breaks	20 minutes for around 50 guests 30 minutes for 50 + guests
Dinner	30 minutes per course
Reception	(prior to dinner) 30–60 minutes
Reception style dinner	60–120 minutes
Moving attendees	> 100 guests = 5 minutes; 100–500 guests = 10 minutes; 500–1,000 guests = 15 minutes

20.3.5. Accompanying Persons' (AP) Programme

- Focuses on combining business and leisure
- Spouse programmes
- Kids – programme, venue facilities

20.4. WORKING WITH A PROGRAMME COMMITTEE

- Adhere closely to the programme-planning timeline and deadlines
- Report to the committee chair and staff liaison immediately if a deadline cannot be met
- When contacting speakers, follow the guidelines set forth by the committee with respect to content and format expectations, fees, manuscripts and handouts

- Report immediately to the staff liaison and chairperson if the committee assignments are inappropriate or cannot be completed within the time frame allotted.

20.4.1. Speaker Arrangement

Most of the sessions at a MICE event require speakers to give a speech, from a paper presentation to a keynote address. To arrange speakers, event planners can work with the programme committee or work with other stakeholders to find suitable speakers. (See Figure 20.2.) Speaker bureaus are organizations that list a range of speakers, from professors to past presidents such as Bill Clinton, and their speaking fees.

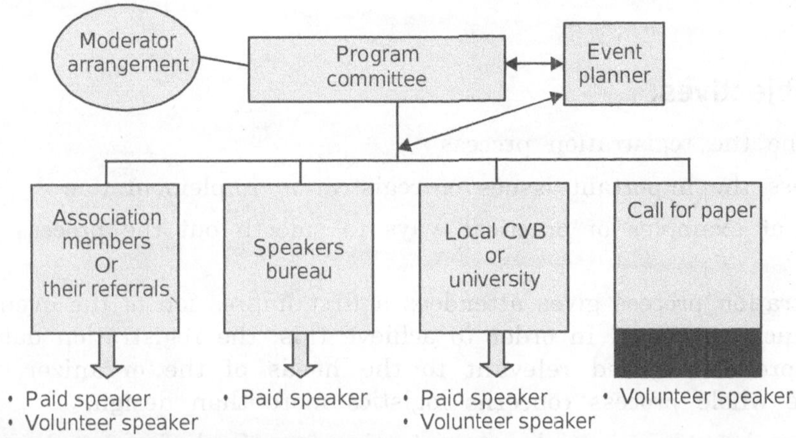

Figure 20.2: Speaker arrangement flow chart.

Activity

Think of the information and specific credentials you will need from your guest speakers and the relevant details and background information that the speakers will need to be briefed on.

CHAPTER 21

REGISTRATION

Learning Objectives:

- Outline the registration process
- Discuss the important issues of registration implementation
- Look at examples of practical ways to smooth out the process

The registration process gives attendees a first impression of the event. It therefore needs to be quick and easy. In order to achieve this, the registration data needs to be accurate, comprehensive and relevant to the needs of the organizer, sponsors and exhibitors. The whole process concerns logistics more than design.

The registration process involves registration fees. Such fees can be all-inclusive or allow a minimum fee with optional add-ons (*e.g.*, conference dinner, tours etc.). As a result, the planner needs to take payment collection and tracking into consideration.

21.1. ADVANCE REGISTRATION

Most of the MICE event can be registered in advance. The advantages of advance registration include:

- Simplifying on-site traffic
- Generating cash flow prior to the event
- An early indication of marketing strengths and weaknesses
- A guaranteed number of reserved tickets for special functions
- Allowing all materials to be ready for immediate and convenient pick-up at the event.

When processing advance registration, the following has to be clear:

- Who can register in advance
- Fee for each category (full member, student etc.)
- Materials and function attendance rights included in the fee
- Deadline for receipt of registration
- Policy for cheques, credit cards and other forms of payment

- Cancellation and refund policies
- On-site registration fees and location.

21.2. REGISTRATION TYPES

There are many methods of registration: mail, phone, fax and Internet (on-line). Registration methods and payment methods are interlinked. For mail registration, payment has to be settled by cheque. For fax/Internet registration, payment has to be settled by credit card. However, both cheque and credit card payments carry the risk of being rejected due to insufficient funds. Cheques take longer to clear but there is no risk of charge back. Both have processing charges that need to be considered. For instance, Visa cards may have a transaction fee of up to 3%.

21.2.1. Confirmation

Once the registration forms and fees are received, the attendees need to be confirmed. Initial confirmation should be immediate, with detailed follow-up within 48 hours. The confirmation should indicate event dates and times, fees paid, registration ID, on-site registration location and time, refund policies, as well as other useful information.

Registration forms:

- Can be either part of the brochure or a separate insert
- Include such details as:
  - ➢ Personal information
  - ➢ Registration fees and dates
  - ➢ Payment options
  - ➢ Cancellation and refund policies
  - ➢ Contact information
- The use of **bold** and *italics* should be reserved for important information only
- AVOID THE USE OF CAPITAL LETTERS
- Fill in blank spaces and offer alternatives
- Avoid applying a glossy finish – they are difficult to write on.

21.3. REGISTRATION INFORMATION

When processing a registration, the registrant will process the personal information of the attendees as well. Therefore, please bear in mind that:

- Data security and privacy protection are critical in conference registration
- Privacy laws in effect in many countries make organizers liable to legal action if attendee privacy is violated
- Registrants have to be aware of the use of their personal information and give consent to it
- Measures must be taken to ensure the safety of personal information
- The sale of registration lists to third parties is prohibited.

21.4. ON-SITE REGISTRATION

In general, 40% to 70% of attendees register early, with the remainder registering on site. On-site registration has to be as fast as possible to avoid long waits and queues. Each staff member with computer access needs to register 25 to 30 attendees on average per hour. In order to keep a smooth flow of traffic, the organizer needs to brief registration staff and plan a workable set-up for the registration site.

The common set-ups include:

Registration with a straight queue – Each desk handles a separate group of attendees. For example, one group might include attendees with surnames starting from A to E. This simple set-up is clear for attendees. However, each registration desk may not have an equal workload. Some lines may be crowded with too many people during peak periods. Media representatives,

VIPs and people with special needs also need to stand in the same queue to register.

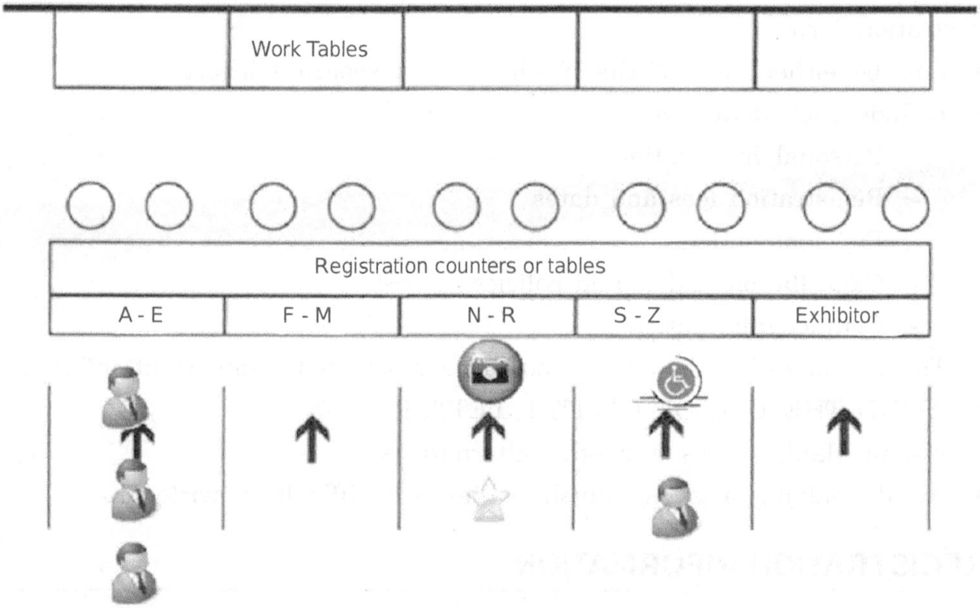

Figure 21.1: Registration with a Straight Queue.

Registration with a Serpentine Queue – All registration desks can handle any attendee on a first-come-first-serve basis. All attendees, including media representatives, VIPs and people with special needs, stand in one single queue in a serpentine format to save space. Each desk will share the same workload. Therefore, all registrant information will be distributed to and collected by all registration staff members with desks. However, the setting may not be convenient to everyone, particularly for those with special needs.

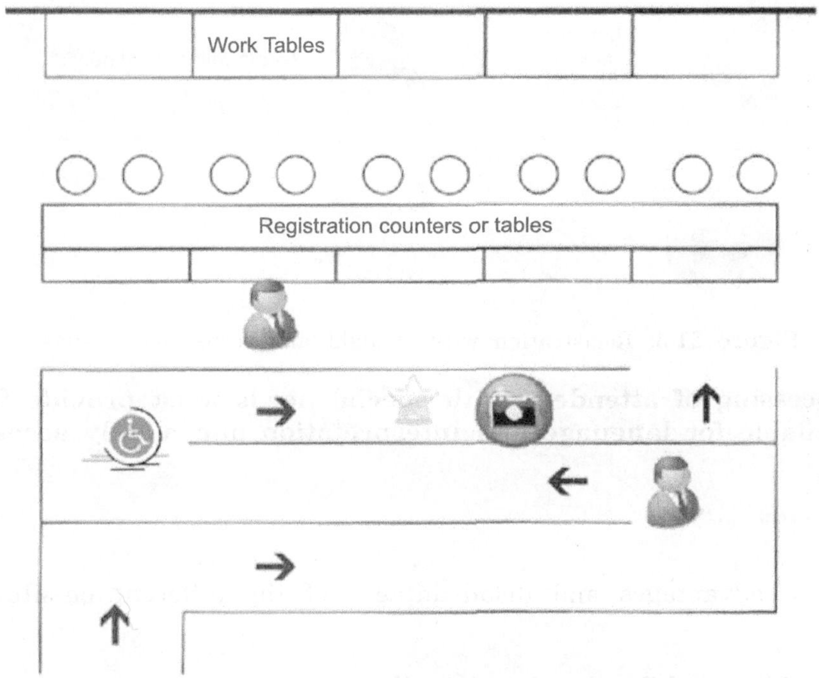

Figure 21.2: Registration with a Serpentine Queue.

Registration System with Both Straight and Serpentine Queue – This involves a mix of two queues: A straight queue for media representatives, VIPs and people with special needs; and a serpentine queue for regular attendees. In this way, attendees will be registered on a first-come-first-serve basis and occupy less space even during peak periods. VIPs and media representatives do not need to wait for too long a period. It is also more convenient for those with special needs.

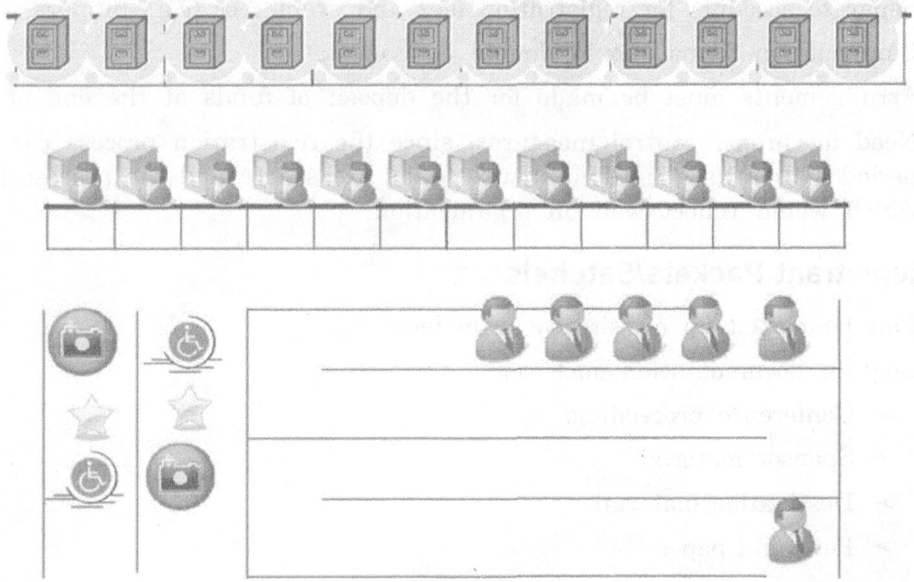

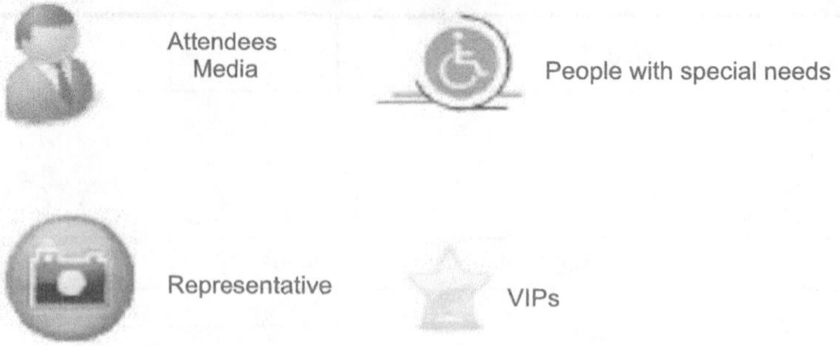

Figure 21.3: Registration with straight and serpentine queues.

TIP: Processing of attendees with special needs must provide for trained staff available for language and interpretation and a fully accessible area on site.

Activity

Discuss the advantages and disadvantages of the different on-site registration setups.

21.4.1. Advantages of On-line Registration

- Reduces the time required to register each attendee
- Allow for quick analysis of attendee trends
- Eliminates repetitive errors
- Cost involve are small through the use of software or website.

21.4.2. Payment Collection

- Separate accounts for registration fees and event fees (*e.g.*, dinners, receptions)
- Confirmation forms should double as receipts
- Arrangements must be made for the deposit of funds at the end of each day
- Need for proper control measures, since the registration process can be hectic period – there is a need to ensure funds are secure and the process is smooth, which would reflect well on organization.

21.4.3. Registrant Packets/Satchels

- Can be picked up on site by attendees
- Contain documentation such as:
    - ➢ Conference proceedings
    - ➢ Sponsor material
    - ➢ Destination material
    - ➢ Pens and paper

- Name badges and payment receipts are typically placed on separate tables
- Name badge:
  - ➢ Safety pin/clip/stick on/plastic pin/magnetic
  - ➢ Lanyard

Develop a Floor Plan that Includes

- Hospitality area
- Information
- Lost and found
- Messages
- On-site registration desk(s)
- Advance/pre-registration desk(s)
- Publications for display/sale
- Registration material storage/distribution
- Session/event tickets
- Transportation.

Items that Need to be Included

- Signage
- Tables
- Stanchions
- Kiosks
- Chairs
- Easels
- Telephones/Internet connection
- Computers and printers
- Entrance and exit paths.

CHAPTER 22

ON-SITE LOGISTICS

Learning Objectives:

- Examine the operation and understand importance of the pre-con, daily logistic meeting and the post-con
- Understand the key to on-site management

22.1. ON-SITE MANAGEMENT

Precise communication is critical. Therefore, three types of staff meetings need to be held in order to keep the communication flowing:

- Prior – This conveys precise expectations to all site facilities
- During – These are daily meetings to review logistics
- After – These are feedback forums from the various parties

22.1.1. Pre-Event Meeting

Prior to the event, all staff members need to be fully briefed on all activities at the event, their requirements and staff expectations. The **pre-con** is a meeting between the event staff and venue staff, along with the key staff of outside contractors. These include GM (for large conventions), event manager and staff, food and beverage department (banquets/catering), and AV – either in-house or contracted.

Depending on the specifics of the meeting, other staff may need to be present for part of the meeting. The pre-con reconfirms all written and verbal details, discusses arrangements, addresses any questions and resolves outstanding issues. It is typically held 24 hours before the event starts.

22.1.2. Daily Logistics Meeting

Each day, there will be a meeting for staff to confirm the event's daily logistics.

This is especially important for conventions incorporating multiple facilities. These meetings are attended by convention service, F and B and AV personnel from each hotel and venue. The purpose of these meetings is to inform everyone about the events of the day, cancellations or additions to the program, changes to F and B and A/V orders, and provide a review of previous activities while identifying areas of improvement.

22.1.3. Post-Event Meeting

Following a meeting with the event staff, a **post-con** is an arrangement for the event staff to meet with the venue staff and key staff of outside contractors. The purpose of this meeting is to solicit feedback in order to plan for future events with the venue and meeting team. This meeting will also detail services that were delivered well and then move on to discussing problem areas.

22.1.4. Wrap-Up

To conclude the event, the following tasks need to be completed after the event:

- Return rented equipment
- Store reusable signs and other supplies
- Settle bill payments (including the decision on tips and gratuities)
- Prepare financial reports
- Prepare thank you letters
- Analyze attendee and supplier feedback

Activity

Brainstorm what needs to be prepared for a post-con.

22.2. COMMUNICATION! COMMUNICATION! COMMUNICATION!

To smoothly manage the on-site operation, communication between event staff, the supply staff and the attendees is important. Below are a few reminders:

On-site Office Operation – There should be an office for event staff to congregate, access private phones, and store and retrieve event materials.

Staff identification is required to gain access to this office. Large conventions or exhibitions may require an additional:

- On-site office
- Offices for the event manager and staff
- A speaker-ready room
- A press/PR office

Information Kiosk and Message Centre – This can be combined with the lost and found area to save on space and for added convenience. It should be a physical location central to attendee traffic flow (for example, near the registration area). It should also be equipped with:

- Telephone and Fax
- Computer with on-line service
- Message pads and pens
- Local maps
- Restaurant guides

- General tourist info
- General event info

Signage (Temporary, Permanent and Electronic)

- Office and service areas
- Directional assistance
- Identification of function rooms
- Ground transportation vehicle and stops
- Sponsor related
- General event information

Communication Systems

Business equipment can be rented if not owned, or a "one-stop shopping" service contract can be negotiated. Equipment used may include:

- Telephones
- Fax machines
- On-line services
- Wireless communication
    - Pagers for staff
    - Walkie-talkies
    - Cell phones
    - Personal digital assistants (PDAs)

CHAPTER 23

RISK MANAGEMENT

Learning Objectives:

- Understand the steps to risk management
- Identify the main areas of risks
- Work out an emergency plan

Risk management is the process of foreseeing, preventing or minimizing potential costs, losses or problems for the event, organization, partners and attendees.

23.1. NINE STEPS TO RISK MANAGEMENT

1. UNDERSTAND CONTEXT: Consider event type, management, stakeholders and general environment
2. IDENTIFYING RISKS: Look for the hazards
3. DECISION: Decide who might be harmed and how
4. EVALUATING THE RISK: Evaluate the risks and decide whether the existing precautions are adequate or whether more should be done
5. CONTROL: Control problems that may arise
6. MITIGATING ACTIONS: Consider action that can minimize impacts
7. SPECIFIC EVEN RISKS: Consider risk details
8. RECORDING: Record your findings
9. REVIEW: Review your assessment and revise it if necessary

23.2. MAIN AREAS OF RISK

- **Administrative:** Organizational structure and office layout should minimize risk to employee
- **Marketing and public relations:** The promotion and image of the event
- **Health and safety:** Risks associated with food hygiene and sanitation. Accidents, health problems, fire, social disturbances and anticipated emergencies
- **Crowd Management:** Crowd flow, alcohol sales and noise control
- **Security:** Crime and terrorism
- **Transport:** Deliveries, parking and public transport carry many potential hazards
- **Financial:** Loss of revenue sources, theft and loss of assets; costs that exceed projections; litigation and unanticipated costs
- **Management:** Goal displacement, takeovers or management failure
- **Environmental:** Causing a negative impact on the environment, community and economy; natural hazards (earthquakes, floods etc)

23.2.1. Types of Common Emergencies

- Medical emergencies
- Demonstrations and confrontations
- Severe weather
- Strikes
- Fire
- Bomb threats or terrorist activity
- Mechanical problems
- Speaker cancellation
- Meeting supplies delayed in transit
- System failure
- Transportation breakdowns

23.2.2. Set up an Emergency Plan

To draw up an emergency plan, the planner can start by completing a vulnerary assessment form (see Table 20.2 for an example). By looking at each type of emergency and its possible impact on the event (the lower the score the better), the planner can consider the probability of the emergency and plan countermeasures for each of them accordingly. The planner will then use that item to draft an emergency plan in order to work out the details. (See Table 23.1)

The **lower** the score the better

Table 23.1: Sample Vulnerary Assessment

Vulnerary assessment form

Type of Emergency	Probability	Human Impact	Property Impact	Business Impact	Internal Resources	External Resources	TOTAL
	High 5<->1 Low	High Impact 5 <--->1 Low Impact			Week 5<->1 Strong Resources		
Mechanical problems	2	1	2	1	1	1	8
Guest speaker cancellation	3	1	1	3	1	1	10
Fire	2	5	5	5	1	1	19
……							

Emergency Plan

Table 23.2: Sample Emergency Plan

Type of Emergency	What can happen	Procedure to be followed	Who is Responsible	Outside Contact	Insurance	Public Relations Response (Media)
Mechanical problems	Breakdown of on-site equipment	Prior detailed inspection, back-up equipment	On-site programme co-ordinator	Venue duty manager	Insurance policy set up with venue	Public relations team to follow up with press release
Guest speaker cancellation	Speaker is absent	Show video tape or arrange for back up speaker with schedule	Programme co-ordinator	Speaker's agent or representative	Not applicable	Public relations team to follow up with press release
Fire	Evacuation and event cancellation	Wait for fire fighters, aid in rescue efforts, inform participants	On-site Programme co-ordinator, first-aid team	Police and fire department, venue security department and duty manager	Insurance policy set up with venue and with individual organization	Public relations team to answer questions from reporters and media

- The **outside contact,** such as police or firemen, does not work for the organization but works with the MICE event

- **Insurance** options should be arranged and the contact of an insurance agent should be listed
- A contact person to handle the **media** should be listed

Activity

Use the below case of Ministerial Conference to set up an emergency plan. First, fill in the vulnerary assessment form above and calculate the risk to the event. Then, copy the column, "Type of Emergency," to your emergency plan and work through each column.

Vulnerary Assessment form

Types of emergency	Probability	Human Impact	Property Impact	Business Impact	Internal Resources	External Resources	Total
	High 5<->1 Low High Impact 5 <--->1 Low Impact Week 5<->1 Strong Resources						

Emergency Plan

Type of Emergency	What can happen	Procedure to be followed	Who is Responsible	Outside Contact	Insurance	Public Relations Response (Media)

CHAPTER 24

MARKETING

Learning Objectives:

- Understand event information sources
- Identify popular promotional tools for MICE events
- Work out how to increase publicity for a MICE event

When promoting an event, the planner may want to consider what resources are available. The planner can then identify and capitalize on the existing strengths of the event. Typically, it will be easier to promote the event when there is a:

- Strong event history
- A good geographical cluster of members
- Loyal membership
- An energetic event committee
- Strong government support
- Financial reserves
- Good communication tools

24.1. EVENT INFORMATION SOURCES

Usually, attendees may learn about the event from:

- Event Publicity
- Friends and colleagues
- Prior events
- Professional trade journals
- Posters

24.2. PROMOTIONAL TOOLS

Typical promotional tools include:

- Direct Mail
- Advertising

- E-Marketing
- Publicity
- Sales Promotion
- Promotional trips/convention attendance building
- Others — Posters, Stickers and Banners

24.2.1. Direct Mailing

Direct mail includes postcards, brochures, exhibitor prospectus, event invitations, promotional flyers and personalized letters posted directly to potential attendees. However, the success ratio is often quite low. The percentage of returned mail to "lost mail" depends on the accuracy and size of the mailing lists. The organizer needs to monitor the return and success rate in order to understand how many people they are actually reaching. Bulk mail is cheaper but more time consuming as addresses need to be sorted.

24.2.1.1. Number of Direct Mailings

Preliminary, first, second and third announcements are required to inform, attract and remind attendees. The mailing lists are often sourced from international associations, in-house lists or purchased lists. Three or more notices may need to be sent out, depending on the:

- Importance of the event
- The number of prospects
- Status of the recipients
- Mail screening process
- Worthwhile additional information
- The program's complexity
- Price/profit per attendee
- Competition

24.2.2. Advertising

Advertising is designed to inform, persuade, remind, add value and otherwise attract potential attendees who fit into the event's target market. It is not used a lot in the promotion of meetings because of the costs involved. Options include:

- Print (magazines, newspapers, trade journals)
- Broadcast (network TV, cable, radio)
- Electronic (Website banner ads, blogs and sponsored e-mail messages)
- Outdoor signage (billboards, bus boards, building banners)

24.2.2.1. Advertisements

Mass media advertising costs more and may not guarantee dollar-for-dollar returns compared with direct mailing. It is useful in gaining exposure or prestige for the event. However, it is not justified unless the event is public.

Crucial success factors depend on:

- The size and impact of the advertisement
- Visual effects
- Copy
- Media considerations – cost, prime-time, premium coverage, readership/viewer profile, circulation/audience size.

24.2.3. E-Marketing

E-marketing has become increasingly popular due to its cost-effectiveness.

However, planners need to consider the target audience's access to fax/e-mail/Internet. The key is to reach the right people with the right message. Keep in mind that e-mails can be forwarded to others. They can also be expanded to include on-line questionnaires and surveys.

24.2.4. Publicity

Publicity is a marketing tool that involves the public relations arm of marketing. It includes **press releases**/coverage/editorial/advertorial. Press releases should be newsworthy and sent to all major press, trade journals and associations. A **press kit,** which includes letters, media release, fact sheet, brochures, graphic standards, tickets and posters (if applicable), should be prepared and distributed to journalists and reporters. **Public relations** is the organization's ongoing interaction with the media before, during and after the meeting event.

Activity

Think of how you can stir up news for an event and when. Try creative methods.

> ***Press Room***
>
> **Typically at larger events, a press room, set up on site, will include work areas with phone lines, fax machines, copiers and Internet connection, as well as refreshments. A separate area within the press room can be used for interviews and press conferences. Usually, the room is large enough to accommodate an area for public speaking. Press kits containing newsworthy material on the various sessions, speakers, products or services should be made available in advance and in the press room.**

CHAPTER 25

EVALUATION

Learning Objectives:

- Explain the evaluation methods
- Identify evaluation planning issues
- Understand the suitable tools and timing for evaluation

25.1. WHAT IS AN EVALUATION?

An evaluation is the systematic process of placing a value on an event. It often employs quantitative measures and techniques. It is a process of critically observing, measuring and monitoring the implementation of an event to accurately assess its outcome. Feedback on an event, its application and its results come from a variety of sources and are gathered through numerous data collection methods. It is essential to report the evaluation results to key stakeholders.

25.2. WHY EVALUATE?

You evaluate in order to:

- Identify and solve problems
- Find ways to improve event management
- Determine the value of the event and its programs
- Measure successes or failures
- Identify costs and benefits
- Identify and measure impact
- Satisfy the sponsors and authorities
- Gain acceptance/credibility/support for future events
- Determine the meeting's success in accomplishing its objectives
- Identify the strengths and weakness in event management and its design process
- Compare the meeting costs with their benefits
- Decide on who should participate in future meetings

- Identify which participants most appreciated and gained the most from the meeting content
- Reinforce the major points made to the participants
- Gather data to assist in marketing future meetings
- Determine if the meeting was the appropriate solution for that specific need.

25.3. EVALUATION PLANNING

When planning for an evaluation, the following questions should be asked:

- What is the purpose of the evaluation?
- What data will be collected?
- What are the levels of evaluation? (Data can be collected at one or more levels of evaluation)
- When will the data be collected?
- How will the data be collected?
- Who will collect the data?
- Who will analyze the data?
- Who will use the data?

25.3.1. Needs Assessment for Evaluation (10 steps)

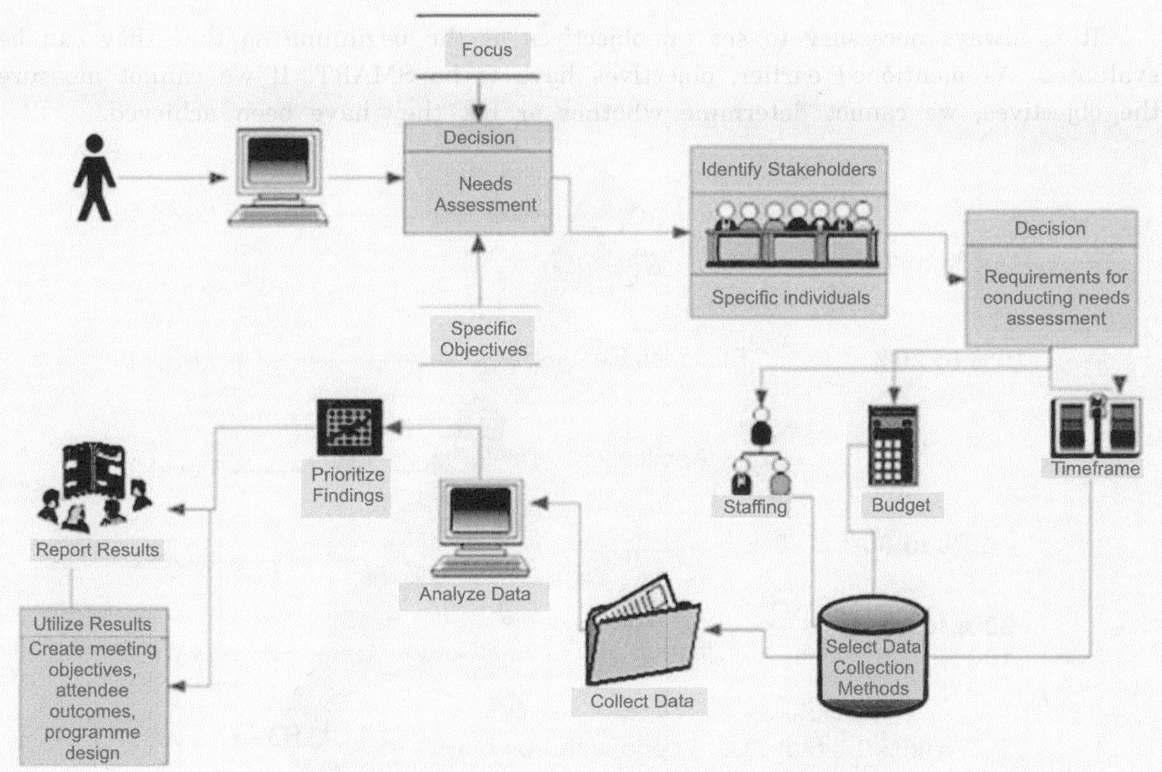

Figure 25.1: Flow chart of Assessing Needs.

High-profile and costly meetings may require a thorough assessment of needs, while for other types of meetings, a needs assessment every two to three years might be sufficient. The ten steps to follow in conducting a needs assessment are:

1. Deciding to complete a needs assessment;
2. Developing a focus and outlining specific objectives of the needs assessment;
3. Identifying the meeting stakeholders and specific individuals to be involved;
4. Determining the time frame, budget and staffing required in conducting the needs assessment;
5. Selecting the data collection methods;
6. Collecting the data;
7. Analyzing the data;
8. Prioritizing the findings;
9. Reporting the results;
10. Using the results to create meeting objectives, attendee outcomes and aid in programme design.

25.3.2. Six Level of Objectives and Measurements

It is always necessary to set up objectives at the beginning so that they can be evaluated. As mentioned earlier, objectives have to be SMART. If we cannot measure the objectives, we cannot determine whether or not they have been achieved.

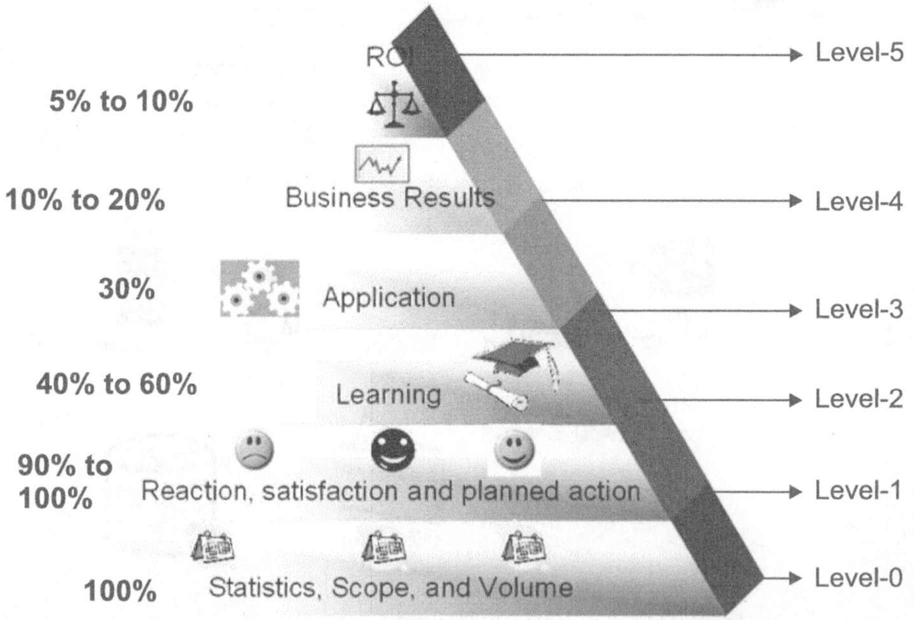

Figure 25.2: Six levels of objectives and how often they are used (Adapted from PCMA 2006).

Level 0 – Statistics, Scope, and Volume

Measures meeting statistics as well as the scope and volume of meeting attendance, press coverage, budgetary measures and so on. This level of objectives can be measured before, during and after the event.

Example Objectives:

- Attain 500 paid attendees at $795 per attendee
- Generate $200,000 in net profit from the annual conference
- Sell 200 trade show booths at $2,000 each by Nov. 1.

Level 1 – Reaction, Satisfaction and Planned Action

Measures participant satisfaction with the meeting and records the participant's planned actions. Monitoring and post-event evaluation can help measure objectives at this level.

Example Objectives

- Over 80% of attendees would recommend the conference to others
- Attendees would rate the hotel experience and food and beverage at an average of 4.3 or above out of 5.0
- Over 80% of attendees will indicate an intention to use new the sales strategies within two months after corporate training.

Level 2 – Learning

Measures changes in knowledge, skills, attitudes and professional contacts that resulted from the meeting. Monitoring and post-event evaluations can measure the objectives at this level.

Example Objectives

- Participants successfully demonstrate negotiation techniques when role playing at training workshops
- Score of over 75 out of 100 on new sales strategy quiz administered at the end of the sales meeting.

Level 3 – Application

Measures changes in behaviour following the meeting. Monitoring and post-event evaluation can measure objectives at this level.

Example Objectives

- Participants use new customer interaction skills in 90% of relevant situations within three months of training
- 75% of the action plan (developed during the meeting) was achieved within three months after the retreat.

Level 4 - Business Results

Measures changes in business impact. Post-event evaluation can measure objectives at this level.

Example Objectives:

- Increase sales from existing customers by 5% within nine months of the managerial meeting
- Save one or more hours a week on routine administrative tasks within three months of the training seminar
- Attain 20 new association members within nine months of the strategic meeting.

Level 5 - Return on Investment (ROI)

Compares benefits with meeting costs. This level of objectives needs to be measured before, during and after the event.

Example Objectives

- Achieve a 25% return on investment within 12 months of the meeting.
- Attain a 2:1 BCR on the meeting within 12 months (that is, for each dollar spent on the meeting or event, $2 was generated).

25.4. WHEN TO EVALUATE?

Pre-event assessment – before the event:

- Formative – undertaken during feasibility studies; include needs assessments, learning about tourist and resident markets, creating the product

Monitoring the event – during the event:

- Process evaluation – evaluates whether the plan has been implemented as planned

Post-event evaluation – after the event:

- Outcome evaluations are conducted after the event to evaluate its impact and overall value.

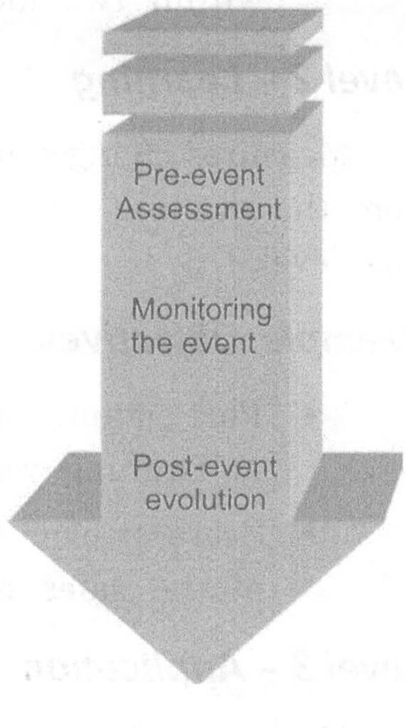

25.4.1. Types of Research

- Secondary research
- Research reports from previous events
- Research bureaus
- Web searches
- Journal databases
- Primary research
- Data collection
- Staff observations

- Stakeholder observations
- Debriefing meetings
- Questionnaires and surveys
- Other evaluation methods
  - ➢ Group evaluation
  - ➢ Chairman's overview
  - ➢ Reports by functional managers
  - ➢ A SWOT analysis conducted by the group
  - ➢ Identification of implications and priorities
  - ➢ Formulation of action plans.

Activity

Matching Exercise

- Which research methods can be used at each stage
  - ➢ Pre-event
  - ➢ Event-monitoring
  - ➢ Post-event

25.4.2. Data Source

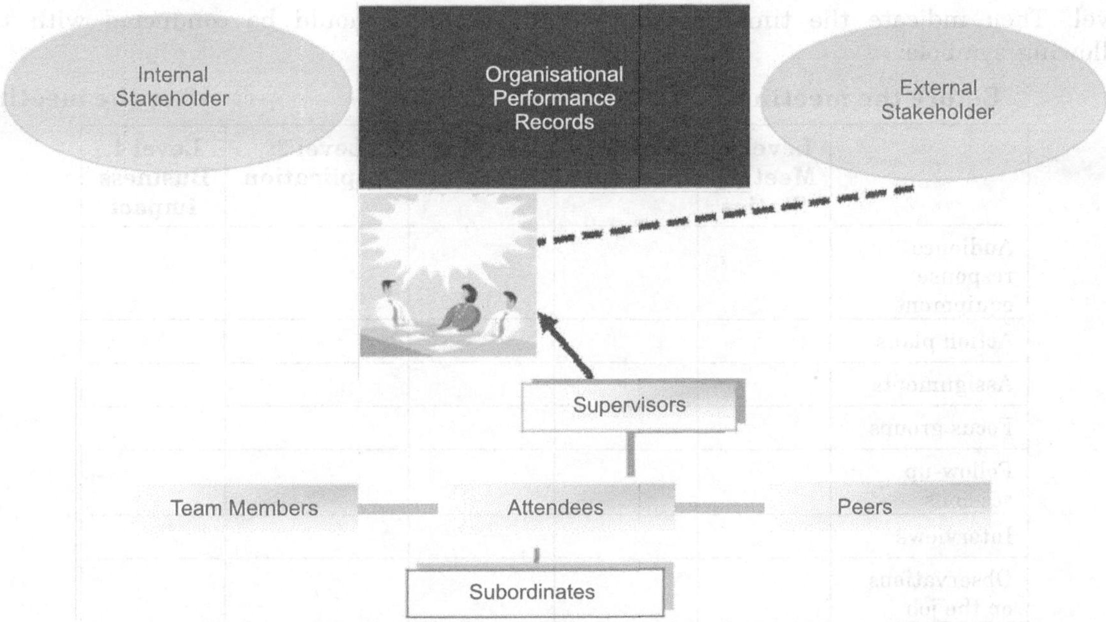

Figure 25.3: Data Source.

Since most MICE events have an educational purpose, there are different methods of collecting data for the event.

25.4.3. Data Collection Methods

- **Audience response equipment**
- **Action plans:** Developed at the meeting and implemented afterward.

It reflects the benefits gained by attendees from the meeting, including a report on attendee successes.

- **Assignments**
- **Focus groups:** Are small group interviews with a facilitator.
- **Follow-up sessions:** Are sessions after the event to discuss additional information about the event.
- **Interviews**
- **Observations on the job:** Evaluates whether attendees are applying what they learned from the event.
- **Performance contracts:** Developed before the event after the attendees and their supervisors agree on certain outcomes.
- **Performance records monitoring:** Examines the attendee operational data and performance.
- **Questionnaires:** A set of questions given to attendees via Internet, telephone or in survey format.
- **Tests**

Activity

Decide which data collection method would be suitable for measuring which objective level. Then indicate the time in which such research should be conducted with the following symbols:

☺ **Before the meeting** ☺ **During the meeting** ☺ **After the meeting**

	Level 0: Meeting Statics	**Level 1: Reaction**	**Level 2: Learning**	**Level 3: Application**	**Level 4: Business Impact**
Audience response equipment					
Action plans					
Assignments					
Focus groups					
Follow-up sessions					
Interviews					
Observations on the job					
Performance contracting					
Performance records monitoring					
Questionnaires					
Tests					

An Evaluation Example

2013 Medical Tourism Congress

Feedback Questionnaire

Thank you for participating at the 2013 Medical Tourism Congress. To assist us in making future conferences more useful to you, we would appreciate it if you would complete this evaluation form and return it at the registration counter.

Is this your first Medical Tourism Congress?

☐ Yes ☐ No

How did you learn about this conference?

☐ XXX website ☐ Association

☐ Colleague/Friend ☐ University

☐ Journals/Magazine ☐ Others ________________

Overall Congress	Strongly Agree	Agree	Neutra l	Distance	Strongly Distance
• The congress provided many networking opportunities	5	4	3	2	1
• The congress provided opportunities to exchange ideas and experiences with delegates	5	4	3	2	1
• The congress programme was well organized	5	4	3	2	1
• The information gained from the congress is valuable	5	4	3	2	1
• The congress theme and topics really interested and inspired me	5	4	3	2	1
• The speakers and Presenters communicated their topics effectively	5	4	3	2	1
• The speakers are knowledgeable in their respective area	5	4	3	2	1
• The local representatives were professional and helpful	5	4	3	2	1
• My time at the congress was well spent	5	4	3	2	1
• Given a choice, I would attend the next World Congress	5	4	3	2	1

(Page 1 of the example)

Which topic and/or speaker impress you most? Please list all of them

____

____

____

Congress Dinner (if Applicable)	Strongly Agree	Agree	Neutral	Disagree	Strongly Disagree
• Venue of Congress dinner was well selected	5	4	3	2	1
• Food arrangement was appropriate	5	4	3	2	1
• The rundown was conducted smoothly and efficiently	5	4	3	2	1
• The program was impressive and entertaining	5	4	3	2	1

Agency Visit (if Applicable)	Strongly Agree	Agree	Neutral	Disagree	Strongly Disagree
• The visit was well-organized	5	4	3	2	1
• The visit was Informative and relevant to my area of work	5	4	3	2	1
• The duration of visit was appropriate	5	4	3	2	1
• The program was Impressive and entertaining	5	4	3	2	1

Comments and Suggestions

Please give us your comments and suggestions that help us improve future congress.

____

____

____

____

Thank you for taking the time to complete this evaluation. Your feedback is invaluable.

(page 2 of the example)

25.5. REPORTING THE RESULTS

Key issues to be considered:

- Determine the most effective format to reach different stakeholders/readers in order to increase the likelihood that they will be read
- Results can be shared face to face, through memos, newsletters, company Intranet, e-mail blasts or articles
- Negative or average results?
  - ➢ Use them as an opportunity to recommend changes for future meetings
- Use the results as a chance to demonstrate critical thinking.

Table 25.1: Reasons for Sharing Results Evaluation

Target Audience for Results Evaluation	**Reasons for Sharing Results**
Top executives and organizational leadership	Secure approval for the meeting, build credibility for the meeting staff and stimulate interest in the meetings
Attendee supervisors	Gain support for the meeting and enhance reinforcement of the meeting's content
Participants All employees or	Increase the effectiveness of future meetings Demonstrate accountability for expenditures association members
Prospective meeting attendees and association members	Use as a marketing tool for future meetings

CHAPTER 26

TRENDS

Learning Objectives:

- Look at the latest statistics for global MICE
- Identify trends in MICE
- Work out an emergency plan

26.1. WHERE MICE EVENT MANAGEMENT IS HEADING

- Understand the specific purpose behind every meeting and event
- Design every aspect of a meeting or event to reflect and respect the participants' varying learning styles and requirements
- Maximize participants' pre-event and on-site experience to stimulate their interest in learning
- Organize venues and deliver services in ways that better meet the strategic and educational objectives behind an event.

26.2. STATISTICS

26.2.1. Number of International Convention Per Continent

- Meetings in Europe dropped from 61% in 2003 to 59% in 2004, to 58% in 2005, and to 57% in 2006
- Asia's market share remained stable at 18%
- North America's market share also remained stable at 11%
- Latin America's market share again grew 1% to 8%.

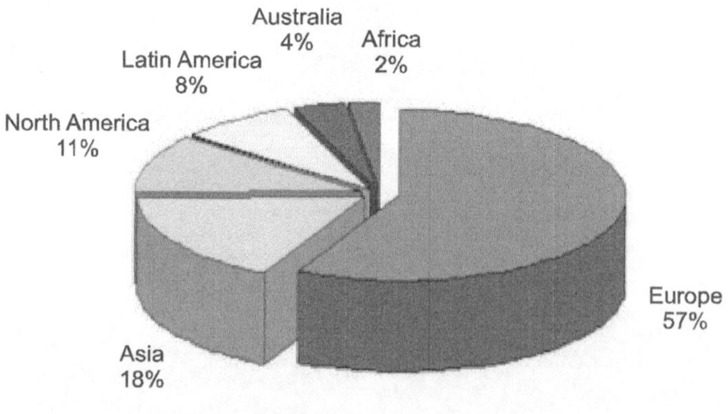

Source: ICCA 2007

Figure 26.1: Percentage of international conventions.

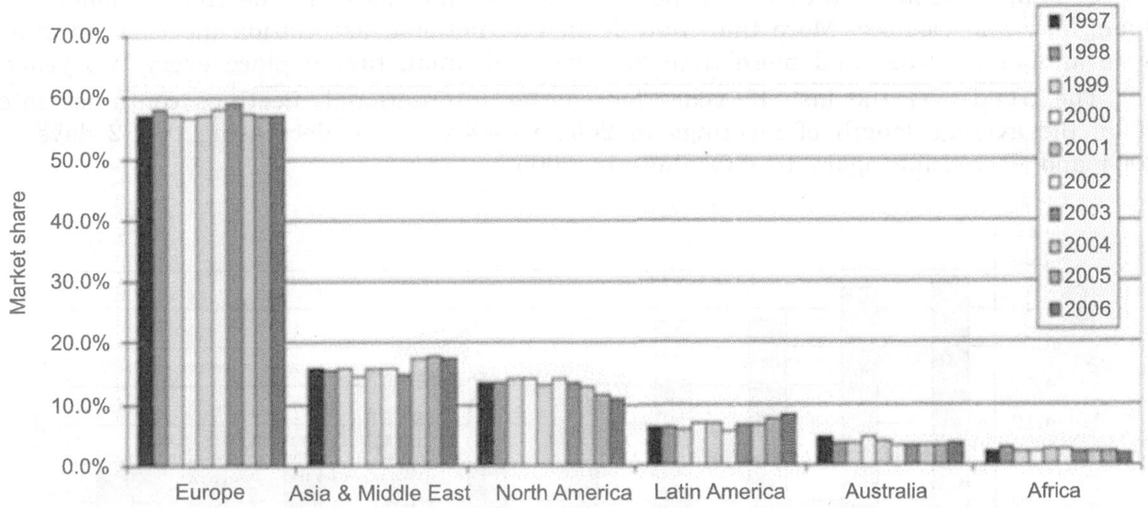

(*Source: ICCA 2007*).

Figure 26.2: Number of international conventions per continent (1997–2006).

26.2.2. Number of International Conventions Per Country

- In 2004 and 2005, the United States and Germany ranked first and second, respectively, in 2006
- U.K. now ranks third, with France following at fourth.
- The U.K. and France both climbed one place compared with their 2005 rankings at the cost of Spain
- For the first time, a Latin American country is represented in the top 10, with Brazil taking seventh place in 2006.
- Austria and Australia have swapped places and are ranked eighth and ninth, respectively.

26.2.3. Seasonality

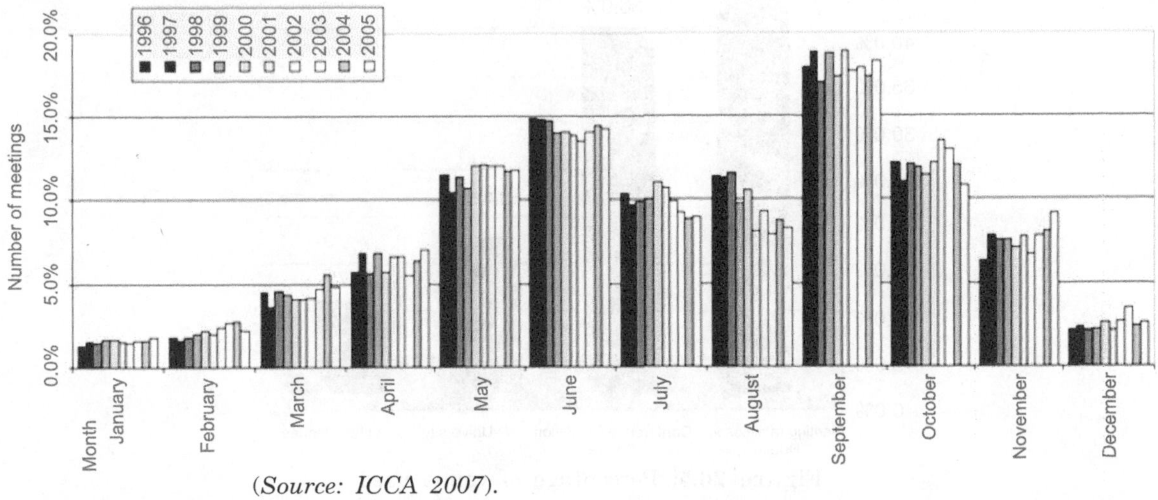

(*Source: ICCA 2007*).

Figure 26.3: International Conventions held in different months.

September remains the most popular month for international meetings, followed by June, May and October. More than half of all international association meetings in 2005 were annual meetings and more than 20% were biennial, taking place every two years.

The trend over the last 15 years for shorter international meetings continues into 2005; the average length of meetings in 2003 was 4.27 days, decreasing to 4.2 days in 2004 and decreasing again to 4.08 days in 2005.

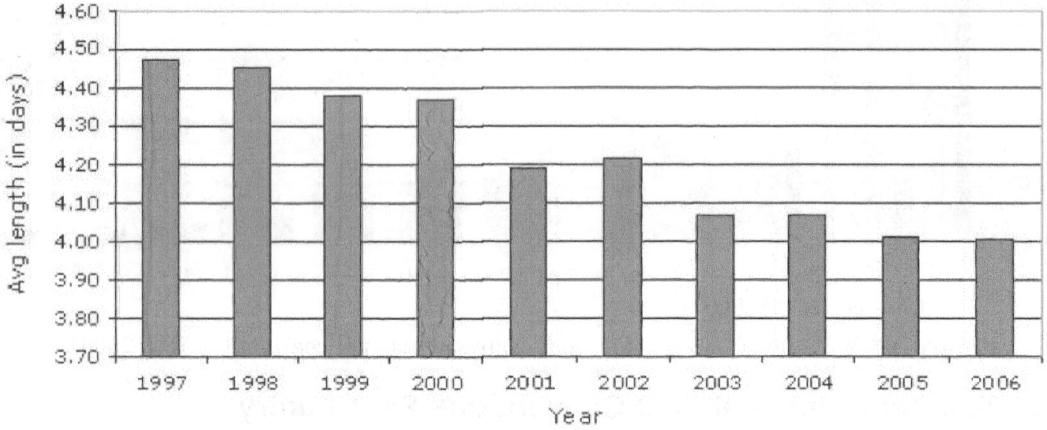

Figure 26.4: Average length of stay for international conventions.
Source: ICCA 2007.

26.2.4. Convention Venue Used

In 2005 and 2006, hotel meeting facilities have taken over from conferences and exhibition centres as the most popular type of venue to organize an event. The use of conference and exhibition centres dropped further in 2006 by 2% and the use of hotel facilities rose by 0.8% to a record 40.9%. The use of universities as congress venues has also risen (1.5%). Other venues include castles, boats etc.

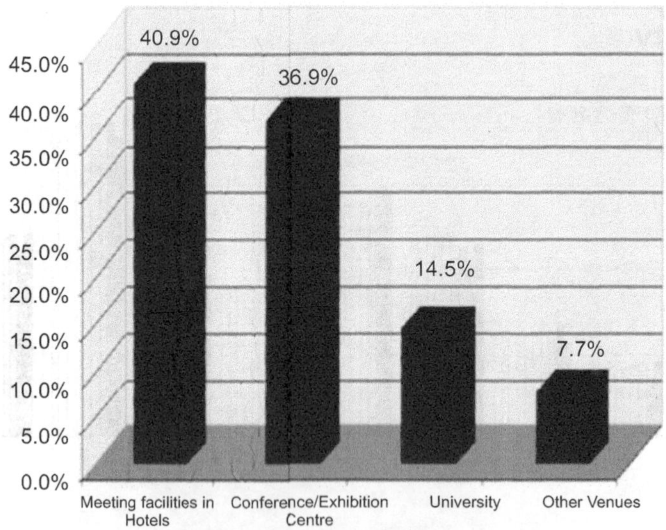

Figure 26.5: Percentage of venue used.
Source: ICCA 2006.

26.3. THE INDUSTRY IN INDIA

According to the ICPB, direct expenditures by event organizers reached $1.4 billion in 2006 (See Figure 26.7 for percentage of the expenditures) and direct expenditure by convention and exhibition visitors climbed to $8.2 billion (also See Figure 26.8 for percentage of expenditures).

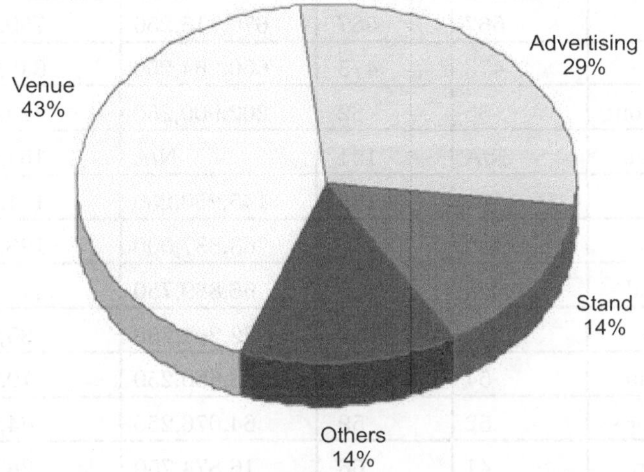

Figure 26.6: Direct expenditure by event organizers 2010.

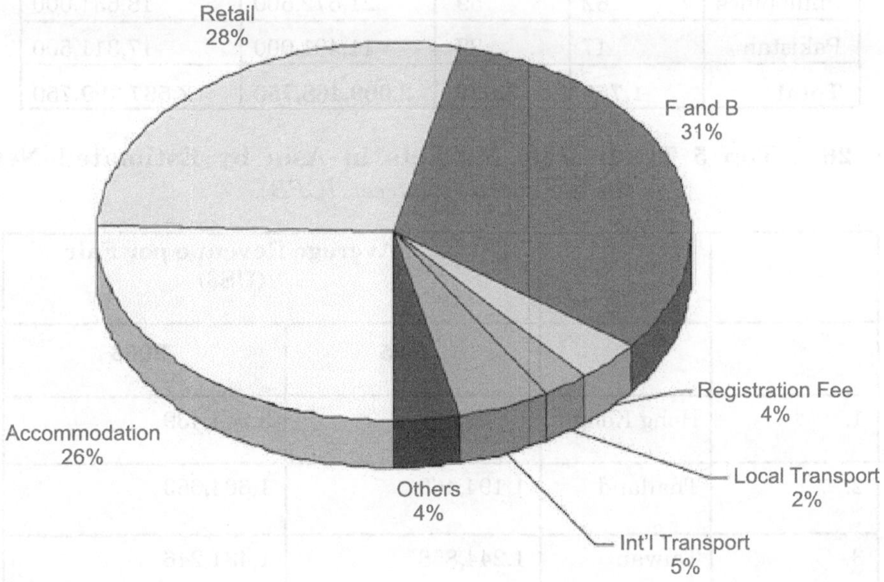

Figure 26.7: Direct expenditure by convention and exhibition visitors 2010.

Trade fair markets in Asia by estimated revenue also reported an increase (See Table 26.1). India remains at the top of the trade fair market; although it does not have the largest convention and exhibition centre in Asia (See Tables 26.2 and 26.3).

Table 26.1: Trade Fair Markets in Asia by Estimated Revenue. (*Source: ICPB*).

	No. of Exhibitions		Estimated Annualised Revenues (US$)	
	2005	**2006**	**2005**	**2006**
China	567	587	670,715,250	759,823,000
Japan	473	475	600,264,250	648,069,250
Hong Kong	55	82	202,900,250	323,444,000
Australia	N/A	151	N/A	154,600,250
Korea	139	140	145,250,250	131,792,500
India	130	158	63,887,000	128,437,750
Thailand	56	69	66,889,750	110,721,750
Taiwan	58	60	72,201,750	85,874,750
Malaysia	54	57	38,680,250	70,907,750
Singapore	52	59	64,076,250	64,023,750
Vietnam	41	56	16,874,750	28,260,500
Indonesia	55	54	34,755,500	25,502,000
Philippines	62	59	21,572,500	18,631,000
Pakistan	17	32	11,401,000	17,311,500
Total	**1,759**	**2,039**	**2,009,468,750**	**2,567,399,750**

Table 26.2: Top 5 Trade Fair Markets in Asia by Estimated Net Square Metre Sold (*Source: ICPB*).

		Average Revenue per Fair (US$)	
		2005	**2006**
1.	Hong Kong	3,689,095	3,944,439
2.	Thailand	1,194,460	1,604,663
3.	Taiwan	1,244,858	1,431,246
4.	Japan	1,269,058	1,364,356
5.	China	1,182,919	1,294,417

Table 26.3: Number and Size of International Conventions and Exhibition Centres in Asia

	Number of Centres		Total Gross Indoor Size in m^2	
	2006	**2007**	**2006**	**2007**
China	61	66	2,313,506	2,423,984
Japan	12	12	362,403	404,834
India	11	11	253,123	244,353
Thailand	4	5	191,322	199,122
Korea	5	10	135,533	166,493
Hong Kong	3	3	132,440	132,440
Singapore	2	2	124,000	124,000
Australia	N/A	7	N/A	107,913
Taiwan	2	3	47,710	95,868
Macau	N/A	2	N/A	76,714
Malaysia	3	3	49,244	58,954
Pakistan	1	2	6,690	30,690
Indonesia	2	3	11,610	29,712
Vietnam	1	2	7,134	15,904
Philippines	1	1	8,300	8,300
Total	**109**	**131**	**3,643,015**	**4,110,981**

Activity 1

Describe India's ranking within the international exhibition market, based on the above statistics.

Activity 2

Based on the following figures, find out the following about India's MICE sector:

- Number of exhibitions
- Number of convention
- Number of arrivals per convention and exhibition
- Percentage of attendees from China

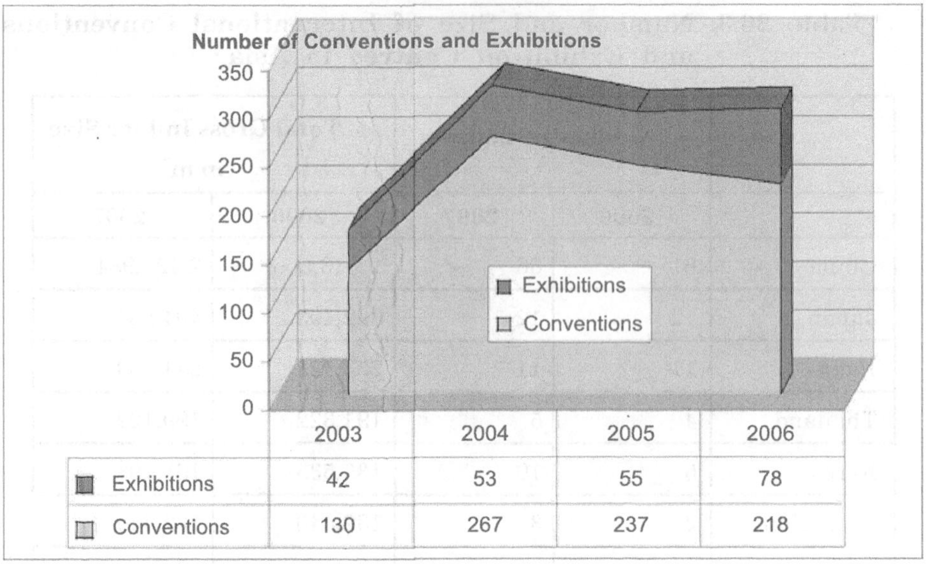

Figure 26.8: Number of conventions and exhibitions (2003–2006). (*Source: ICPB*).

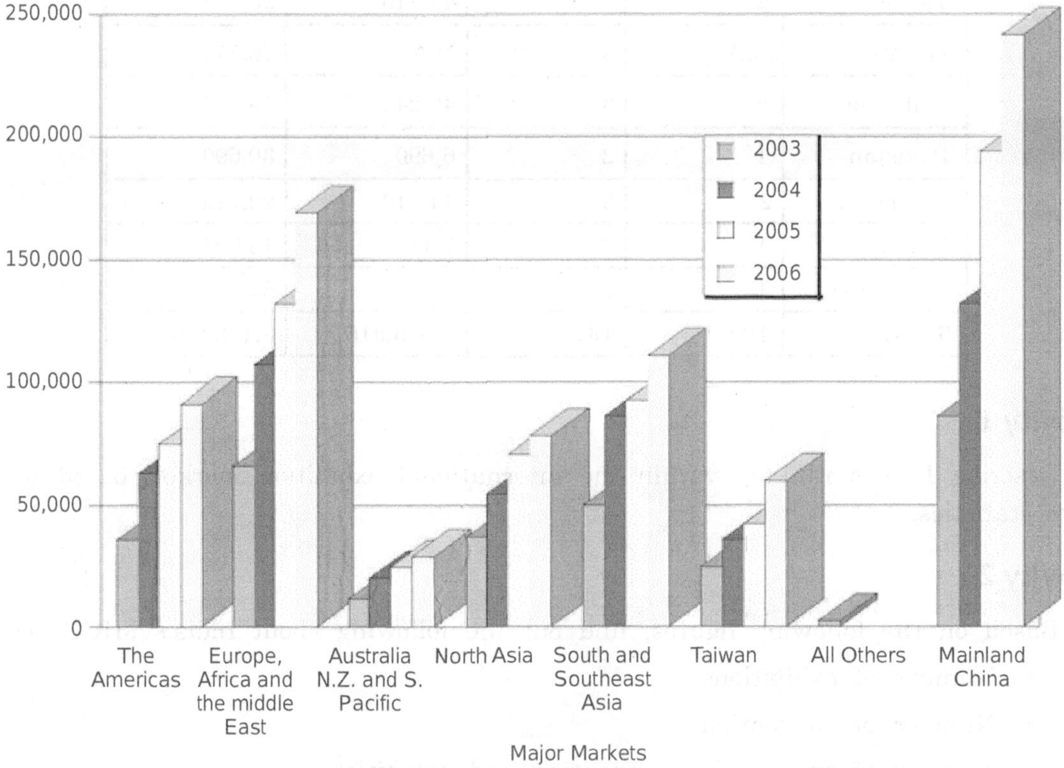

Figure 26.9: Number of convention and exhibition arrivals (2003–2006). (*Source: ICPB*).

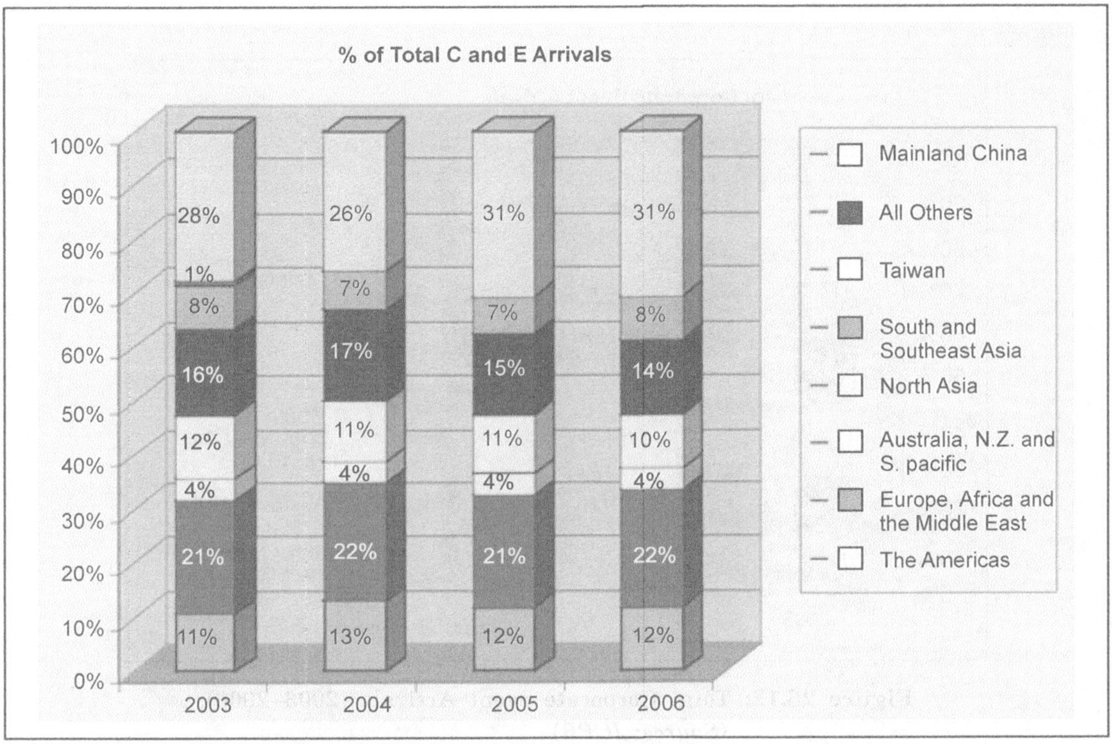

Figure 26.10: Total convention and exhibition arrivals (2003–2006). (*Source: ICPB*).

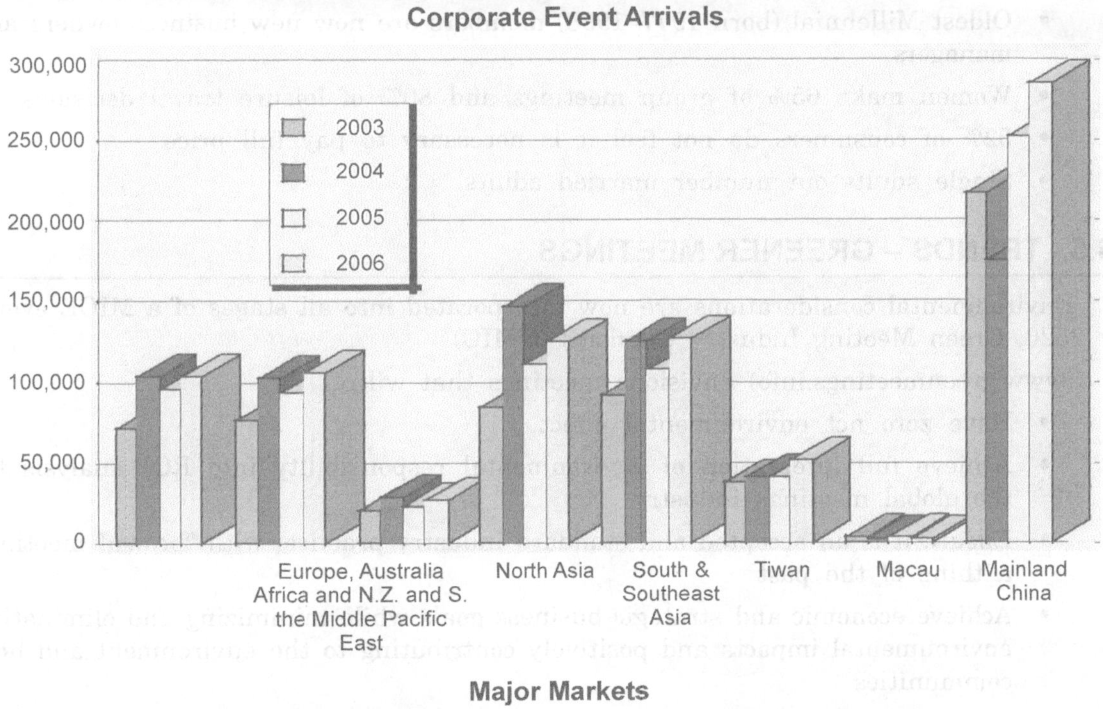

Figure 26.11: Number of Corporate event Arrivals (2003–2006). (*Source: ICPB*).

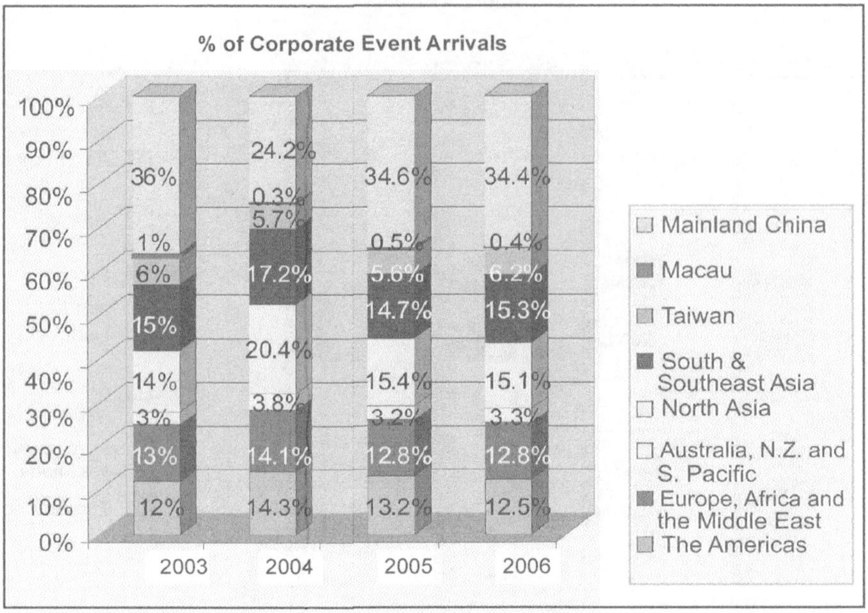

Figure 26.12: Total Corporate event Arrivals (2003–2006). (*Source: ICPB*).

26.4. TRENDS – CHANGING DEMOGRAPHICS

- Oldest Millennial (born 1977–1998) members are now new business owners and managers
- Women make 65% of group meetings and 80% of leisure travel decisions
- 92% of consumers do not feel it is necessary to pay full price
- Single adults out number married adults.

26.5. TRENDS – GREENER MEETINGS

Environmental considerations are now incorporated into all stages of a MICE event. By 2020, Green Meeting Industry Council's (GMIC)

(www.greenmeetings.info) envisions meetings that will:

- Have zero net environmental effect
- Achieve full integration of environmental responsibility into ROI analysis for the global meetings industry
- Ensure it is an accepted and standard industry practice, with "brown" meetings a thing of the past
- Achieve economic and strategic business goals while minimizing and eliminating environmental impacts and positively contributing to the environment and host communities
- Meet minimum green meeting practices as set out by the GMIC.

The National Recycling Coalition (www.nrc-recycle.org) also provides comprehensive guidelines for green meetings in all hospitality areas such as:

- Criteria for site selection
- Printed and promotional materials
- Recycling minimum guidelines
- Exhibits and trade shows
- Food and beverage
- Sleeping rooms.

26.6. TRENDS – TECHNOLOGY

Event managers now need to have expertise in computers. Consumers demand high-tech communications, ticketing and services for events. The Internet has become a necessary tool in marketing, and its full potential in the events sector is yet to be realized. Technology can overwhelm other aspects of the event and affect its appeal. There are ethical issues involved in database marketing, particularly with respect to corporate sponsors.

Face-to-face meetings will still be the preferred method for training and events. Webinars, webcasts/podcasts and virtual meetings are gaining in popularity because they:

- Reduce travel costs
- Do not require additional software
- Allow for less time away from the office

47% of respondents from MPI's FutureWatch 2007 indicated that they expect an increase in virtual meetings

Activity

Discuss the following two questions.

- Will communication advances replace the need for meetings and exhibitions?
- Will virtual events increase or decrease consumer demand for "real" events?

26.7. TRENDS – SPECIAL-PURPOSE EVENT VENUES

- Cities want major convention centres, arts and cultural complexes, and sports facilities – all of which lead to an emphasis on event programming and marketing.
- Venues are becoming larger and more expensive.
- Special venues for festivals are being created.
- Facility managers are also required to be event managers or co-ordinators.

26.8. OTHER FACTORS: CULTURAL DIVERSITY

- Meetings are becoming increasingly multicultural.
- Future challenges will involve:
  - Marketing to different ethnic or racial groups
  - Taking into account cultural sensitivities.

26.9. MAKE BUSINESS EVENTS MEMORABLE, RELAXING AND FAMILY FRIENDLY

- There is a growing desire to bring the family along on business trips.
- Meetings at sea are growing in popularity
- Spa, golf, tours, festivals... all should be available within reach
- Culinary, ecotourism and heritage themes should be available at selected destinations
- Unique destinations and locations include:
  - Academic venues
  - Museums
  - Cruise Ships
  - Cultural venues
  - Entertainment venues.

Activity

Examine each trend and think about:

1. How will it affect the industry?
2. Is there a deeper meaning behind these trends?
3. What do the results imply?
4. Do you have any suggestions?

TOURISM IN INDIA 2013

CHAPTER 27

TOURISM IN INDIA

27.1. INDUSTRY OVERVIEW

27.1.1. Background

Tourism is driven by the natural urge of every human being for new experiences, and the desire to be both educated and entertained. The motivations for tourism also include religious and business interests; the spread of education has fostered a desire to know more about different parts of the globe. The basic human thirst for new experience and knowledge has become stronger, as communication barriers are getting overcome by technological advances. Expenditure on tourism induces a chain of transactions requiring supply of goods and services from the related sectors. The consumption demand, emanating from tourist expenditure also induces more employment and generates a multiplier effect on the economy.

Tourism in India is broadly classified by its regions - North, East, West and South Indian tourism. Each part of India offers identifiable differences from the rest of the nation. The creation of niche tourism products like medical tourism, wellness tourism, religious circuits, adventure tourism, cruise tourism, and caravan tourism has served to widen the net of this sector. Inbound tourism is booming and the country is going all out to lure more travelers from around the world. Contrary to perceptions across the world that tourism in India is still confined to traditions, the country is opening up with trendy tour packages and affordable air travel deals to woo inbound visitors from every segment.

27.1.2. Present Scenario of Tourism in India

The Indian Tourism sector is one of the largest service industries in the country in terms of its contribution to the Gross Domestic Product (GDP) and Foreign Exchange Earnings, as well as for providing employment to millions. The sector in fact is expected to generate around US$ 42.8 billion (INR 1,897.7 billion) by 2017, according to an industry research. The amount of foreign direct investments (FDI) inflow into the hotel and tourism sector during April 2000 to April 2013 was worth US$ 6,664.20 million. Foreign tourist arrivals (FTA) during the Month of June 2013 stood at 0.44 million as compared to FTAs of 0.43 million during June 2012, registering a growth of 2.5 per cent and the domestic tourism is expected to increase by 15 per cent to 20 per cent over the next five years.

Tourism in India is witnessing widespread growth on the back of increasing inbound tourism by the burgeoning Indian middle class, rising inflow of foreign tourists and successful government campaigns for promoting 'Incredible India'. Infrastructure development holds the key to India's sustained growth in the Tourism sector. Further the government has also allowed 100 per cent foreign investment under the automatic route in the Hotel and Tourism related industry. Significantly, the country has the potential to become a major global tourist destination, with the Tourism sector expected to contribute around INR 3,414.8 billion (US$ 77.0 billion) by 2021. India is currently ranked 12th in the Asia Pacific region and 68th overall in the list of the world's attractive destinations.

Foreign tourist arrivals in the country have increased substantially during the past decade motivated by both, business and leisure needs and are further expected to grow at a compound annual growth rate (CAGR) of around 8 per cent during 2010–2014. Visitor exports are a key component of the direct contribution of the sector.. By 2021, international tourist arrivals are forecast to total 11,149,000, an increase of 6.1 per cent pa generating expenditure of INR 1,344.7 billion (US$ 30.3 billion). The country has received 3.3 million foreign tourists during the period January to June 2013.

27.1.2.1. Drivers Behind Increase in Tourist Traffic

The main driver for increase in tourist traffic to India has been the following factors:

Domestic Tourist Traffic

- Rapidly increasing purchasing power of the middle class
- Better road connectivity
- Evolving lifestyle.

International Tourist Traffic

- Value for money/economical holiday destination
- Business cum pleasure destination
- Development of Kerala and Rajasthan as the most popular tourist destinations in India with their distinctive brand image
- Opening of the sectors of the economy to private sector/foreign investment
- Reform in the aviation sector such as Open Skies Policy has led to better connectivity with many countries with India
- Success of "Incredible India" campaign and other tourism promotion measures.

27.1.3. Forms of Tourism in India

India offers various tourism options due to its vastness and diversity, attracting tourists from all over the world. The country boasts of natural treasures like mountains, ocean, seas, deserts, rainforests, valleys etc. on one hand, while world-class healthcare infrastructure on the other, which provides varied kinds of tourism options such as adventure and rural tourism, sustainable tourism/eco-tourism, cruise tourism, golf tourism and medical tourism to the travelers.

27.1.3.1. Rural Tourism

The Ministry of Tourism started the scheme of rural tourism in 2002-03 with the aim to showcase art, rural life, and culture and heritage to the tourists at various rural locations and villages. The Ministry intends to help the local community economically and socially, together with facilitating interaction between the local population and tourists, through this scheme. On 28 February 2011, 169 rural tourism sites in 28 States/Union Territories have been sanctioned by the Ministry of Tourism. This segment has also been winning accolades in the international circuits as well. For instance, the Rural Tourism Project at Hodka village in Kutch District of Gujarat won the Pacific Asia Travel Association (PATA) award for the year 2010 under the Heritage category.

27.1.3.2. Cruise Tourism

Cruise tourism is emerging as one of the most dynamic segments of the leisure industry globally. India with its vast and beautiful coastline, forests and undisturbed idyllic islands, rich historical and cultural heritage, can be a fabulous tourist destination for cruise tourists. The Cruise Shipping Policy of the Ministry of Shipping was approved by the Government of India on June 28, 2008. The objectives of the policy are to make India an attractive cruise tourism destination with the state-of-the-art infrastructural and other facilities at various parts in the country; to attract the right segment of the foreign tourists to cruise shipping in India; to popularize cruise shipping with Indian tourists.

27.1.3.3. Adventure Tourism

Adventure travel involves exploration or travel to remote, exotic areas. Adventure tourism is rapidly growing in popularity as a tourist seeks different kinds of vacations.

27.1.3.4. Sustainable Tourism/Eco Tourism

Sustainable Tourism growth is in the process of evolving the Sustainable Tourism Criteria for India. In recent years tourism industry in India has registered a considerable growth. A Steering Committee with representatives from all the sectors of the tourism and hospitality industry of India has been constituted to develop draft Sustainable Tourism Criteria which would eventually be adopted by the different sectors of the industry.

27.1.3.5. Wellness Tourism

Wellness tourism is about travelling for the primary purpose of achieving, promoting, or maintaining maximum health and a sense of well-being. Health Tourism holds immense potential for India. The Indian systems of medicine that is Ayurveda, Yoga, Panchakarma, Rejuvenation Therapy etc., are among the most ancient systems of medical treatment of the world.

27.1.3.6. Medical Tourism

India is one of the most lucrative medical tourism markets in the world. The sector is witnessing remarkable growth on the back of Government support through policies and initiatives, low cost, less waiting time and healthcare infrastructure. The growth in India's medical tourism market will be a boon for several associated industries, including hospital industry, medical equipments industry and pharmaceutical industry.

27.1.3.7. Religious Tourism

This segment of tourism has been growing in popularity. Bihar, for instance, holds a very important position in such a touristic destination as it has association of five religious circuits of country. The Buddhist Circuit, a pilgrimage route including sites of significance related to the life of the Buddha, is sacred to 500 million Buddhists and also attracts non-Buddhist tourists interested in historical heritage sites. The four main sites are Bodhgaya in Bihar, Sarnath and Kushinagar in Uttar Pradesh. The Shirdi-Shanishignapur circuit in Maharashtra clocked over 10 million tourists between October 2011 and March 2012. Apart from Shirdi, the most favoured destination, and Siddhivinayak temples, other places that drew the crowds were Trymbakeshwar in Nashik and Tuljadevi in Osmanabad.

27.1.4. Sub-segments of Tourism Industry

The tourism industry in India can be categorized under three major sub segments as depicted below:

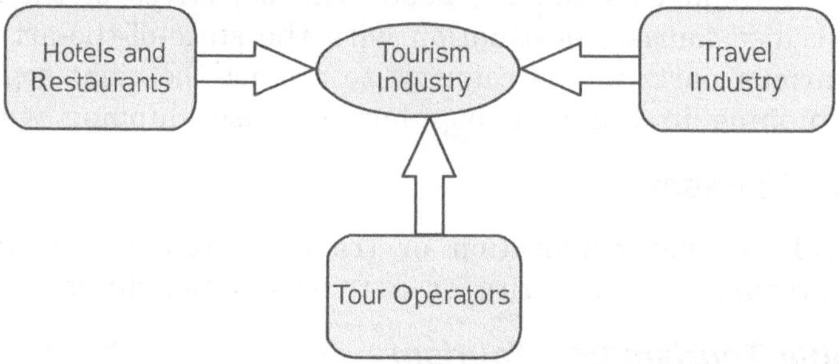

27.1.4.1. Hotels and Restaurants

The Hotels and Restaurants Industry has contributed between 1.2% and 1.5% of the GDP over the last seven to eight years. The Ministry of Tourism estimates that there are more than 8,700 hotels at 54 key locations across the country with a total room supply of about 174,000 including hotels in the classified, approved but not classified, and licensed by the state governments but not approved categories.

Major players

In the large/luxury hotels segment there are about 11 long-standing players such as ITC Hotels, Asian Hotels, The Oberoi Group of Hotels, Hotel Leela Ventures, ITDC, Indian Hotels, The Park Hotels and international players like Hilton Hotels, Marriott International, Le Meridien Hotels and Resorts, and Radisson Hotels and Resorts. There are about 16 listed hotel groups in the mid-segment including Bharat Hotels, Oriental Hotels, Nehru Place Hotels, Jaypee Hotels, Piem Hotels, and Taj GVK Hotels.

In addition, there are more than 90 listed hotels and resorts in the small/mid-sized segment including Country Club, EIH Associate Hotels, Kamat Hotels, and Mahindra Holidays and Resorts. Apart from these, as mentioned earlier, there are a number of guest houses and hotels, particularly in the budget and small hotel segments, which are primarily run by localized players.

27.1.4.2. Tour Operators

The tour operators, tourist operators and adventure tour operators in the country follow strict guidelines. As per the estimate of Ministry of Tourism, there are nearly

6,000 travel trade companies and firms comprising of tour operators, travel agents, and tourist transporters

Major players

- Thomas Cook India Pvt Ltd
- Cox and King India Pvt Ltd
- Kuoni India Ltd

27.2. GOVERNMENT POLICY

27.2.1. Government Initiatives

Government of India, the government has allowed 100 per cent foreign investment under the automatic route in the Hotel and Tourism related industry. The terms hotel includes restaurants, beach resorts and other tourism complexes providing accommodation and/or catering and food facilities to tourists. The term tourism related industry includes:

- Travel agencies, tour operating agencies and tourist transport operating agencies.
- Units providing facilities for cultural, adventure and wildlife experience to tourists
- Surface, air and water transport facilities for tourists
- Convention/seminar units and organizations

As a facilitative measure to make Tourism sector in India more attractive the following initiatives are taken by Government:

- The Government has launched a Scheme of 'Visa on Arrival' (VoA) from January 2010 for citizens of five countries, viz. Finland, Japan, Luxembourg, New Zealand and Singapore, visiting India for tourism purposes. The Government has now extended this Scheme for the citizens of six more countries, namely Cambodia, Indonesia, Vietnam, Philippines, Laos and Myanmar from January 2011. During the period January-June 2011, a cumulative figure of 5774 VoAs were issued, with a total of 865 and 770 VoAs issued in the months of May and June respectively.
- The Ministry of Tourism has launched a scheme for development of nationally and internationally important destinations and circuits through Mega Projects. As on 4.2.2011, 38 mega projects have been identified, out of which 26 projects have already been sanctioned.
- To overcome the bottlenecks of multiple inter – state road transport barriers, Ministry of Tourism has been advocating implementation of seamless travel for commercial tourist vehicles. This would facilitate smooth movement of tourist traffic and avoid delays and inconvenience to tourists.

Mega Destinations/Circuits Identifies in different States:

S. No.	States	Name of the Mega Projects
1.	Andhra Pradesh	Charminar area of Hyderabad, Tirupati Heritage Circuit, Kadapa Heritage Tourist Circuit.
2.	Assam	National Park Mega circuit covering Manas, Orang, Nameri, Kaziranga, Jorhat, Sibsagar and Majouli.
3.	Bihar	Bodhgaya-Rajgir-Nalanda Circuit.
4.	Chhattisgarh	Jagdalpur-Tirathgarh-Chitrakoot-Barsur Dantewada-Tirathgarh Circuit.
5.	Delhi	Illumination of Monuments Circuit.
6.	Goa	Churches of Goa.
7.	Gujarat	Dwarka-Nageshwar-Bet Dwarka Circuit Shuklatirth-Kabirvad Mangleshwar Angareshwar.
8.	Haryana	Panipat-Kurukshetra-Pinjore.
9.	Himachal Pradesh	Eco and Adventure Circuit (Kullu-Katrain-Manali).
10.	Haryana and Himachal Pradesh	Panchkula-Yamunanagar (Haryana)-Paonta Sahib (Himachal Pradesh) Circuit.
11.	Jammu and Kashmir	Mubarak Mandi Heritage Complex Naagar Nagar Circuit (Watlab via Hazratbal, Tulmullah, Mansbal and Wullar Lake), Srinagar Spiritual and Wellness Destination Leh – Ladakh.
12.	Karnataka	Hampi.
13.	Kerala	Muziris Heritage Circuit connecting historically and archaeologically important places of Kodungalloor.
14.	Madhya Pradesh	Spiritual and Wellness Destination of Chitrakoot.
15.	Maharashtra	Vidarbha Heritage Circuit Aurangabad.
16.	Manipur	INA Memorial.
17.	Orissa	Bhubaneswar- Puri-Chilka.
18.	Punjab	Amritsar.
19.	Rajasthan	Ajmer- Pushkar, Jodhpur- Bikaner-Jaisalmer.

20.	Sikkim	Gangtok.
21.	Tamilnadu	Mahabalipuram, Pilgrimage Heritage, Madurai-Rameshwaram-Kanyakumari), Thanjavaur.
22.	Uttarakhand	Haridwar-Rishikesh-Muni-Ki-Reti Circuit.
23.	Uttar Pradesh	Agra Circuit, Varanasi-Sarnath-Ramnagar.
24.	West Bengal	Ganga Heritage River Cruise Circuit.
25.	Tripura	Mega Lake Circuit including Mata Bari.

27.3. FUTURE POTENTIAL

The Tourism sector is expected to perform very well in future and the industry offers an interesting investment opportunity for long-term investors. The India travel and tourism industry ranked 5th in the long-term (10-year) growth and is expected to be the second largest employer in the world by 2019. This means that the sector's share of total national investment will increase from 4.7 per cent in 2011 to 4.8 per cent in 2021.

27.3.1. Capital Investment in Travel and Tourism

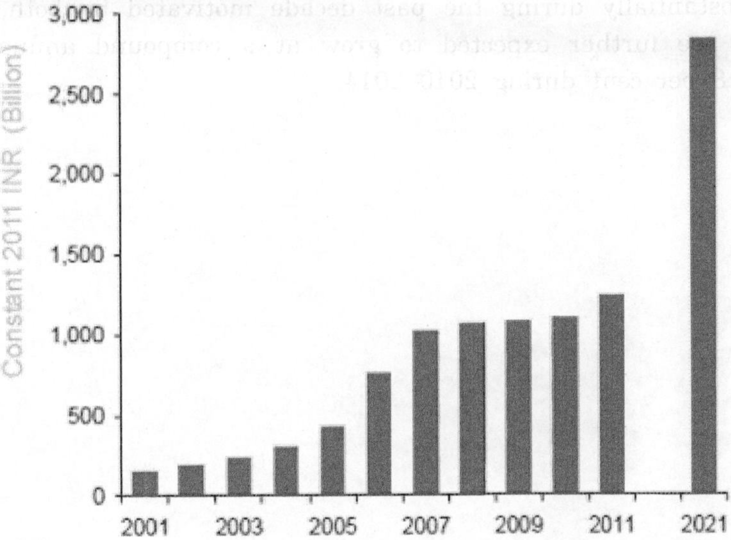

The hospitality consultancy HVS India and World Travel and Tourism Council (WTTC) has pointed out that in next 10 years, the Indian hospitality sector will need an additional supply of 180,000 rooms, a capital investment of $25.5 billion for constructing them and manpower of 211,000 to operate these additional hotels. From the current 810 million travelers, both domestic and international, India is slated to host 1,747 million travelers in 2021. Some of the key policy changes mentioned in the white paper include grant of infrastructure status to the industry, hotel sector to be included within the interest subvention schemes and rationalization of taxes which includes service tax, luxury tax, VAT/sales tax, tax on transportation etc. Also, the public-private partnerships (PPP) for the conservation of heritage sites, setting up of single nodal agency for all hotel project approvals and higher budgetary allocation for tourism by the state governments.

The Tourism industry in India provides opportunities in diverse fields such as tours and travel circuit, hospitality and hotel sector and development of specialized tourisms such as medical tourism, rural tourism, golf tourism, cruise tourism, adventure tourism, eco tourisms, and wellness tourism.

The WTTC predicts that by 2021, global travel would reach 1,362 million travelers. India, according to WTTC, is expected to account for 0.8% of those travelers or 11.1 million international travelers. The Tourism sector is witnessing fast growth due to the ever-growing number of participants in allied businesses such as hotels, tour operators, airlines, shipping lines, among others. Therefore, the sector is expected to witness high growth in the near future and offer varied opportunities to the investors in all these areas of businesses. In fact, the hotel industry is one of the major areas wherein investors can look for long-term opportunities. Foreign tourist arrivals in the country have increased substantially during the past decade motivated by both, business and leisure needs and are further expected to grow at a compound annual growth rate (CAGR) of around 8 per cent during 2010–2014.

INDIA—GLOBAL CONVENTIONS DESTINATION

CHAPTER 28

INDIA—GLOBAL CONVENTIONS DESTINATION

28.1. INTRODUCTION

Article 28.1 sets the background for the study by listing the research objectives, defining the scope of conventions, and identifying the various segments that constitute the conventions market. An overview of the methodology including data sources and analyses is also provided to help understand the research process. As outlined in this section, the methodology consists of a mix of primary and secondary sources, the former comprising of surveys and personal interviews with various stakeholders in the industry and the latter relying on published reports, academic studies, official documents, and web-based resources. The data collected in the course of this study has been used to develop performance and impact related tables, matrices, and charts in later sections.

The Introductory Article starts with a section listing the background for the study and the research objectives. The second section highlights the issues related to defining the conventions business for estimating its size and scope. A definition for the study and use it as the basis for segmentation of the market by type in the third section. The fourth section focuses on the methodology adopted for the study. It highlights the sources of data and the analysis carried out as part of the study. Finally the fifth section summarises the remaining chapters of the report.

28.1.1. Objective

The MICE (Meetings, Incentive, Conventions and Exhibitions) business is a large revenue generator for many economies across the world. However, there is a common feeling that India has not really been able to capitalise on this opportunity to that extent. The Ministry of Tourism and the India Convention Promotion Bureau (ICPB) initiated this study through the Indian Institute of Management Bangalore (IIMB) to explore various dimensions of the World and Indian Convention market and identify areas where India can effectively position its services, based on its inherent capabilities, as well as developing necessary skill-sets to address emerging areas of importance in this industry.

The objectives of this study are:

- Identification of various segments in the worldwide conventions market and developing an attractiveness matrix for these segments as applicable to India.
- Estimating the market size of different geographical segments- viz. Asia, Europe, Americas, Australia and South Pacific, Middle East and South Africa.
- Identify India's competitive position to explore and evaluate India's capability to exploit the booming conventions market and also to identify key focus areas for developing the required capabilities/infrastructure, including short as well as long-term perspectives. This would entail a study of convention infrastructure already available in the country.
- Comparison of allied/related conference infrastructure in major cities in India and other world destinations- highlighting learning from established/upcoming popular convention destinations in the world. Target centres for the research included 6 Metros viz. Mumbai, New Delhi, Bengaluru, Kolkata, Hyderabad, and Chennai and 4 other centres viz. Goa, Jaipur, Agra, Kochi.
- Analysis of two case studies highlighting successful conventions held in India along with two case studies of unsuccessful bids from India. Developing a roadmap for ICPB for developing conventions business in India, and enumeration of roles that can be played by the government as well as ICPB and its members in developing the conventions business in India.
- This roadmap should highlight directions towards development of marketing processes and organisational changes that can aid ICPB in addressing the emerging issues.

28.1.2. Definitions Applicable for the Study

One of the major issues about capturing information on the World Convention Industry is the lack of clarity about the exact definitions of various MICE components; as such estimates of the market vary widely in terms of numbers. The broad categorisations, which are accepted by the industry, are those of International Congress and Convention Association (ICCA) and Union of International Associations (UIA, or Union Association Internationale (UAI) in French speaking regions).

The UIA's definition of international meetings includes events organised or sponsored by 'international organisations' like non-governmental organizations (NGOs) and intergovernmental organizations (IGOs). They cover events of any size and events having a fixed city or country. In addition, the UIA definition covers meetings of significant international character organised by national organizations and national branches of international associations and which meet the following criteria:

- Minimum participation of 300
- Minimum foreign participation to the tune of 40%
- Minimum number of nationalities as 5
- Minimum duration of event as 3 days.

The ICCA definition for international association meetings specifies the following criteria:

- Minimum attendance by 50 delegates
- Must be organised on a regular basis (one-time events are excluded from classification)
- Should rotate among at least 3 countries.

This study has widely used the ICCA definitions. However, whenever UIA information has been used, it has been mentioned clearly. As mentioned earlier, clarity regarding definitions is lacking and even information available for this industry is collected at varying levels. While some countries make a conscious effort to segregate information on Conventions, Meetings and Exhibitions/Trade Shows and Fairs separately, there are others who collect information under the common MICE head.

This study has tried to segregate these revenues into different segments, as applicable to Conventions and conferences market.

The definition used for national/domestic conventions/Conferences is slightly different from the ICCA definitions. The study has focussed on conferences/conventions that have delegate figures of at least 100 and which have been organised by some national (or at State-level) level associations. For this study only conferences/meetings, which take place regularly are considered. One-time events are not considered.

28.1.3. Key Segments

The following diagram captures the different segments in the Conference Industry. However, this segmentation approach is a top-down one-and can be considered as capturing the broad classification of different types of meetings.

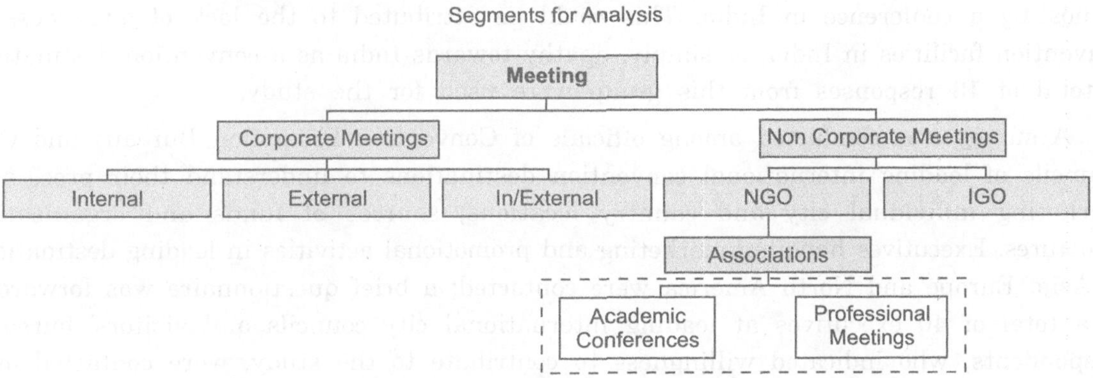

Figure 28.1: Classification of Meetings.

Most associations host regular conferences/meetings, which can range from purely academic conferences to professional meetings. Many of these meetings *e.g.*, medical conferences are sponsored by corporates. These are either bi-annual or annual in nature and typically rotate between destinations. These can be further segregated into different industry-specific segments.

28.1.4. Methodology

The study has been based on a large number of information sources including a mix of primary and secondary sources. Primary sources mainly comprised of surveys and personal interviews with various stakeholders in the industry, whereas secondary sources included a range of information sources, websites of various agencies, published industry data from ICCA and UIA, Journal articles in tourism and hospitality management as well as several other publications in related areas.

Primary Sources

Consumer Survey: A Survey was conducted among international conference visitors to India over the Internet as well as in person at several conferences in Bengaluru, New Delhi and Thiruvanathapuram. A large share of the responses was, however, filled up over the Internet (web-survey) made available online to a select group (625) of international conference visitors. The focus was to understand various factors driving the choice of an international venue, specifically India, as well as expenditure patterns. This survey was also used to capture several perceptual dimensions among potential conference delegates who have not yet visited India. A total of 75 responses were used for the study.

Customer Survey: This survey was targeted towards organisers around the world, to gauge their expectations and understanding of India as a potential conference destination. The aim was to get a qualitative understanding of perceptual blocks as far as India is concerned. This was followed up by several interviews with individual organisers. The survey questionnaire was sent, in 3 waves, to 100 ICCA members. The response to this survey was limited, as most of them mentioned that they had no plans of hosting a conference in India. This could be attributed to the lack of awareness of convention facilities in India, or simply, apathy towards India as a convention destination. A total of 13 responses from this group were used for the study.

A survey was conducted among officials of Convention Promotion Bureaus and City Councils of leading international convention destinations to understand their process of marketing individual city and country locations, sources of funds and organisation structures. Executives handling marketing and promotional activities in leading destinations in Asia, Europe and North America were contacted; a brief questionnaire was forwarded to a total of 40 executives at leading international city councils and visitors' bureaus. Respondents, who indicated willingness to contribute to the study, were contacted over phone for interviews. A total of 8 responses were found useful for the study.

Personal Interviews were conducted with domestic Professional Conference Organisers (PCO), tour operators and senior executives in leading hotel chains to get their views on the Indian market and suggestions for improvements. This interview also covered some of the premier ICPB Members. The primary focus for these interviews was to understand the Indian Conventions Market, how it has evolved over the past decade, and their individual views about the market development activities. Further, views were sought on their perception about the role of the government in promoting conventions as well as of ICPB, including their assessment of ICPB's performance in promotion of conventions of India. Findings of 14 interviews have been analysed for this study.

Personal interviews were conducted among organisers of past events, (with medical practitioners and other professionals) as well as future events about the various aspects of hosting a conference, their understanding of the impact of conferences on the local economy, help they require from a nodal body like ICPB as well as the Ministry of Tourism. The interviews also focussed on issues and challenges faced by conference organisers and ICPB's possible role in alleviating some of them. These interviews have been summarised under the Case Studies Section of the report. Total number of interviews used for this study was 11.

Finally, interviews were conducted with participants at domestic conferences. These included 22 professionals including doctors, educators and business managers.

Table 28.1: Summary of Primary Sources Covered for this Study

Sl. No.	Primary Data Collection Initiatives	Responses used
1.	Consumer Survey - Conference Visitors (International Conference Attendees)	75 Delegates (Combination of Web-Surveys and Personal Administration) individual mails sent to 625 participants
2.	Customer Survey- Focussed towards International PCOs	13 (Professional Organisers)
3.	Survey Conducted among Convention Bureaus and other City Promotion Councils	8
4.	Personal Interviews with Domestic Professional Conference Organisers (PCOs), tour operators and senior executives in leading hotel chains	14
5.	Interactions with ICPB Members	6
6.	Organisers of international events	11
7.	Conference participants (domestic visitors at various conferences)	22 (Doctors, Educators, and Business Managers)

Secondary Sources

Industry Reports from ICCA and UIA as well as International Association of Convention and Visitors' Bureau (IACVB). These reports provided general information on world trends as well as specific geographical markets. Some of these reports also provided details about future market development activities for various cities in the world.

Websites of Convention and Visitors' Bureaus worldwide-these helped in identifying individual positioning strategies for cities as well as countries and gathering possible/ applicable insights for ICPB in the Indian context. Some of the websites have user-friendly features, e.g. the website of Brussels City provided a detailed MICE toolkit, which could be used by a potential organiser to plan an event.

Journal Articles from Online Databases, *e.g.*, EBSCO, Taylor and Francis, ProQuest, etc. on Tourism, convention and hospitality management. These articles provided insights from academic research, which had earlier focussed on various socio-economic variables for evaluating the impact of tourism on local economies.

Professional journals published in India, especially in areas of Pharmaceuticals, Medicine and Surgery, and Information Technology for information on upcoming/past events. A large number of conferences were categorised from the lists available in the journals.

Reports from the Ministry of Tourism including the International Passenger Survey (IPS), Tourism Satellite Account (TSA) study. These studies were used for insights on Business Tourism trends in India and to capture the direct as well as indirect impact of tourism on the Indian economy. The TSA methodology was adopted to assess the impact of convention tourism in the country. The analysis of this section is based on the National Income Statistics information of 2002. The International Labour Organisation (ILO) Reports on Tourism employment offered an extensive understanding of the role of tourism in employment generation. These reports have investigated the employment-related and other dimensions of tourism for Asian countries like Thailand, Singapore including Oceania.

Annual reports of Visitors' Bureaus as well as India Convention Promotion Bureau for comparison across contexts.

Analysis of Data

Primary data collected through interviews as well as through surveys conducted among consumers and customers, and secondary information collected from various sources, viz. journals, industry reports, websites were used in tandem to arrive at conclusions. The coded data of the International Passenger Survey (provided by the Ministry of Tourism) was analysed for understanding several trends in business tourism on the basis of which conclusions were made. The insights from the consumer survey, which was conducted among international visitors to conferences in Bangalore, New Delhi and Thiruvananthapuram along with responses from the web based questionnaire (same questionnaire was made available to respondents over the Internet) were extremely important for arriving at several perceptual issues as well as creating the Importance Performance (IP) Matrix. The Economic Multiplier Effect from Business Tourism was developed from the analysis of raw data of the IPS. Finally, the gap analysis as well as the recommendations was the culmination of the primary surveys, insights from various interviews with professional conference organisers, and eminent professionals from the various areas. The summary of the analysis is presented next page:

Table 28.2: Summary of Analysis Carried out on the Basis of Primary and Secondary Studies

Insight(s)	Data Source	Analysis
Trends in Business Travel	Primary Survey, Raw Data from IPS	Various Cross Tabulations and Pivot Tables were created to analyse broad trends including expenditure patterns in the business tourism market.
Perceptual Maps	Primary Survey-Consumers, Interviews with PCOs	International Consumer Survey was analysed for their perceptions of India vis-à-vis other Asian Destinations and then similar exercise was repeated for destinations within the country.
Economic Multiplier Effect	Raw IPS Data (pertaining to the 2002 Information) + Tourism Satellite Account (TSA)	An extensive re-look at the I/O analysis and then analysing impact on related industries to isolate Direct and Indirect impacts.
Gap Analysis	Primary Survey, Case Studies from interviews	Key variables were isolated through the consumer survey, then case studies were analysed on the basis of these parameters.
Recommendations	Primary Survey, Case Studies and Policy documents from other destinations and various analyses	Macroeconomic data was analysed for major convention destinations for comparison. Smaller economies separated from larger, more developed economies to identify clusters and map India's potential position in the medium and long term. Effect of public investments analysed with the help of research papers in related area, focussing on substitution effects of public investment.

Chapter Summaries

The rest of the report is organised in the following order:

Article 28.2 The World Convention Market—This chapter summarises the broad trends in the world market, which have emerged in the last few years. A detailed explanation of the bidding process is provided for better appreciation of the complexity of this process, which is extremely critical for bringing convention business into the country.

Articles 28.3 and 28.4 Prominent Convention Destinations in Asia / World—These chapters provide a fairly detailed overview of 14 major convention destinations in the world including eight from Asia and six from Europe. This is further supplemented with a tabular analysis of 10 more world destinations.

Article 28.5 The Indian Conventions Industry—This chapter focuses on the emerging trends in the conventions business in our country. A detailed analysis on the basis of consumer surveys has been incorporated to understand the relative importance of several variables used by consumers in their choice of a convention destination. An entire section has been dedicated to the understanding the economic impact of conventions- to have clarity about the Direct and indirect impacts of tourism. Following this, a brief inventory of available facilities and attractions has been prepared for 10 major conventions destinations in India. The learning from the consumer surveys and interviews are summarised under the section for gap analysis.

Article 28.6 titled 'ICPB - Future Directions'—This chapter utilises the conclusions from the preceding analyses to provide recommendations focusing on ICPB and the Ministry of Tourism.

28.2. THE WORLD CONVENTION MARKET

Article 28.2 provides an overview of the world conventions market. Longitudinal data from published sources and reports have been used to identify trends in the conventions market. Data on tourism reveal that conventions or meetings tourism accounts for roughly 20 percent of all international arrivals and is projected to grow at around 10 percent per year over the next decade. ICCA sources point to 14,000 events worldwide of which there were 4,099 meetings in 2005. India accounted for 47 meetings and ranked 36th in the world, with New Delhi hosting the largest number within the country. While the top city-wise convention destinations in 2005 were mostly in Europe, a geographic shift is evident in recent years towards cities in Asia and Oceania, with growing importance of cities such as Singapore, Seoul, and Shanghai. Certain sectors emerge as more important, in particular medical sciences, followed by others such as science, technology, industry, and social sciences. The majority of these events are hosted at conferences or exhibition centres, followed by hotels, and universities. An analysis of the trends further reveals that the frequency of conferences is going up; that they tend to be of shorter duration, and that the lead times for organizing them is becoming shorter. The bidding process, which results in the selection of destinations for hosting conventions, is very important. It consists of gathering information about market segments and offerings by competing venues, understanding the customer, preparing a bid document, site inspection, participation by specialists and other professionals, and a bid submission, which if successful is then followed by a post bid evaluation and finally hosting of the convention. In the case of major international conventions, where lead times are long, hosting may be based on rotation across destinations.

This article provides an overview of the broad market trends that have emerged in the last few years by highlighting the market shifts as well as changes in customer segments. One of the key aspects of competing in the international markets for conventions is to manage the bidding process effectively. The last section of this chapter helps understand the bidding process and the dynamics of this business for marketing the services.

28.2.1. Market Overview

Worldwide, the role of tourism to jumpstart fledgling economies has been well explored; many of the smaller Caribbean nations, Mauritius, Maldives, Cyprus have proven that even with low levels of natural resources and industrialisation, countries can develop economically with the help of the tourism sector. Business Tourism is a significant part of tourism because of the greater per capita expenditures compared to leisure tourism. MICE tourism is a segment of the business tourism and conventions and meeting tourism is again a sub-segment of business tourism. Convention or Meetings Tourism accounts for approximately 20% of all international arrivals and is expected to see annual growth of 10% over the next decade. Overall planners expect the worldwide number of meetings to grow 7% in 2006 (Future Watch, 2006).

ICCA currently tracks close to 14,000 events worldwide; out of which, international meetings add up to 5,269 meetings in 2005. The market has grown from 4,500 meetings at the turn of century to over 5,269 in 2005. The US accounted for 376 of these meetings in 2005, while India bagged 47 and was ranked at the 36th position in the world. While the US attracted nearly 680,000 visitors for the meetings, India played host to 33,000 visitors in the same year. The top destinations for conventions as far as cities are concerned are Vienna, Barcelona, Singapore and Stockholm, while New Delhi hosted the largest number of meetings in India.

Table 28.3: Geography Wise Share of Conventions

(Source: ICCA, The International Association Meetings Market, 2005)

Continent	2000	%	2001	%	2002	%	2003	%	2004	%	2005	%
Africa	113	3%	110	2%	133	3%	126	3%	133	2%	128	2%
North and South America	913	20%	868	19%	929	19%	951	19%	984	18%	952	18%
Asia, Middle East and Pacific	888	20%	906	20%	981	20%	923	18%	1,171	21%	1,132	21%
Europe	2,579	57%	2,570	58%	2,921	59%	2,996	60%	3,188	58%	3,057	58%
Total	4,493	100%	4,454	100%	4,964	100%	4996	100%	5,476	100%	5,269	100%

28.2.2. Market Highlights

Till the early nineties, North America and Europe had dominated the conventions and conference markets. The US still holds the top spot for the highest number of meetings as a single country destination. However, since 1999, the market has moved towards newer destinations in Asia and Oceania. Europe accounts for the maximum share with about 57.1% of all international meetings in 2005. However, there is a constant decrease in the share of Europe, while Asia and Oceania are gaining. This growth in Asian and Australian conventions is in spite of rising concerns over future travel because of rising oil prices. According to industry experts, this steady shift in conferences/conventions venue can be attributed to the emergence of several strong Asian economies, *e.g.*, India, China apart from Korea and Japan. The revised estimates of the Asian Development Bank indicate strong growth in the Asian economies, to the tune of 7.7% in 2006—with the larger economies of India and China growing even more rapidly, around 8–10%. This economic upsurge in these countries means that top venues in Asia, including, Singapore, Hong Kong and Bangkok have continued to outperform most other venues as far as conventions are concerned.

Medical Sciences remains a popular area for international meetings accounting for about 33.2% of all meetings. The other top sectors are Science (12.9%), Technology (8.6%), Industry (6.7%) and Social Sciences (4.2%). As far as seasonality is concerned, the industry worldwide shows seasonality, with September, October and November being the busiest periods for convention tourism. Both expenditure heads, average fees per delegate and average expenditure per delegate per meeting have hovered around USD 500 and USD 1600 for last few years. Most organisers worldwide still prefer to host meetings at Conference/Exhibition Centres (55%), Hotels come second with (25%) and Universities and others account for the rest.

Meetings and conventions offer high value added in terms of delegate expenditure and also serve the dual purpose of promoting international relations. It is a highly profitable form of tourism as most delegates are subsidized and tend to use costly accommodation and often travel before and after the event. In addition, by organising during the off-seasonal months, one can remove the seasonality effects of leisure tourism. Thus undesirable social effects of seasonal tourism such as migration, temporary employment, and job instability can be avoided. These events can also be termed as "knowledge tourism" as they promote the exchange of ideas, technology and commercial knowledge that contribute to an intangible but important source of value add to the economy of the host country. The MICE sector also helps increase local government and private sector investments that result in improvements in the general hospitality environment of the destination country.

28.2.3. Emerging Trends

Smaller conferences-Shorter durations—The trend for smaller and shorter meetings is growing because Companies are maintaining firm controls over their conference related spending Time constraints result in delegates attending only those parts of conferences they really need to Frequency going up—As meetings become shorter and smaller they are also being held more frequently because:

- The accelerating rate of changes in business and in society as a whole means that associations and corporations have to hold more meetings, to ensure that their members or employees can keep up with developments.

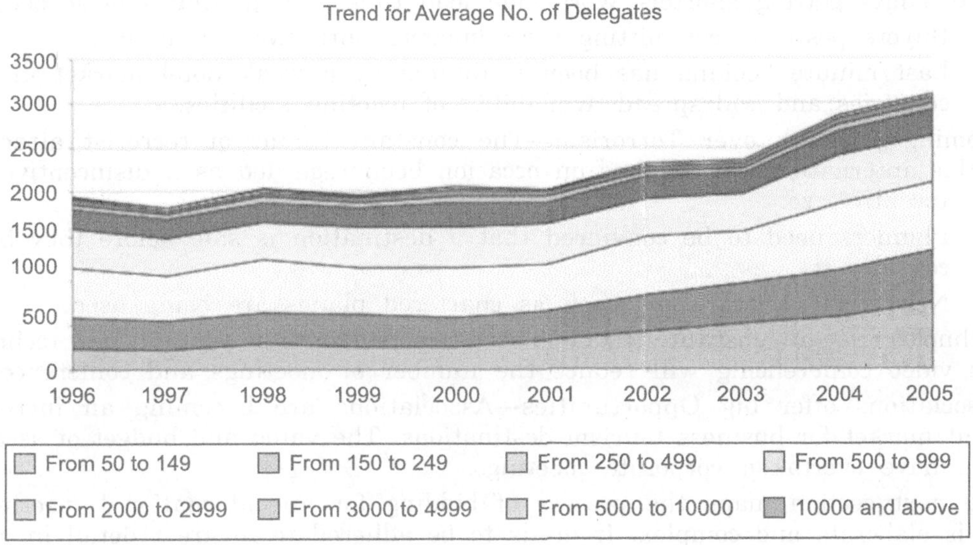

Figure 28.2: Size of Conference (No. of delegates) over the last decade. (*Source: ICCA Report, 2006*)

- The one big annual hit in the form of the yearly staff conference is no longer effective in helping companies meet their corporate objectives.

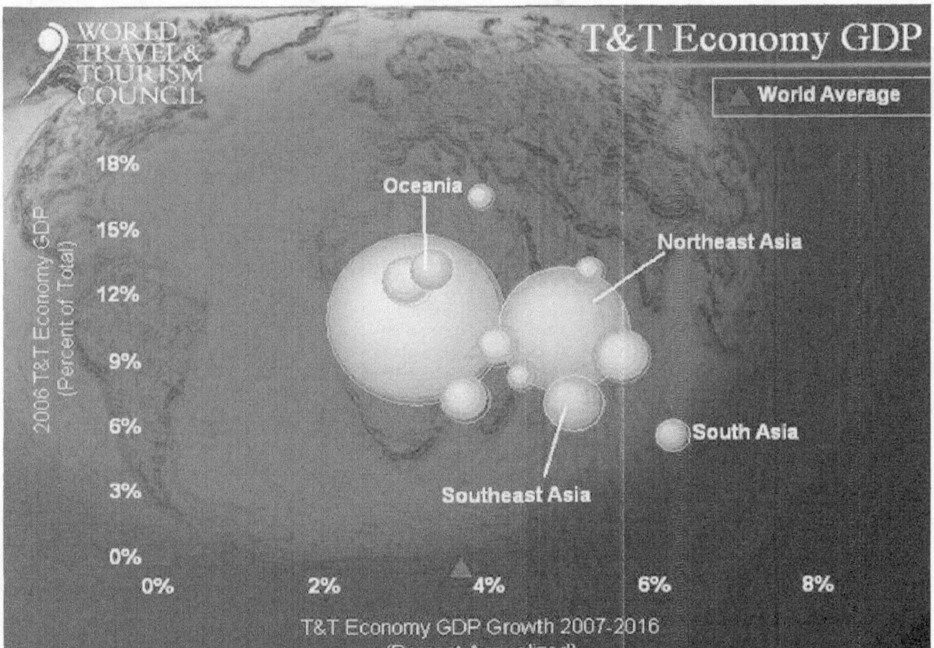

Figure 28.3: WTTC: Asian Economies outperform others- although Tourism Economies are small (*Source: World Travel and Tourism Council Presentation*)

Lead Times getting shorter- Worldwide lead times are getting shorter because:

- Buyers postpone committing their budgets until the last minute
- Last minute booking has been facilitated by a weak hotel market in several countries and widespread availability of meeting facilities.

Looming concerns over Terrorism—The constant threat of terrorist attacks has meant that international travel has on occasion been regarded as a disincentive rather than an incentive, so:

- Planners need to be convinced that a destination is safe before they begin to consider it
- New forms of transport such as chartered planes are being used.

Technology yet to substitute travel—There is no evidence as yet that new technologies such as video conferencing will reduce the number of meetings and conferences.

Associations offer big Opportunities—Associations are becoming an increasingly important market for business tourism destinations. The value and budget of association meetings have overtaken corporate meetings.

The next section maps the process of bidding for an international meeting. The process is elaborate and complex. It needs to be adhered to in great detail in order to attract conventions to a city/venue.

28.2.4. Inviting Convention Business-the Process

Most large international conventions are allotted to different destinations by rotation on the basis of competitive bidding. The entire process predates the actual event by 5–8 years and in some extraordinary cases by 10–12 years. The selection process can take close to a year and individual organisers need to put up an impressive presentation and upstage the competition in every way.

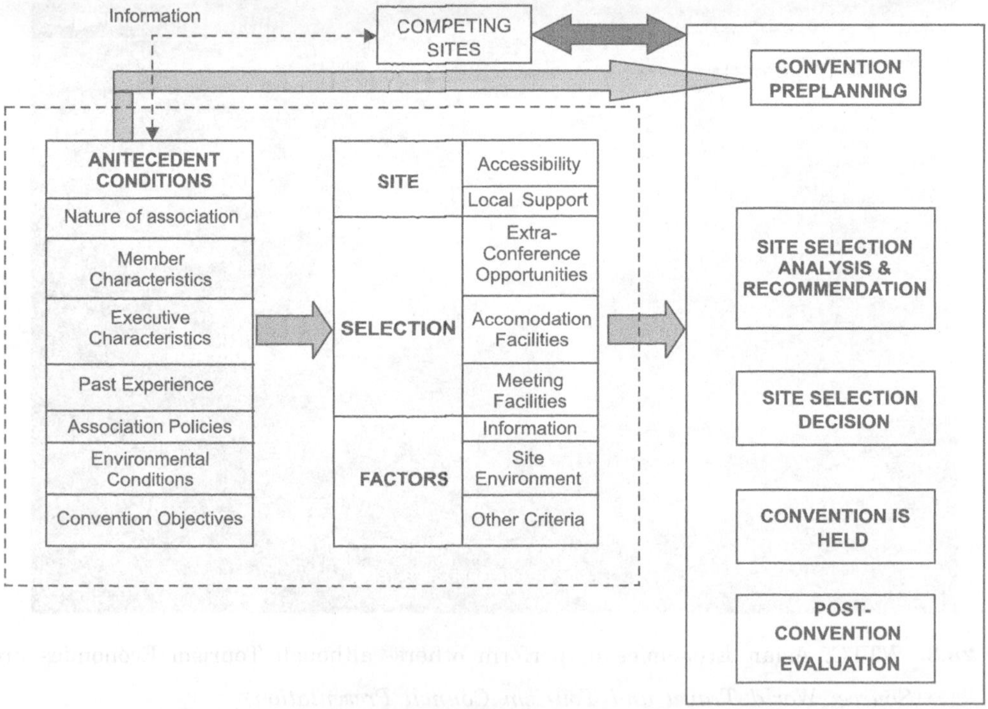

Figure 28.4: The Bidding Process for Conventions.

28.2.5. Key Aspects of the Bidding Process

Market Intelligence—the first step of the bidding process starts with gathering information about market segments and collecting data on competitive offerings from other venues domestic as well as international. This provides a comprehensive understanding of market dynamics, customer segments and competitive strengths and weaknesses. Often gathering historical data on similar conventions as well as association/ delegate profiles can provide interesting insights to venue managers.

Understanding the Customer—the Host Organisation– this process is the heart of the convention business, understanding the rationale behind hosting a convention/meeting and what the host organisation wishes to achieve through this event. A thorough understanding of the customers' expectations leads to better match in the bid document.

Developing a Committee—gathering necessary expertise is the key; a committee consisting of specialists (domain or industry, marketing as well as project management) needs to be formed to ascertain that a proper match is ensured between expectations and execution.

Preparation of the Bid Document—the actual bid document can take any form; however, the document should be persuasive, brief, and yet comprehensive. The aspects highlighted should focus on how the host organisation would gain through a larger delegate presence and exposure in the host destination, what the venue can offer to the delegates for entertainment and as a memorable stay, and what benefit the local economy could potentially derive by hosting the meeting. A balanced view of these dimensions is expected.

Site Inspection—convincing the hosts– although not explicitly stated in most cases, this aspect of the bidding process is one of the most critical– as this provides the venue manager with an opportunity to showcase his strengths, as well as convince the host organisation about the measures taken to address any weaknesses. Some of the more popular convention venues plan for periodic site inspection visits by the host organisation members to make this statement. Many venues use this opportunity to show that the government (city/state/national) is rallying behind such conventions, which in turn lends credibility to the venue.

Bid Submission—the final bid submission for international meetings is usually attended by a team comprising of professionals, host-organisation officials and venue managers put their best foot forward for this occasion. Typically, the local diplomatic mission lends a helping hand to the delegation along with other members in the decision-making bodies.

Post Bid Evaluation—this phase is involved more with following up on strict timelines for the convention, as well as regular reporting to the parent organisation body.

Hosting the Convention—a successful hosting of an international meeting requires excellent co-ordination and planning among various associates; the key in this phase is to ensure that the delegates have a memorable time. Word of mouth is very critical to the long-term success of a particular venue. Visitors to prominent destinations like Vienna and Singapore have often come back with pleasant memories, which they share with other colleagues leading to the popularity of these venues.

28.3. PROMINENT DESTINATIONS IN ASIA

Articles 28.3 and 28.4 provide a summary of eight leading conventions destination from Asia and six leading destinations from Europe. These destinations include Singapore, Shanghai, Kuala Lumpur, Bangkok, Hong Kong, Seoul, Jakarta, Vienna, Frankfurt, Paris, Barcelona, Geneva and Stockholm. The discussion in these articles focuses on each destination's, convention centre and related infrastructure and other facilities such as the availability and cost of accommodation, recreational and tourism opportunities, accessibility, local transport, shopping, etc. The discussion also provides a synopsis of the size of the conventions market for these selected cities based on the number of events hosted in the recent past. It highlights the role of the local convention promotion bureau in developing these cities as convention destinations to underscore the importance of organized efforts in marketing a location to attract conventions. There is also a brief overview of other world destinations in terms of their ratings on convention facilities, accessibility, other attractions, and policy environment with respect to the conventions industry. The highlights that emerge from this global overview are that all major convention destinations have pro active city promotion bureaus of boards which are professionally managed and well funded, that there is a lot of focus on convention specific as well as supporting infrastructure, of which transport infrastructure and accessibility are of foremost importance.

This article provides an overview of some prominent destinations in Asia and then the World conventions market. Among the Asian destinations, the study focuses on Singapore, Shanghai, Kuala Lumpur, Bangkok and Hong Kong, which are already established and well known in the conventions market followed by Seoul and Jakarta, which are emerging as strong contenders in the Asian market. In the world market, the top destinations include, Vienna, Frankfurt (the Trade Show capital of the world), Paris, Barcelona, and Geneva, and Stockholm, a destination that is growing in popularity. A table summarising additional ten key world destinations is presented towards the end of the article.

28.3.1. Singapore, Republic of Singapore

Singapore, the city-state is located at the southern tip of the Malayan Peninsula. The island has emerged as one of the most successful growth stories in the world economy. This Asian Tiger is often considered to be the financial capital of South-East Asia. The country has prospered as a business destination as well as a tourist destination, although the island is not blessed with any great natural beauty. It has become synonymous with shopping along with Dubai because of the hugely popular Singapore Shopping Festivals and a very proactive tourism promotion board. Worldwide, Singapore is viewed as a tourist friendly destination.

Suntec City, Singapore's primary Convention and Exhibition centre is one of the best convention centres in the world. Suntec City is located in the Central Business District of Singapore and occupies an area of about 12 hectares. It is an integrated MICE centre with five office towers, 5,200 hotel rooms, a shopping mall with about a thousand shops, three hundred restaurants, a theatre complex and most importantly convention space totalling about seven million square feet.

Suntec City is a case study on how to turn around operations in the MICE sector. In its early days it was not very successful at attracting potential visitors. However, it defined a niche and presently attracts 95% occupancy through its FSP (Facilities Service Provider) concept with "The Worlds Best Host" vision. This has led to multiple initiatives such as the setting up of an incubation centre for start-ups, a community web portal, car parking aesthetics, a ball room, a concourse, the largest banquet kitchen in Singapore, interpretation in 14 languages, and theatres at the bay. Individually these improvements may not amount to much, but collectively what they signal to potential customers is that every possible small little detail would be taken care of to make their stay during the conference engaging and entertaining. It is this philosophy of being a service provider par excellence that has helped Suntec to be successful in achieving a remarkable turn around.

Singapore shares the top honours in the world convention market with Vienna, having hosted 125 international meetings in 2005 and close to 50,000 visitors during international meetings. However, the number of delegates/ visitors for tradeshows and exhibitions is much larger than this figure.

Today, Singapore stands for its political and economic stability and a strong financial system, which is important in the context of the Asian currency crisis. Although the city-state suffered a decline in inbound tourism during the outbreak of SARS, it has witnessed a strong recovery in numbers in the past two years.

Although an island, Singapore is easily accessible through road and railway network with the mainland (Malaysia). Singapore can boast of a truly world-class airline, Singapore Airlines, which is extremely popular world over for its outstanding service quality. Singapore Airlines connects Singapore to a large number of cities all across the world. Changi Airport is considered by many to be an architectural marvel and can aptly be called an 'Airport City'. A number of cruises operating in the South China Sea– Japan Sea and the Indian Ocean are now currently connecting Singapore as an important destination, and bring a large number of tourists to Singapore every day.

Singapore is known for its shopping extravaganza, and a stroll on its most famous shopping locale, Orchard Street is a must for all tourists. Other shopping locations are Arab Street, Holland Village and Little India. For families, Sentosa Island offers a great getaway with children, along with a host of attractions for the international traveller. This city is also known for its restaurants and cuisines-a heady mix of Chinese, Malay, Indian and other South East Asian cuisines.

Recent Conventions

Name of Convention	Date(s)	No. of Delegates
3 GSM World Congress Asia 2006	October 16–20, '06	4,000+
GlobalTRONICS 2006	October 10–13, '06	3,000+
61st Annual Meeting of the Board of Gov. IMF	September 14–20, '06	23,000

Source: Secondary Research involving various sources.

Singapore has hosted several large conventions focussing on the technology and retails sectors in the last few years. With the successful hosting of the IMF summit in September 2006, it has entered the sphere of Inter-governmental conventions too.

The Singapore Tourism Board or STB is considered to be one of the most proactive tourism promotion boards in the world. Apart from promoting Singapore as a great tourist destination, it also promotes the city as an attractive convention/exhibition destination. The Singapore Exhibition and Convention Bureau (SECB) actively promotes the city as a business destination to leading associations and also encourages private professionals, e.g. doctors, academics as well as professional associations to bid for bringing conventions, exhibitions and trade-shows to the city. Even Suntec City offers the organising individual/association comprehensive services, which includes bid assistance, arranging for visits of the parent international organisation officials, financial and professional assistance for preparing bids, and total event management.

Although the city is growing at the rate of 20% in terms of meetings and conference volume, it does not need capacity/infrastructure enhancement, as the current infrastructure will be able to sustain the volumes. However, the city continues to develop new customised promotions targeted at associations and professionals with various incentives to bring their conferences to the city. The SECB offers customised support to business event organisers, corporations and associations under the "BE IN SINGAPORE" incentive scheme. This endeavour is to encourage many in the industry to develop new channels in—the market for business events development, to help International Organisations who wish to establish a presence in Singapore as part of their expansion into the Asia-Pacific region.

28.3.2. Shanghai, Peoples' Republic of China

Shanghai is the commercial hub of China. It is situated in the middle of China's East Coastline, and is the capital city of the province by the same name. It is the most populated city in China with a population of 17.42 Million. It is the largest economic and trade centre and a comprehensive industrial base of the country. Shanghai Port is the leading port in China and the third largest in the world. It is also the largest cargo port in the World. Exports comprise mainly of machinery, electronics goods, garments and textile products and machinery and imports include electronics products, paper pulp, wool, oil products and plastics.

Shanghai, as most other Chinese cities facing the economic boom, is trying to come out from its 'Red' image. Today's China, as many would agree, showcases its capitalist best, when it comes to attracting foreign investments. The City has witnessed an unprecedented boom in real estate and infrastructure related investment and this has made it attractive to foreign investors. Being the economic hub of the Chinese resurgence, Shanghai ranks high as a convention destination. According to ICCA 2005 estimates, for the future (2006–17) number of meetings, China ranks 10th in the world and Shanghai ranks 30th in the world, along with Brussels.

The Oriental Riverside Conference Centre (housed in the Hotel by the same name) is the largest convention facility in the city. The Grand Ballroom can accommodate up to 4,000 persons for a dinner and the Auditorium up to 1,000 persons for meeting, where simultaneous translation can be provided in 10 different languages. The centre also has 21 meeting rooms with capacities ranging from 10 to 300 persons, ideal for the smaller breakout sessions along with main schedule. The adjoining hotel has 259 rooms, 4 restaurants and 3 bars, fitness facilities, along with tennis courts and a bowling alley, for visitors' relaxation. Shanghai boasts of a large number of 3–5 Star accommodations and most hotels offer very competitive rates of 250 RMB ($42)-2000 RMB ($250) for a night's accommodation, which offer good value for money for the international traveller. A large number of these hotels also double up as Convention and meetings facilities, and can cater to 1500 + delegates, *e.g.*, Everbright Convention Centre and Hotel, Worldfield Convention Hotel. Over 80,000 delegates visited Shanghai for international meetings in 2005.

Shanghai is one of the most well connected cities in Asia along with Tokyo and Kuala Lumpur. Comprehensive Air, Rail and Sea routes connect it to most cities in the world. The city has its own airline, Shanghai Airlines (connecting to 27 Chinese cities), along with being a major hub of Air China—is also a Star Alliance member, which means it connects major European and North American cities almost seamlessly. This city has been a well-known port on the China Sea for several centuries. Shanghai has grown into a modern port with substantial investments from private and public enterprises. The city is also well connected to other parts of China, through an extensive network of road and rail, and air. The city's mass transit system is well developed, and the metro-rail systems enable easy and speedy transit from the airport to the city centre.

Shanghai has a number of tourist attractions with a modern flavour, like the Oriental Pearl TV Tower, Nanjing Road, Yuyuan Garden, Shanghai Museum, Bund and the famous Jade Buddha Temple. Shanghai is also a paradise for gourmets where one can taste all the different cuisines in the world. Shanghai is also known for being a 'shopping paradise' for all economic classes; with rows of shops and large modern shopping malls packed with large collections of merchandise serving as a feast to eyes, meeting the demands of different classes of domestic and foreign customers. In the recent past, various colourful festivals depicting Chinese lifestyles have been well appreciated by visitors.

Recent Conventions

Name of Convention	Date(s)	No. of Delegates
Hong Kong University Alumni Global Convention	November 2–4, '06	600+
20th International Project Management Association	September 25–26,'06	500+
28th International Conference on Software Engg.	May 20–28, '06	600+

Source: Secondary Research involving various sources.

Shanghai is gaining popularity in the Asian academic research arena as a venue for technology related conferences, with delegate sizes of 600–700. Local universities play an active role in hosting conferences in Shanghai.

The Chinese government actively promotes its major cities, Beijing, Shanghai as well as Hong Kong (SAR) and Macau (SAR) for international conventions. Each city is promoted through individual city and convention promotion bureaus, which receive endowments from the government.

The past decade can by symbolised as the decade of infrastructure growth in China, with substantial investments in transport infrastructure, (roads, airports, ports) as well as real estate growth, especially quality accommodation and convention facilities. This momentum is expected to continue in the next few years.

28.3.3. Kuala Lumpur, Republic of Malaysia

Kuala Lumpur (or KL as it is popularly known as), Malaysia's capital is synonymous with the world-famous twin Petronas Towers. Again, a land of cultural mix, with ethnicities divided among Malays, Chinese and Indians, it is a hotbed of culture. Considered by many as the symbol of Asian's rising stature in world business– many visitors are in awe of the country's strong growth in manufacturing as well as service sectors. The country's market-oriented economy, supportive government policies and a large local business community that is ready to do business with international corporations have made Malaysia a highly competitive manufacturing and export base. Malaysia is slowly making its mark in the Information Technology sectors too.

Owing to the colonial presence of the British till the sixties, English is widely used in Malaysia, especially in business, which facilitates the world investors' communication with local personnel and suppliers. The various chambers of commerce and trade associations enjoy memberships of corporations from different countries. These organizations are invaluable sources for general business information, advice and assistance, and complement the role of government agencies. A well-developed financial and banking sector has enhanced Malaysia's position as a dynamic export base in Asia.

The Kuala Lumpur International Convention Centre (KLCC) is located at the City Centre, with the Petronas Towers in the background, which adds to the glamour. The total area of the complex is around 100 acres. The entire layout is divided into 4 major areas, with a total space of 9,700 square metres for exhibition and capacity to cater to 3,500 visitors. The plenary arrangements are also impressive, with a capacity of 3000 delegates in two levels. All seats are provided with advanced multimedia kits and a wide range of translations is available. An impressive set of accommodations is available, either on-site at the KLCC or at walking distances from the convention centre. While 1400 rooms are available at KLCC itself, another 3700 rooms are available within small distances from the convention centre. KL hosted 38 international meetings in 2005 attracting 16,500 visitors for meetings alone.

Malaysia is very accessible through Air, Sea and Overland routes. Although Kuala Lumpur is not accessible directly by sea, the peninsular region had historically been a centre of vigorous maritime business. The country's flag bearer, the Malaysian Airlines, with a large fleet of planes connects Kuala Lumpur to most of the key destinations in the world. It is currently flying for the top honours in service quality. The Malaysian government has invested a substantial amount of money in developing world-class roads all over the country, which also help in providing access to other regional centres in the country. The city has a well-developed mass transit system similar to other major cities like Shanghai and Singapore, which enables visitors to arrive at the convention centre easily from the railway station or the airport.

As mentioned earlier, the city is almost synonymous with the Twin Petronas Towers. Visitors come to KL every year in large numbers just to have a glimpse of this architectural and engineering marvel. Genting Heights, located in the East of the city, is another crowd puller. In the city, Batu Caves, The Kuala Lumpur Bird Park (the largest aviary in the world), Merdeka or Independence Square, and Menara Tower are other attractions for visitors. Kuala Lumpur has become an attractive destination for shoppers too; the city has also launched its own version of a shopping festival. The government has also decided to ease out visa restrictions for nationals from most countries to facilitate tourist visits to the country.

Recent Conventions

Name of Convention	Date(s)	No. of Delegates
Graphite 2006	Nov 29–Dec 2, '06	300
Asian and Oceanian Epilepsy Congress 2006	November 16–19, '06	2,100
Federation of Gynaecology and Obstetrics	November 5–10, '06	8,000

Source: Secondary Research involving various sources.

The city has emerged as a strong contender for medium to large medical conferences; it has also hosted several international summits/meeting on electronics as well as manufacturing technologies.

The Malaysian Tourism Board promotes business tourism and MICE through its convention promotion division. Although this division maintains a low profile, the KLCC actively launches various marketing programmes to promote the centre. Within a very short time, Kuala Lumpur has reached the 30th rank in international meetings.

Currently, the city has not fully utilised its available convention infrastructure. The traffic to the city is slowly building up. Recently, the Malaysian government has decided to develop the 3rd federal territory of Putrajaya in the Selangor territory as the next administrative region. The Putrajaya Convention centre is expected to boast of 135,000 square metres of floor area over nine levels with state-of-the art facilities on completion. The government is also focussing on Genting Highlands for improving convention infrastructure. This would mean a set of 3 major convention centres around the same region.

28.3.4. Bangkok, Kingdom of Thailand

Bangkok is the capital city and the largest city in the Kingdom of Thailand. Since the shifting of the capital from Thonburi to the east bank to Krung Thep (or Bangkok) in 1782, the city has grown in importance over the next two centuries. The city was the centre of the American army build-up during the Vietnam War and since then Bangkok has adopted many American ways. The population stands at 7 million for the city proper and 10 Million over the metro area. It is one of the most densely populated cities in South East Asia and has surpassed Singapore in terms of the size of its economy.

The country was badly affected in the nineties during the Asian Crisis. However the government has taken several precautions to prevent a similar crisis. The city's real estate growth is still continuing, although at a slightly slower pace compared to the pre-Asian Crisis period. Tourism and business was further affected during the Bird Flu crisis as it hit other cities in the region. The recent crisis was a political one, a coup leading to the ouster of the charismatic Prime Minister, Thaksin Shinawatra. Though this coup could have undermined Thailand's image as a well-functioning democracy (under the guidance of the Royal crown) and a safe tourist destination, in reality, tourism was really not affected at all.

Queen Sirikit National Convention Centre is Thailand's premier exhibition and conference centre. The centre has been built to cater to national and international events and has played host to some of the biggest events ever to take place in Thailand. These include the World Bank/IMF Conference of 1991 and the 10th Session of the United Nations Conference on Trade and Development (UNCTAD X) in 2000.

Another important convention facility is the IMPACT Exhibition and Convention Centre, A 60,000 square meter, international-standard exhibition and convention venue in Muang Thong Thani, just outside Bangkok. The centre consists of 8 halls and provides modern facilities for exhibitioners and conferences. These include more than 100,000 exhibition spaces, a car park that caters to 15,000 cars and a wide range of public utilities and facilities (including multi-cuisine restaurants and other amenities). Over the last few years, the centre has catered to some of the highest profile business events staged in Thailand, including the BOI Fair, the Science and Technology Fair and Bangkok's Motor Expo.

A large range of accommodations, comprising of hotels and serviced apartments are available around the city—with 3 star accommodations available at 1300 TBT or $30 (Thai Baht TBT~ 1.30 INR) onwards and 5 star accommodations going up to 7000 TBT or $180. Business visitors have a plethora of choice. Although Bangkok was well served by the city buses, the need for a mass transit system was felt, and recently the Skytrain (called by many—the 'BTS') and the metro (underground) has revolutionised travel in the city. The city has some interesting alternatives; the ubiquitous taxi is complemented by another marvel, the Tuk-Tuk. Besides these, the city's Khlongs also offer visitors an alternative mode of travel in boats and small river boats on the Chau Praya.

Bangkok stood at 16 in the world for International Meetings; the city had hosted 56 meetings and close to 28,000 visitors. However, the domestic and near East clientele is much larger. 2006 has been remarkably successful for the TCEB. During 2006, Thailand hosted 1,579 conferences, which include domestic as well as international meetings and incentives and attracted 223,752 visitors and generated TBT 1.3 billion ($35 million) in revenues, while 143,719 visitors attended conventions held in Thailand, which generated another TBT 1.1 billion ($28 million).

Bangkok is the one of the key tourist destinations in the region. The city boasts of one of the largest airport complexes in the world. The erstwhile primary airport, Don Mueang Airport was one of the busiest in the world and catered to 38 million passengers every year, will be used for domestic flights over a phased manner. On September 28, 2006, the new Suvarnabhumi Airport was inaugurated-however, since then it has hit upon some operational difficulties. It is considered as the pride of Thailand. This airport has a large 8,000-acre area, 2 runways and 5 concourses, and considering the other expansion projects, which are projected over the next 3–5 years; this airport is expected to build up capacity to cater to 100 million passengers every year. The national airliner, Thai Airways connects Bangkok to most prominent international destinations, and is considered one of the most popular airliners due to its high level of service quality. Low cost airliners have started operating in the Thai skies and connect other important cities in the region. Although a large number of cruises operate in the region and other destinations in Thailand, Bangkok is not on the list because of its inland location.

Most people travel to Thailand for its world-famous beaches. However, the country has many other attractions too. The city of Bangkok is famous for its temples, waterways and palaces. The world renowned Emerald Buddha (Wat Phra Kaew) is the chief attraction, apart from that, Wat Arun, Wat Pho (reclining Buddha), Wat Mahathat are other shrines worth a visit. The ancient capital of Ayutthaya (named after the Indian kingdom of Ayodhya), Thonburi and the current Royal Palace are important pieces in the fabric of Thai history. Another interesting aspect of Bangkok is the number of network of narrow canals called Khlongs connecting the Chau Praya River. Some of the more important canals have their own floating markets, which offer the visitors (and the residents along the canals) a host of culinary options in exotic food. Bangkok is a delightful city for food lovers. Its street stalls are known for their '100 Culinary Secrets' and low prices. Over the last decade, Bangkok has become known for cheap electronic goods shopping too, mostly cheap imports from China.

Recent Conventions

Name of Convention	Date(s)	No. of Delegates
7th Asian Pacific Industrial Engg & Management	December 17–20, '06	300
International Parliamentarians' Conference (IPCI)	November 21–22, '06	300
2006 Conferences on CIS-RAM (Cybernetics)	June 7–9, '06	600+

Source: Secondary Research involving various sources.

Academic conferences form a substantial part of Bangkok's convention business. In recent times, high technology conferences have been hosted in the city. This city still remains one of the key destinations for Incentive Meetings for many corporate visitors.

The Thailand Convention Exhibition Bureau (TCEB) is engaged in promotion of conventions and exhibitions in Thailand. TCEB has launched a plan to encourage entrepreneurs and their staff. The government plans to attract 870,000 visitors and earn revenues of 59 billion TBT ($ 1.55 billion) in 2010 through MICE business. TCEB encourages collaboration between local and foreign entrepreneurs and provides them with financial support and other essential resources. As a way of expanding into new markets and increasing business opportunities, the TCEB participates in several major events, including international conferences and industry seminars. The TCEB has joined in project bidding for 25 conferences, winning eight contracts, with another 13 under consideration. TCEB has also extended its support to 90 meetings and 75 future projects. It also organised 363 exhibitions - 241 domestic and 122 international – attended by 187,823 visitors, generating TBT 1.3 billion ($ 34 Million) in revenues.

The bureau has ambitious plans for developing human resource capabilities for catering to the MICE industry's requirement. TCEB plans to develop seminars and workshops designed for staff and entrepreneurs through collaboration with domestic and international educational institutions who can develop curricula that matched the requirements of the MICE industry. It will also offer scholarships to staff and entrepreneurs for higher studies. TCEB is looking forward to greater use of ICT and electronic media and communication tools to improve its operations and management. This will include data collection, financial management and accounting, budget management, human resources and communications management. It also plans to establish a MICE Information Research Centre, in order to provide entrepreneurs with useful information for better decision-making. Effective information and knowledge distribution will be run through a newly established call centre and the bureau's existing website (www.tceb.or.th).

28.3.5. Hong Kong (S.A.R.)

Hong Kong is a unique blend of Chinese and British legacy. The island nation was transferred from British control to China in 1997. Although the city has lost some of its sheen to other 'upstart' Asian destinations, it has managed to hold onto its unique, mystic charm that attracts visitors from all over the world. The city-state has expanded beyond its natural boundaries of Hong Kong and Kowloon Bays and reclaimed new territories from the sea. The 'City of Lights' is also known for its yearlong celebrations, shopping and dining options.

Hong Kong has been known since the late 17th century as an excellent port and harbour, which attracted many felons to its shore. Under the British, the port flourished and still today remains one of the most important ports in the world. The city enjoys excellent air connection to all major destinations in the world—Thanks to the services of Cathay Pacific and the recently launched services of Air China. The Hong Kong International Airport had been adjudged the best airport for the 5th consecutive time, between 2001 and 2005. Hong Kong's city transport system is considered world-class, and provides excellent mobility across the city-state.

The Hong Kong Convention and Exhibition Centre (HKCEC) is a modern structure, larger than any other convention centre in Asia outside Japan. This centre has five exhibition halls, two ballroom-style convention halls, two theatres, 52 meeting rooms of different sizes, and two large foyers for pre-function gatherings plus supporting amenities, which include food and beverage arrangements. Apart from this impressive structure, the city offers a wide range of accommodation and smaller conference venues (about 30,000 square metres of exhibition space and 14,000 Guest rooms), which can suit different requirements (Ref. Appendix 2). Hong Kong is only to next to Singapore in the Asia Pacific Region, having been host to 95 International Meetings (and 60,000 participants) in 2005 alone.

Most visitors come to Hong Kong to feel the blend of the orient and occident, a legacy from its historical past. For visitors, the attractions are the memorable cruises on the South China Sea and the spectacular views of the city and the harbour, Theme parks for children, a cultural walkthrough of Chinese festivals around the year and excellent shopping and dining experience. HKTB has been actively promoting Green tourism with its focus towards environmentally conscious tourists.

Recent Conventions

Name of Convention	Date(s)	No. of Delegates
3G World Congress & Mobility Marketplace	December 4–7, '06	1,500
CASBAA 2006	October 24–27, '06	1,200+
INFORMS International Conference	June 25–28, '06	800

Source: Secondary Research involving various sources.

The Hong Kong Tourism Board (HKTB) promotes the conventions business through its MICE site. Any organiser or association or individual planning to host a conference, exhibition or trade fair needs to fill a simple Request for Proposal (RFP) document on the website- choosing his own set of venues from Hong Kong, Kowloon and other New Territories. A number of Conference Managers, Hotels and other service providers are connected through the Web-partner program under HKTB, who can then contact the customer with their offers. The HKTB also offers customised services to organisers to help in preparation of bids for international meetings and conferences.

The city now has a new airport and since 2002, an ambitious plan is underway to upgrade the infrastructure facilities– 1,600 projects at a total cost of about 600 billion HK dollars (77 billion US dollars) over the next 10 years, ranging from better town planning, enhancing Hong Kong's position as a transport and logistics hub, promoting tourism, and improving the environment. A cable car system linking Tung Chung and Ngong Ping was completed in 2005 together with the Disney theme park. These projects are expected to bring the less developed tourist attractions to the mainstream.

28.3.6. Seoul, Republic of Korea

Korea, the Land of the Morning Calm, has always possessed a unique charm– a global superpower in the making, yet strongly rooted to its cultural roots. Since the formation of Korea, it was the capital of the United Korea, and it has remained so, except for a small period during the Korean War. Seoul is the 10th largest city in the world with a population of 11 million and the capital of South Korea. Historically, Korea has always been under the influence of two major imperial powers in the region, viz. Russia and Japan. Following the crushing defeat of the Czarist forces in 1905 by the Japanese, Korea came under the control of the Japanese and remained so till their defeat in 1945 under the attack from Allied Forces. The post WWII period has been a blessing and curse for Korea as such-while the country was divided into American and USSR spheres of influence, into North (Communist) and South (Capitalist) Korea- South Korea has shed its feudal past and leapt into the twenty first century.

This intriguing country is considered to become one of the key convention destinations in the Far-East. Although not a traditional a tourist hotspot, Seoul has made significant progress in promoting the city as the choice destination for trade shows, exhibitions and conventions.

The largest convention centre in Seoul is the COEX convention centre. It was originally named KOEX (Korea Convention and Exhibition Centre), this building was established in 1979 to accommodate more than 100 separate conventions, exhibitions, conferences and events. In 1988, the name was changed to COEX (Convention and Exhibition Centre). This convention centre also has shops where delegates can shop for clothes, visit tailors, dine at various Korean or continental style restaurants, or can have a few drinks at one of the bars. Visitors can also enjoy latest movies at the Megabox Cinema, which is one of the newest and largest movie theatres in the capital. A newer facility is the 5-storeyed ASEM centre. This facility, as the name suggests was built for the Asia Europe Meeting scheduled in 2000. This can seat about 6,000 delegates. The SETC, Agro-trade Centre (AT Centre) and Seoul Women's Plaza are other main convention centres.

While these are the main convention facilities, some of the top-end hotels also have banquet facilities with capacities of accommodating 500+ delegates. Seoul also has a number of top quality accommodation options around the various convention venues; the COEX Intercontinental Hotel is located right in the convention complex area. Besides this facility, there are close to 10,000+ rooms available falling under the star categories. However, room tariffs are slightly higher than in other Asian destinations- ranging from $100– $ 325.

Connectivity to Seoul is still a problem, considering the fact that the national carrier Korean Air does not have extensive connections to major international destinations. Most visitors have to use other airliners, which translates into a transit flight through some of the other Asian countries. Star Alliance partners like Singapore Airlines, Lufthansa, Thai Airways, Air Canada, Polish Airlines, Asiana, are some of the better options to Seoul. The Domestic airliners connect 15 cities in the country. Though there are ferries via Incheon in the west, that mode of transport is not usually used by international visitors.

Seoul blends its ancient heritage with the new economic boom almost seamlessly. The main city is surrounded by a set of inner and outer ranges- each having 4 separate mountains. The ancient royal palaces of the Joseon Dynasty viz. Gyeongbokgung, Deoksugung, Changdeokgung, and Changgyeonggung, the royal ancestral shrine of the Joseon Dynasty, along with Huwon (the Rear Garden) next to Changdeokgung are noted for their beautifully landscaped gardens and traditional Korean structures.

One of the most popular areas for international visitors, Insa-dong, which is located in downtown Seoul, is lined with antique shops, art galleries, traditional teahouses, and restaurants as well as bookstores. It is a place that beckons both casual shoppers and serious collectors.

The most important aspects of Seoul are its mass transit systems. Seoul boasts of a subway system, which is one of the most efficient subway systems in the world. It is very tourist friendly too, with English signage all around to help the international visitor. The subway criss-crosses the entire city and very few places are beyond the reach of the subway system. Supplementing this subway, is the efficient bus system, which further is classified into Blue, Red, Green and Yellow lines, catering to various routes (covering different cities, city centre to outskirts, etc.). The KTX, or the super-fast service (Korea's answer to Japan's bullet train), connects Seoul to the city of Pusan, another important convention destination.

Seoul ranks 8th in the world in terms of International Meetings, having played host to approximately 48,000 international visitors in 2005. A total of 77 international meetings were held in this city. This is the first time Seoul has featured in the list of top 10 cities in the world, and the rise has been rapid by any standard.

Recent Conventions

Name of Convention	Date(s)	No. of Delegates
VLDB 2006	September 12–15, '06	700
72nd World Library and Information Congress	August 20–24, '06	N/A.
SportAccord 2006	April 3–7, '06	900+

Source: Secondary Research involving various sources.

One of the key aspects of the rapid infrastructure development in Seoul and Korea in general, is the proactive approach taken up by both the Korean governments. When the government decided to bid for the 1988 Olympics at Seoul, there were widespread apprehensions even among various ministries. The government pushed for Infrastructural development, which resulted in many of the forward-looking projects. The 1988 Olympics were followed by the 2002 Soccer World Cup- (co-hosted with Japan) and 2002 Asian Games in Busan. These mega international events brought about the confidence, that Seoul and Korea were ready for large-scale international events. Convention centres were also planned to sustain this vision Korea as the venue for international mega-events. With the economic growth of Korea fuelling the inbound business traffic, this has become a reality.

The Seoul Convention and Visitors' Bureau (SCVB) is a fairly new, but a forward looking organisation, which is involved in promoting Seoul conventions with large scale support from the metropolitan government of the city.

Through active intervention from Seoul City council, two more large convention facilities are expected to be completed by the year 2010, viz. the Seoul International Finance Centre and Sang-Am Convention centre. Further, under the banner of "Vision Seoul 2015," an intensive cultural enhancement project has been undertaken for establishing new arts and performance centres, promoting cultural industries and recovering historic relics. The plan includes completing construction of the Seoul Performing Arts Centre on Nodeul Island in the Han River. Construction will begin in 2008 on the facility. It will be modelled after the world-renowned Opera House in Sydney, Australia. These initiatives are expected to bring more tourism revenues to the country. The city will also erect more facilities in culturally disadvantaged areas to balance access to culture in the city, notably between the booming Gangnam (south of the Han River) and derelict Gangbuk (north of the river). An estimated 7.6 trillion Won (US$7 billion) will be spent on the project and among its many aims will be providing financial support for aspiring artists.

28.3.7. Jakarta, Republic of Indonesia

The Republic of Indonesia has been in the news in the recent past for all the wrong reasons, first the Asian crisis, then the ouster of the Presidents Suharto and Habibie, which left the country in a crisis. The Bali bombings put Indonesia on the terrorism map. Since then, the country has never been able to come out of economic and political controversies- the country's growing pan-Islamic terrorism is also a cause of concern for many moderates in the country as well as visitors from the western hemisphere and Australia. However, in spite of these problems, the country has been trying hard to promote its leisure and business tourism opportunities. Jakarta, the capital city of Indonesia, like other Southeast Asian capitals is the ideal mix of convergence of civilisations, Chinese, Javanese, Arab and Indian along with the recent invasion of American media. The country's mixed heritage comes from its occupation by various foreign forces at different periods, Hindu, Arab, Chinese, and most recently Dutch, who departed the shores as late as 1949. Jakarta is situated on the island of Java, which has a population of 124 Million and is one of the most densely populated islands in the world.

Jakarta's chief convention facility is the Balai Sidang Convention Centre in the western part of the city. The modern convention centre offers a range of services for the business visitors. The centre has a 5,000-seat Plenary Hall, 4,000 square metres Assembly Hall (flexibility of having 3 rooms), Exhibition Halls with a combined space of approximately 9,600 square metres, and a large lobby offers organisers a plethora of choice. At present, a large number of hotels offering a wide range of accommodation are also available in the city—some of these hotels also have smaller convention halls, which cater to the domestic meetings. According to the ICCA report, Jakarta hosted 7 international meetings in 2005.

The city is accessible by Air and sea routes, from most destinations—but the accessibility is limited. A large number of flights are routed through Singapore (Singapore Airlines) and Bandar Seri Begawan (Royal Brunei) and Bangkok (Thai Airways) to these islands. The national airline, Garuda Airlines connects most of the domestic centres, as well as destinations in Australia, New Zealand, Japan, South East Asia and London/ Amsterdam in Europe. The current financial condition of this airline is critical and rising debt is a threat to the survival of this airliner.

The country boasts of a large number of isolated islands (close to 17,000 in the archipelago) many of them uninhabited. While most visitors do not venture beyond the islands of Java and famous island resort of Bali, restricting themselves to the Buddhist Temple at Borobodur and Mt. Luwu, the country has much to offer to the discerning visitor. The jungles of Borneo for eco-tourism, the gorgeous beaches, snorkelling and the Hindu temples of Bali and Java, trips to volcanoes in Java, and wonderful beaches in other exotic islands.

Recent Conventions

Name of Convention	Date(s)	No. of Delegates
Better Air Quality (BAQ) 2006	December 13–15, '06	1100
IDC Asia Pacific InfraVision Conference	November 16, '06	400
International Geo-sciences Conference	August 14–16, '06	500

Source: Secondary Research involving various sources.

Convention business is promoted through the Indonesian Trade Promotion Centre (ITPC-http://www.itpcla.org), however, the focus is not very strong and individual centres, especially Jakarta Convention Centre carries out its own promotional campaigns targeted towards businesses and academics at the University of Bandung. The majority of revenue for the convention centres comes from domestic organisers, as Jakarta has lost out on many of the international meetings since 1994. However, the city is slowing signs of resurgence registering steady growth since 2002.

The Indonesian government has often come under attack because of its poor record as far as infrastructure development is concerned. Widespread corruption during erstwhile

President Suharto's rule has often been cited as the main cause. However, the Asian Development Bank, a key stakeholder in infrastructure projects in the country, has applauded recent efforts from the federal government. As far as convention facilities are concerned, the government is planning to promote Yogyakarta, another proposed city for the development of convention facilities, although no plans have been confirmed.

28.3.8. Highlights from Asian Destinations

The analysis of prominent convention destinations in Asia helps us identify a few key success factors as listed below:

- Destinations like Singapore and Hong Kong are currently at the top of the world market, as they have managed to merge the best of both worlds—the meticulous planning of the western world, with the courtesy and hospitality of the eastern world.
- Most Asian destinations were primary tourist destinations, which later developed into large economic centres and the convention business was developed around this economic development. Yogyakarta (Indonesia) and Putrajaya (Malaysia) are two exceptions, where two cities are being developed to cater to the conventions market, unique in the Asian context.
- Convention and Visitor Bureaus from cities like Seoul, Hong Kong and Singapore are extremely proactive, and they work closely with various government agencies to provide a delightful experience to its visitors
- Cities like Shanghai and Hong Kong have taken the top down approach of building convention infrastructure in the respective locations—following the European model of development; since the infrastructure has been developed to a substantial level already in these cities, one would witness more aggressive marketing in the near future for the utilisation of these facilities. While Cities like Singapore, Bangkok and to some extent Kuala Lumpur have adopted the Public-Private partnership model.

28.4. PROMINANT NON-ASIAN DESTINATIONS

This section highlights some of the popular European convention destinations in the world. A brief summary of other popular destinations across the world is provided at the end of this section.

28.4.1. Vienna, Republic of Austria

Founded way back in 500 BC as a Celtic settlement, Vienna emerged as a flourishing European city in the thirteenth and fourteenth centuries. Since 1805, Vienna has been the centre of European politics and hosted one of the most significant conferences in history in 1815, which was subsequently known as the "Congress of Vienna". It had become the seat of power of the Austro-Hungarian Empire and following its fall became the capital of the new state of Austria. For a brief period, it lost its glory under the Anschluß (or Union) with the Third Reich and the capital of All Germany was shifted to Berlin. However, since the end of WWII, Vienna has regained not only its glory as the political capital of Austria, but also as the artistic and cultural capital of Eastern Europe. Due to its geographical position, it has been the melting pot of West European, Caucasian, Turkish and South Slavic cultures.

The last few decades have seen Vienna taking up a more moderate political role, trying to strike a balance between the capitalist Western Europe and its eastern communist neighbours. This in turn meant that Vienna received its share as a 'neutral' venue for various political and industrial events during the WWII era.

The chief convention centre in the city is the Reed Exhibitions Messe Wien Congress Centre. The capacity of the Congress Centre is quite impressive, with some 54,000 square metres of space across the 4 Halls. Apart from these halls, the site also offers large exhibitions spaces. Apart from the Mesee Wien, there are other large centres like the Austria Centre Vienna, Hofburg Kongresszentrum Wien, Hofburg Redoutensäle Wien, Wiener Stadthalle all offer flexible space for exhibitions/trade shows as well as conferences/ conventions. This inventory of convention centres is further supplemented by a large number of top hotels in the city—inside as well as outside the city centre, which can also host conferences of medium sizes, comprising of 300-500 delegates. A network of 300+ hotels in the city, also ensures that international visitors can have adequate choice as far as budget and comfort options are concerned.

According to ICCA 2006 report, Vienna tops the world list of convention destinations with 129 international meetings (a significant 20% increase over 2004), attracting over 76,000 visitors. In terms of number of visitors, Vienna came in second to Paris.

Vienna is well connected through all major hubs in Europe; North American passengers can reach Vienna easily with a small stop over at Amsterdam, Paris, Frankfurt or Milan. Because of the Schengen agreement shared by 15 nations in Europe for unified visa regulations, visitors can travel within these countries easily, which has encouraged visitors to visit these countries. Most Star Alliance Airline partners connect Vienna—apart from the National Air, which has Vienna as its hub. As far as Rail connections are concerned, Vienna is again well connected to all major cities in Europe. European roads are well developed, which also facilitates connectivity between major cities in Western Europe.

The chief attraction of Vienna is the Imperial Hofburg Palace, seat of the Habsburg Empire. Other important attractions are the baroque Schönbrunn and Belvedere Palaces along with Sisi Museum, The Spanish Riding School, where one can witness the elegance of the world-renowned Lipizzaner horses. The city council offers a 72-hour Vienna Card priced at €16.90 or $22 (or Vienna Ala Carte), where visitors are offered unlimited access to all public transportation as well as special rates (discounts or free access) for museums and other venues (numbering 210). For Music and art lovers, the cities galleries and theatres offer a splendid fare-chief attractions being Wiener Konzerthaus, Volkstheater Wien, Die theatre Wien, Museum of Fine Arts, Liechtenstein Museum, Austrian Gallery in the Belvedere Palace, etc. Vienna is also known as the Coffee Capital of the world, coffee lovers from all over the world congregate here for enjoying the ambience in this city.

The city's local transportation network of buses, trams and trains (U-Bahn, S-Bahn and Lokalbahn), called Wiener Linien offer comprehensive access to all major venues in and around the city.

Recent Conventions

Name of Convention	Date(s)	No. of Delegates
HP Software Universe 2006	December 12–15, '06	N/A
FENS Forum 2006 (Neurosciences)	July 8–12, '06	5,000
6th European Congress against Epilepsy	May 30- Jun 3, '06	3,000

Source: Secondary Research involving various sources.

One of Vienna's specialities is medical conference; apart from that, the city regularly hosts a mix of academic, high technology and travel meetings/conventions.

Vienna Convention Bureau (VCB) has been very active in promoting the city and its convention centres in the last decade or so, registering strong growth from 49 meetings in 1997 to 129 in 2005. The Vienna City Council and the Vienna Chamber of Commerce support the promotion bureau financially. The proceeds from various conferences/ Conventions organised at the city are shared by VCB. Additional funds come from various sponsorships. The team is organised across various regional markets where VCB promotes its services, though mostly in Europe, some effort is also focused towards North American countries, especially USA and Canada.

Fortunately, the city has a surplus of convention related infrastructure, be it convention centres or hotels or in terms of accessibility to the city. Rail connections to the city are currently under focus, because of its location in the eastern part of Austria, accessibility has been a problem through non-Schengen countries, *e.g.*, Czech Republic or Poland. The recent inclusion of these countries under the extended Schengen policy would facilitate smooth traffic into the city.

28.4.2. Frankfurt, Federal Republic of Germany

Frankfurt was an early Celtic settlement. During the thirteenth century, this city became powerful as a Reichsstadt (Imperial City) and as such free of control from any of the smaller Germanic principalities. This status allowed Frankfurt to flourish as a major centre of trade and commerce—its strategic location on the bank of river Main also allowed its easy access to other major trade centres in northern Germany.

Frankfurt is the fifth largest city in Germany. All over the world it is commonly known as "Frankfurt" although its full name is Frankfurt am Main. The city is the largest financial centre of Germany. This is one of the top cities of the world. The financial capital of Germany, Frankfurt is often called by the nicknames "Bankfurt" or "Mainhattan" because of its skyscrapers. Over 325 banks are located in Frankfurt. The Frankfurt Stock Exchange is one of the world's most important exchanges. Frankfurt International Airport is among the three busiest airports of Europe. In the new Euro economy, Frankfurt plays an important role- it is the home of the European Central Bank (ECB). Finance, Trade Fairs and Transport are the three pillars of this city's economy. Frankfurt's Fair and Exhibition Centre is one of the largest trade fair centres in the world. About 40 trade fairs are held here annually. Frankfurt plays host to about 16 of the world's most important trade fairs.

Frankfurt can be called the Trade Fair capital of the world. Every year, this city hosts some of the largest fairs in the world; viz. Internationale Automobil Ausstellung (International Motor Show) and the Frankfurt International Book Fair have 100,000 visitors every year. Other large shows include the LinuxWorld Conference and Expo or Musikmesse Frankfurt. The Messe Frankfurt GmbH is one of the largest convention centres in the city. It holds close to 100 large international trade shows/convention every year. In order to cater to this huge visitor traffic, close to 100 hotels are situated in the vicinity of the convention centre. There are close to 150 convention centres in the city with different capacities, ranging from 400 to 15,000 visitors.

Being a key financial destination, Frankfurt has a vibrant business tourism industry, in addition to convention traffic. Because of thriving trade, the city has a large number of quality hotels in a wide range of prices. Frankfurt also can boast of one of the largest mass transport systems in the world, the RMV or Rhein-Main- Verkehrsverbund. The city's main station has been developed recently to receive trains from all over the country and other major cities in Europe. The city also has an efficient subway system, the S-Bahn and the U-Bahn—and the Straßenbahn Trams which ply in and around the main city.

Frankfurt features much lower (77th in the world) in the ICCA Rankings (2006) for International Meetings; however, it is one of the largest destinations as far as Trade Fairs are concerned. In 2005, the city had 2.72 million visitors.

Frankfurt is a major international airport and the second or third busiest airport in Europe, after London's Heathrow and Paris' Charles De Gaulle airport. It also features in the world's top ten servicing 304 destinations in 110 countries around the world. Germany's national carrier, Lufthansa has its hub in Frankfurt for all its flights. The city has another secondary airport, the Frankfurt Hahn Airport, which is somewhat far away (120km) from the city centre. The central location of this city in Europe also makes it easily accessible by road and rail as well as water.

Frankfurt has its share of famous and awe-inspiring historical and modern structures. Some of the historical tourist attractions of Frankfurt are the Archaeological Gardens and Emperor's Hall inside the Roemer. Some modern tourist attractions of Frankfurt are the Banking District and Commerzbank Towers. The city has a number of museums offering a glimpse into its culture and heritage. Some of the local history and culture museums that one should take the time to visit are Göthehaus, Heinrich-Hoffman Museum, and Possman. Göthehaus is the house in which Johann Wolfgang von Göthe, the noted German novelist, lived from 1749 till some years later.

Recent Conventions

Name of Convention	Date(s)	No. of Delegates
Pension Fund Investment World Congress	December 12–14, '06	600
BIO-Europe 2006	November 6–8, '06	1850+
International PHP 2006 Conference	November 5–8, '06	500 (approx.)

Source: Secondary Research involving various sources.

Being the financial capital of Western Europe, the city attracts a large number of conferences related to banking as well as investments. These range from being purely academic conferences to congregation of large corporate entities. Larger (800+ delegates) medical conferences are also hosted in the city; apart from these, the city hosts a large number of trade fairs and exhibitions every year.

The Frankfurt Congress Bureau facilitates the management of requests from potential organisers; along with selection of venues/hotels and supporting the professional convention organisers with analysis of guest data—so that they can position their offering in a more professional manner.

28.4.3. Paris, Republic of France

Paris is the capital of the Republic of France and the cultural and fashion capital of Western Europe and for many, of the world. It is considered to be one of the most romantic destinations in the world. The city derives its name from the Gallic tribes who settled there, although during 'Roman times it was known as Lutetia. Today it is the hub of France's economic activity and the largest city in France. Since the 1970s, many inner suburbs of Paris (especially the eastern ones) have experienced de-industrialization, and the once-thriving cities have gradually become crowded with immigrants and plagued by unemployment. At the same time, the City of Paris (within its periphery ring) and the western and southern suburbs have successfully shifted their economic base from traditional manufacturing to high value-added services and high-tech manufacturing, generating great wealth for their residents whose per capita income is among the highest in Europe. The resulting widening social gap between these two areas and communities has led to periodic social unrest since the mid-1980s, such as the 2005 riots which largely concentrated in the north-eastern suburbs.

A large number of high-end Parisian hotels have large convention facilities, viz. Concorde La Fayette, Accor Paris, Club La Fayette, Club Montparnasse offer convention spaces as well as meeting facilities. Under the Parc Des Expositions programme, several exhibition centres have been constructed around Paris and other major cities in France. The Paris Nord Villepinte is located close to the CDG Airport as well the Le Bourget Airports, and is only 20 minutes away from the city centre, for travel by the Regional railway lines (RER). This facility can handle domestic and international professional events, such as trade shows, fairs, and corporate events (conventions, seminars, workshops, forums, product launches, etc.). Another key feature of this centre is that around 10,000 rooms are available within a distance of 5 minutes from the site, out of which 4,000 are of 4-star standards. Visitors can have options of choosing between large hotel chains as well as private hotels. A further 12,000 rooms are available if one looks over a 20 kilometre radius.

The Charles De Gaulle (CDG) Airport at Paris is one of the busiest Airports in Europe and in the world. The French national carrier Air France connects a large number of International destinations. Besides, various Star Alliance Airline partners have easy access to all corners of the world and large number of flights is routed through CDG. Only Airport handles only a small number of international flights and mostly used for domestic connections. Apart from the airline connections, Paris is well connected by rail and roads. Most Western Europe capitals are connected to Paris via Thalys, Eurostar and Inter City trains.

Paris has a large number of attractions; this city is packed with sights to see and things to do. The city's chief attractions are the famous Eiffel Tower, Arc De Triumph, Louvre Museum, Les Invalides, Grand Palais, Petit Palais, Sacrè Coeur and host of others. High-end shoppers flock to Champs-Elysées, which offers a range of brands from all over the world, and Montmartre, huddled in the crowded immigrant districts offers shopping experience with a difference. For others, the lazy lifestyle of Paris, roadside artists hold a different charm—for everyone, there is something in Paris. The magnificent palace of Versailles is located only a few kilometres from the city centre of Paris.

In 2005, Paris hosted 91 international meetings according to ICCA reports-it had the largest number of visitors-higher than Vienna, a total of approximately 79,000 for these meetings. This figure does not include visitors for the other trade shows and fairs that took place in the city.

Recent Conventions

Name of Convention	Date(s)	No. of Delegates
World Free Zone 2006	December 12–13, '06	400+
EURO-BIO 2006	October 25–27, '06	700+
WI-MAX Summit 2006 + SIP Conference	February 21–24, '06	400+

Source: Secondary Research involving various sources.

The city hosts a large number of Conferences with Social Sciences and Cultural themes, as well as conventions and conferences focussing on technology and world economy themes. Some software and hardware related conferences, which rotate across European cities also form a significant part of the number of events.

The Paris Convention and Visitors Bureau is a not-for-profit association whose main sponsors, the Paris City Council and the Chamber of Commerce and Industry, give their active support to the promotion of the capital. The city council also works closely with various stakeholders, Hotels, venues as well as professional organisers to prepare proposals and submitting to potential customers.

Currently, the focus is not on developing convention infrastructure, as most of it is already available. However, the Paris city council is planning for a more proactive role of the chamber of commerce as well as the council to promote the convention business. The latter has traditionally been more keen to promote the city for the tourism in general, rather than convention related tourism specifically.

28.4.4. Barcelona, Kingdom of Spain

Barcelona is the second largest city in Spain and the capital of the province of Catalonia. There are legends associated with the birth of this city. One of them attributes the foundation to the Carthaginian dynasty, by Hamilcar Barca, father of the great Hannibal in 3rd century BC. The city boasts of a rich cultural heritage, a 2000 year history and has been the centre of Catalan struggle against the Habsburg/Spanish sovereignty. Although in the past the city has witnessed some bitter words being exchanged between Madrid and Barcelona, both parties have managed to tone down the rhetoric in the recent years. This city is also famous for its education institutions as well being the Airbus manufacturing hub for Spain.

The Barcelona International Convention Centre (Centre Convencions Internationale Barcelona) is currently one of the largest facilities in Barcelona. The current available exhibition space in this centre is around 11,200 square metres and houses about 4,000 to 5,000 delegates. There is a cluster of meeting halls, which offer capacities from 60 to 700 delegates. There are close to 25 other smaller convention facilities, which offer facilities catering to 250–1500 delegates. Around the convention venue, there are close to 7,000 3–5 Star rated hotel rooms.

According to the ICCA 2006 report, Barcelona ranks 3rd in the world as far as the number of meetings is concerned, with close to 42,000 visitors for these meetings.

Barcelona is served by El Prat International Airport in the town of El Prat de Llobregat, about 3 km from Barcelona. It is the second-largest airport in Spain and the largest on the Mediterranean coast. The total number of passengers in 2005 was 27 million and it is expected to go up to 30 million in 2006. The airport is connected to the city by highway, commuter train and scheduled bus service. The Sabadell Airport is a smaller airport in the nearby town of Sabadell, devoted to pilot training, advertising flights, Aerotaxi and private flights. Some low-cost airlines, like Ryanair and Martinair, prefer to use the Girona-Costa Brava Airport, situated about 100 km to the north of Barcelona. Spain's national carrier, Iberia connects some of the North American destinations directly to Barcelona or via Madrid. The Barcelona—Madrid air route, called "Puente Aereo" (or Air Bridge), is the busiest in the world. However, international connections to this city, needs to be developed in the long run if the convention business is expected to grow at double digit rates. Barcelona is a major hub for RENFE, the Spanish state railway network, and its main suburban train station is Sants Estació. The AVE high-speed rail system has been extended from Madrid to Lleida in western Catalonia, and is expected to reach Barcelona by 2007. RENFE and the Ferrocarrils de la Generalitat de Catalunya (FGC) run Barcelona's efficient commuter train services.

The most important attraction of Barcelona is the Sagrada Familia, designed by the architect, Antonio Gaudi. It has been under construction since 1882, and it is estimated that this giant temple would take another 30-60 years to complete. This structure attracts close to 2 million visitors every year. Another attraction is the Poble Espanyol de Montjuic- which is a small village, which has a cluster of houses depicting different Spanish styles. Other main tourist spots are; The Barcelona Aquarium, Casa Mila, Barcelona Museum, Picasso Museum, etc.

Recent Conventions

Name of Convention	Date(s)	No. of Delegates
EIBTM	November 28-30, '06	4,000+
e-Challenges 2006	October 25-27, '06	650
ACTE.org	October 22-24, '06	1,000+

Source: Secondary Research involving various sources.

The city hosts a large number of academic conferences, with themes ranging from Management research to manufacturing technologies. Further, the city hosts the annual EIBTM Conventions attracting a large number of exhibitors and delegates from the conventions fraternity—making it a default hub of congregation for professionals in this industry.

The Barcelona Convention Board (BCB) was founded in 1983, one of the pioneer institutions in Spain. The agency actively promotes Barcelona as a key convention destination. Currently, this association has close to 300+ members. The funds for running BCB (close to € 2 million) come from membership fees from members (20%) and Turisme De Barcelona (80%). A significant portion of these funds (about 50%) are spent on promotional activities as well as training for personnel.

The Barcelona International Convention Centre (CCIB) is expected to be further developed in the near future. The Convention Centre is a 67,000-square meter building. It will have the capacity to hold congresses of up to 15,000 people. The modified CCIB auditorium, with a capacity for 3,200 people, will be located in the Forum Building. Both buildings will be connected by a 20-meter-wide underground walkway. The French company, Générale Location, which already operates various congress centres in France, will operate the CCIB. The Convention Centre will fill the city's former shortcomings in the sphere of congresses, as its capacity will make it the largest in Southern Europe. In the past, Barcelona only had centres with a capacity for up to 4,000 people.

28.4.5. Geneva, Swiss Confederation

Geneva is the capital and main city of the Canton of Geneva, which is part of Swiss Confederation. This canton is one of the French speaking cantons in the confederation, situated at the bank of the Lake Geneva. Its close geographical proximity to France meant that its internal politics was regularly affected by French designs—and the last incursion was during Napoleon's time, when this city came under French rule (till 1815). However, since then this city and Switzerland, in general, has maintained the stance of neutrality-because of which the country escaped the destruction during the two World Wars. This neutrality proved to be a strong case to base most of the United Nations' offices out of Geneva and Switzerland. Every year, Geneva and various cities in Switzerland host conferences of great international importance.

Geneva's main Convention and exhibition centre is the PALEXPO centre, a 10km travel from the Geneva city centre with direct access from the international airport as well as the railway station. Other European visitors can access this centre on road, as this is located on the road network connecting Italy, France, Spain and Germany. It has 100,000 square metres of exhibition space and conference facilities for a delegate size of 4,800. Along with 7 restaurants and 8 snack bars in the complex, around 1,500 hotel rooms are available within walking distance from the convention centre. For visitors driving to the exhibition crowd, 4,500 parking slots are readily available and another 3,500 peripheral slots can be made available. Next to the PALEXPO, the Geneva Arena is another conference venue with a capacity of 6,500 delegates. In 2005, the CICG (International Conference Centre, Geneva) was reopened; this centre has a capacity of around 2,200 delegates making it ideal for medium sized congress/seminars. Other smaller but more exotic conference locations are Cartigny Meeting Centre, Interprofessional Centre of Geneva (CIP), Chateau De Bossey, Domaine De Choully, Forum Geneva, and a host of others.

Geneva international airport is connected to major international destinations by 40 airliners. Almost all major airliners connect via Charles De Gaulle (Paris) or the Zurich Airport. The national carrier Swiss also connects Geneva to some of the North Atlantic destinations. Intercity trains connect various locations in France and Italy for the convenience of International passengers. Since Switzerland is not part of the Schengen agreement, separate visa procedures need to be taken care of. However, most European residents can freely travel in Switzerland.

Geneva is famous for the Red Cross and Red Crescent Museum and many other smaller attractions. Cathedral of St. Peter is one of the historic sites, where John Calvin delivered his sermons in the mid 16th century. Other than these, Jet d'Eau (Fountain of Water), Maison Tavel, Museum of Art and History, and of course Lake Geneva are some of the not-to-miss items on every tourist's list.

The city's public transport systems, comprising of trains, buses and Lake Boats are extremely efficient and provide widespread access to all corners of the city. Although the current ICCA report in 2006 ranks Geneva 21st in the world in terms of international meetings (38) and 24,000 visitors, it does not reflect the real picture as Geneva consistently hosts many of the important UN level summits as well as key World Organisation summits.

Recent Conventions

Name of Convention	Date(s)	No. of Delegates
EGP for a Greener Europe	October 13–14, '06	600
EERA/ ECER	September 13–15, '06	450
International Society for Clinical Bio-statistics	August 27–31, '06	500

Source: Secondary Research involving various sources.

Geneva is known all over the world for the large as well as high profile Inter-governmental Meetings. However, the city also hosts a large share of smaller (400-500 delegates) Information Technology, Medical as well as banking/finance/investments conferences and meetings.

The Genève Tourisme bureau has recently changed its name to Genève Tourisme et Bureau De Congres to indicate its commitment to the promotion of conventions in a greater manner. The funds for running this organisation are collected from membership fees from stakeholders as well as a revenue share from events. The bureau works closely with the various convention centres, hotels and other agencies to offer the potential organiser a best possible value. The current budget of this bureau is close to € 2 million or CHF 3 million, a large portion of these funds goes to preparing collaterals for tourism/convention customers as well as other promotional activities.

28.4.6. Stockholm, Kingdom of Sweden

Stockholm is the capital of the Kingdom of Sweden and the largest city in the country. This city was founded across numerous islands joined together by man-made bridges. Some estimate the number of islands to be close to 100,000, which were formed mainly because of glacial movement during the ice ages. When the glacial ice melted, these islands formed an archipelago, on which Stockholm has expanded. It was known since the 12th century as an excellent port and harbour, and as Sweden emerged from the shadows of Denmark as the dominant Scandinavian power, Stockholm's fortunes soared. Today, Stockholm is one of Europe's leading economic regions with its high concentration of information technology, health care industry and research.

Stockholm International Fairs (SIF) is one of Europe's largest convention centres with capacity for conventions with up to 25,000 delegates, offering the latest in modern and flexible facilities and advanced technology. This conference centre has excellent public services. There are 7 restaurants with seating capacity for 2,000 delegates. There are 50 conference rooms, with capacities ranging from 150 to 3,000 delegates in each room. The total exhibition space available is 56,000 square metres. Its proximity to the city centre (15 km, 10 min by train) enables visitors to avail of accommodation facilities ranging from €50-€200 (SEK 450-1,800). Stockholm Globe Arena is another convention centre, although much smaller compared to the SIF; this centre offers a range of conference options, with various sizes. A host of other star level hotels as well as the Arlanda Conference and Business Centre (located close to the Arlanda Airport) have a range of conference facilities, which can cater to 100–800 delegates.

Stockholm's Arlanda Airport is the hub for most Scandinavian airliners; some of the low cost airliners too use this airport. The airport is located 42 kilometres from the city, but is well connected by the Airport train service, as well as a bus service to the city centre. The city has two other airports, the Skavsta and the Vasteras Airports, which cater to other low cost airliners as well as private chartered flights. For visitors travelling over the Baltic Sea, there are ferry options for Stockholm, from Finland, Estonia, Germany and St. Petersburg in Russia. Regular ferries and cruise stop at Stockholm. Scandinavian railways networks are extremely well integrated and visitors can avail of the Eurorail connections to reach Stockholm.

Stockholm has one of the best-preserved medieval city centres in Europe, Gamla Stan, or the Old city of Stockholm attracts the largest number of visitors. The changing of guards at the Royal Palace is also unique, although not as well managed compared to the English experience. Other chief attractions include several museums, notable among them are the Vasa Museum and National Museum, a large part of Sweden's history is linked to the flourishing maritime trade and understandably many maritime historians flock to Stockholm to see these treasures.

The city's excellent local transport infrastructure, the city's subway (Tunnelbana) systems are one of the most extensive (with 110 kilometres of track and 100 stations) in the continent. Apart from these, there are local buses and trams, which criss-cross the city, and most parts of the city centre and the archipelago are accessible to public transport. The local commuter trains merge seamlessly with the Tunnelbana, making it convenient for most travellers from suburban regions. Visitors to the city can also opt for the Stockholm card, which allows unlimited access to public transport for a fixed number of days.

Recent Conventions

Name of Convention	Date(s)	No. of Delegates
Internet Marketing Conference 2006	November 30, '06	500+
Conference on Environmental Law & Justice	September 6–9,'06	350
European Association for Urban History	Aug 30- Sept.2, '06	300

Source: Secondary Research involving various sources.

A large number of conferences and meetings related to Management Research Social Sciences, Art Movements and other cultural themes are hosted in the city. In recent times, a small number of high-technology conferences were hosted.

One of the key highlights of the Stockholm Convention promotion Bureau is that unlike its counterparts, it is largely a privately owned Professional Conference Organiser. The company is owned by MCI SA of Switzerland (2/3rd), Stockholm City Conference Centre and Stockholm International Fairs. The company, set up in 1971, has been promoting the city and its available inventory of convention facilities to a number of customers. The very fact that the majority stakeholder MCI is one of the world's leading companies in the field of association, communications and event management, with presence in 14 countries has also helped the cause.

Table 28.4: Summary of Key Asian and European Destinations from this Section. (High-Medium and Low Rankings are Based on Secondary Research)

City Country	Ocation Political Environment	Tourist Attraction	Accessibility	Prove to Facilities	Govt. Policy	Here too I Facilities	Availability of Affordable Accommodation
Singapore, Singapore	High	Medium	High	High	High	High	High
Shanghai, PRC	Medium	Medium	Medium	High	Medium	Medium	High
Kuala Lumpur, Malaysia	Medium	Medium	High	High	High	Medium	High
Bangkok, Thailand	Medium	High	Medium	High	High	High	High
Hong Kong SAR, PRC	High	Medium	Medium	Medium	Medium	High	High
Seoul, Korea	High	Medium	Low	Medium	Medium	Medium	Low
Jakarta, Indonesia	Medium	High	Low	Medium	Medium	High	High

Vienna, Austria	High	High	Medium	High	High	High	Medium
Frankfurt, Germany	High	High	High	High	High	High	Medium
Paris, France	High	High	High	Medium	High	High	High
Barcelona, Spain	Medium	Medium	Medium	High	High	High	Medium
Geneva, Switzerland	High	High	Medium	High	High	Medium	Medium
Stockholm, Sweden	High	Medium	Medium	High	High	High	High

28.4.7. Other World Destinations

City, Country	Location & Political Environment	Key Tourist Attractions	Accessibility	Convention Facilities	Govt. Policy
Birmingham, UK	Medium	Low	Medium	High	Medium
New York, USA	High	High	Very High	High	Medium
San Francisco, USA	High	High	High	High	Medium
Vancouver, Canada	High	Medium	Medium	High	Medium
Toronto, Canada	High	Medium	Medium	Medium	Medium
Sydney, Australia	High	High	High	High	High
Melbourne, Australia	High	High	High	Medium	High
Dubai, UAE	Medium	High	High	Medium	High
Johannesburg, South Africa	Medium	High	Medium	High	High
Durban, South Africa	Medium	Medium	Medium	Medium	High

28.4.8. Highlights from Non-Asian Destinations

The analyses of all major international destinations help us conclude that the success of these venues stems largely from the following factors:

High level of focus in terms of developing Infrastructure for Convention facilities, often leading the actual trend- *e.g.*, Vienna had invested heavily in convention facilities, even when the market was nascent. While a few of the important convention destinations are well-known tourist hotspots, most of them have been developed as stand-alone convention centres.

Very proactive City promotion bureaus—professionally managed, high quality of Collateral material prepared by professional agencies and employs a full-time market development team, *e.g.*, Brussels, Vienna and Barcelona (Works with prominent Business Schools to train its team of professionals).

Greater access to funds from City Councils, and other members—available funds are close to Euros 1.5 to 2 million for each bureau. This enables the bureau to have access to professionals as well as developing high-quality collaterals. Funds generated by the Bureau can come from conventions facilitated by the bureau itself, thus it has incentive to develop the convention market- (*e.g.*, Vienna—where a share of the tax revenues from conventions held in the city are used by the bureau for promotional activities). This enhances accountability as well as generating necessary funds for developing the target market.

In all the locations, local transportation is well developed as well being well-integrated-visitors can choose between an extensive network of Trains, Trams, buses or the Subway systems. Most of the popular European destinations offer a CITY Card, which allows visitors unlimited travel on any mode of public transport for a fixed number of days, which is extremely convenient for the business visitor/tourist alike.

Stockholm Convention Bureau (StoCon) is an interesting example, where this bureau is run as a professional conference organiser company. However, this City council also plays an active role in its board- Public-Private partnership.

28.5. THE INDIAN CONVENTIONS INDUSTRY

Article 28.5 deals with the Indian conventions industry and constitutes the core of this study. It has various subsections, which discuss the market size and impact of this industry, the city-wise market potential and current state of convention and related infrastructure, and case studies of successful and unsuccessful convention bids, respectively.

The conventions/conference market is estimated at ₹ 4,000–5,500 Crores annually. The entire tourism sector accounts for 2.2 percent of GDP (2005 estimates) of which conventions tourism contributes around 5–7 percent of total tourism revenues, comparable to that in other convention destinations but small in terms of India's potential. Conferences and trade shows are the most important categories of events. A few venues account for the bulk of events and certain sectors such as the medical and pharmaceutical industries predominate. Participation is largely domestic and there is considerable seasonality in the conventions industry.

This article also presents the findings of a consumer survey that was conducted among international delegates in selected cities in the course of this study. The findings reveal that such tourists are relatively high spenders and thus can have sizeable spill over effects on other parts of the economy. The discussion highlights the various channels for such spill over based on primary and secondary evidence and provides estimates for value added and employment multipliers. The analysis estimates a value addition in the range of ₹ 14,000 and ₹ 24,000 Crores per year to the Indian economy with a direct contribution of 0.7–1.2 percent of GDP and a total (direct plus indirect) contribution of 1.4–2.4 percent of GDP. The value added contributions stem from spending on transport, accommodation, recreational facilities, food and beverages, and other tourism. Based on primary evidence regarding the spending pattern of international delegates and existing estimates of the contribution of foreign tourists to employment as well as available employment and business tourism related foreign exchange receipts data, the employment multiplier analysis has been carried out. The results indicate that business tourism can directly add about 13 lakh jobs to the economy in a year and that it has the potential to generate a large number of jobs over the medium term at all skill levels, given projected growth rates for business tourism. Thus there are potentially large effects on local economies, with some Indian cities such as Delhi, Bengaluru, and Mumbai better placed than others in becoming convention destinations and in generating such multiplier effects.

Article 28.5 then highlights the market potential of selected Indian cities, namely, Agra, Goa, Jaipur, Kochi, Delhi, Mumbai, Kolkata, Chennai, Bengaluru, and Hyderabad, in terms of existing convention facilities, transport, accommodation, connectivity, and other tourism attractions. This section also provides the survey evidence on the perception about India as a convention destination compared to other Asian destinations along various dimensions. The survey results indicate that while India tends to compare favourably on costs, business networking and tourism opportunities, it generally compares poorly with most Asian cities on parameters such as connectivity, accommodation, recreational opportunities, and the general state of convention specific as well as supporting infrastructure. The case studies that are presented in Article 28.5 support the findings of the aforementioned perception survey about India. Infrastructural inadequacies, especially with regard to transport, hotels, and convention venues and facilities emerge as the main weaknesses of the Indian conventions industry. In addition, lack of a holistic approach to tourism development, inadequate attention to marketing and promotion of the conventions business by government agencies, and lack of trained manpower are also highlighted as challenges to developing India as a global conventions destination.

The case studies clearly highlight that India has considerable potential in the conventions business and that there are both tangible and intangible benefits from this business, but that there is inadequate appreciation of this potential and of the means through which such benefits can be maximized to the Indian economy. Much of what is occurring in the Indian conventions industry is really an outcome of private effort and not state support, unlike the case in other Asian destinations.

28.5.1. Market Overview

The Indian Convention Industry is currently at a nascent stage, contributing only a small proportion of the world conventions business. In terms of number of meetings, India has a share of 1% and in terms of delegate arrivals/participation, 0.7% of the world figures. In terms of revenue figures, due to lack of agreement on the definition of conventions and conferences as well as absence of records, it is quite difficult to assign a value of this business in the national context. However, this study has tried to cover broad categories and segments of conferences taking place and the rough estimates peg the revenues between ₹ 4,000 and ₹ 5,500 Crores annually for calculation, please refer to Appendix 6. According to TSA (2006), the entire tourism sector contributes to approximately 2.2% to the GDP and convention tourism business in turn contributes

5–7% of the tourism revenues. Although this figure of 5–7% is at par with the other convention destinations, in volume terms, it is small given the potential of India.

However, based on an analysis of secondary information as well as extensive interviews with several professionals during the study, it became apparent that India is at an 'inflection point' as far as the conventions and conferences business is concerned. With the emergence of India as a key economic hotspot along with China, and the country's recent tourism boom (with an increase in inbound travel from several international destinations for leisure, business and medical tourism), convention tourism has enormous possibilities in the country. India's growing strength in the Information Technology arena, as well the booming civilian Airlines industry has prompted prominent international bodies to host trade shows and conventions in the country and similar prominence in the bio-technology area and manufacturing sector is also expected to bring convention revenues to the country in the coming years.

28.5.2. Emerging Trends in the Country

A Consumer survey was conducted among 75 international delegates across several conferences in Bangalore, New Delhi and Thiruvananthapuram. While the consumer survey revealed consumers' perceptions about India as a destination and also revealed information on expenditure patterns for different product/service heads, it also provided details about potential opportunities for Tourism along with the convention market. This survey had collected information mainly on the following aspects: (for details: Ref. Appendix 5 Surveys used for the Study)

- Profile of Conference Visitor, his preference for India as a convention destination on the basis of various parameters. (These parameters were decided on the basis of secondary research on business and conventions travel)
- Expenditure habits, Duration of stay
- His views on the facilities provided at the conference venue and how India can improve to position itself as a global conventions destination?

Data on a large number of Conferences/Tradeshows/Meetings organised between 2003 and 2007 was collected to analyse attendee trends along with effects of seasonality in the Indian market. This dataset contained a total of 2,089 conferences, meetings, exhibitions that were held during the 4-year period across different locations in the country. This data set was created by information provided by ICPB Members, and various secondary sources including Newspaper articles, Journal advertisements, websites of professional bodies, research and academic institutions. For the purpose of this study, the focus was limited to the top 10 conference destinations in the country.

This study utilised the raw data collected for the International Passenger Survey (IPS), which included the information on business visitors. This data was complemented by incorporating the expenditure data collected through the consumer survey carried out specifically for this study.

28.5.2.1. Highlights from the Consumer Survey

Convention tourists spend slightly less than business visitors in terms of total expenditure. However they stay for a shorter duration. Hence, their expenditure/day is many times higher. Among the type of visitors, Repeat Visitors are found to spend slightly more than First time visitors.

Table 28.5: Average Expenditures of Repeat/First time Visitors

(*Source: Consumer Survey, IIMB*)

Average Expenditures	In USD
First Time Visitor	1045
Repeat Visitor	1183
Grand Total	1091

Business and professional tourists are part of a lucrative segment and tend to spend more than average tourists. Business visitors spend close to 10% more than 'Others'.

Table 28.6: Expenditures of Business Visitors

(*Source: IPS, NCAER*)

Average Expenditures (Bus Vs Other)	In USD
Others	1203
Business	1362
Grand Total	1257

Business visitors spend as much time as other tourists in the country. They might possibly have tourist itineraries too as 20 days of average duration of stay seems high 'for business only' visits. The highest duration of stay is attributed to Employment related visitors (44 days), Religion and Pilgrimage and Health and Treatment visitors come next with average stays of 30 days.

Convention Centres account for only 10% of the conventions that are held in the country. However, this figure corresponds to stand-alone convention centres. Convention centres/ halls in major hotels have been classified under the category of "Hotels". "Exhibition Centres" include locations, which have permanent structures (halls, etc.) to host conferences, whereas "exhibition grounds" are locations with no permanent infrastructure for hosting such events. (Please refer to Table 28.6 below).

Table 28.7: Choice of Convention Venues

(*Source: Dataset of Events in India, 2005–2006*)

Year	2005	2006
Commerical Complex	3%	5%
Convention Centre	7%	10%
Exhibition Centre	25%	28%
Exibition Ground	1%	2%
Hotel	49%	49%
Institution	14%	6%

Professional Conference Organisers are the single biggest customer/stakeholder for promoting conventions in the country.

Only 5% of the conferences held in the country attract foreign delegate participation.

The average duration of conferences in India is 3 days. The average participation per event is 226 delegates.

Conference and Tradeshows are the two most important categories of events that happen in India. Between them, they account for 85% of all MICE events.

The top Convention destinations (6 metros + 4 locations) account for 70% of all the conventions organised in the country.

The Medical and Pharmaceutical industries constitute the most important segment; accounting for 38% of all conferences.

Seasonal trends are evident in the scheduling of conferences in India. Most events are organised during the months of September to January; these months account for about 60% of the annual events. This seasonality was evident from the data collected on 2,089 business events held in the country during 2003-07. The adjoining table highlights the events' spread for 2006 (827 events).

Table 28.8: Seasonality in Indian Conference Business
(*Source: Dataset of Events in India, 2003–07*)

Month	No. of Events	Percentage
Jan-06	84	10.2%
Feb-06	56	6.8%
Mar-06	53	6.4%
Apr-06	62	7.5%
May-06	36	4.4%
Jun-06	40	4.8%
Jul-06	44	5.3%
Aug-06	54	6.5%
Sep-06	102	12.3%
Oct-06	62	7.5%
Nov-06	119	14.4%
Dec-06	115	13.9%
Total	827	100%

Discussions with convention organisers revealed that most operators/organisers tend to plan their events around the latter half of the year, which as mentioned earlier, coincides with the peak season of leisure tourism in the country. There is a dominant perception among both domestic and foreign organisers that it would be very difficult to host conventions/conferences during the hot summer months owing to the heat, which would make most international travellers feel uneasy. It is further highlighted that many of the western countries announce an alert about visiting India during the summer and rainy season, because of the prevalence of water-borne diseases and other ailments. Such perceptions need to be addressed by media plan as well as educating operators/organisers. Dubai, which shares similar weather conditions, has managed to develop thriving business tourism and conventions business during its harsh summer months.

28.5.3. Economic Impact of Conventions—The "Multiplier Effect"

Conventions and their Impact

Conventions in many countries contribute to both the regional and national economies. Not only do they contribute economically to their host destinations but also accelerate the growth of overall travel and tourism activities through repeat visits and word of mouth communication. As seen in the figure, the extent of convention infrastructure determines the extent of impact that different events have on the local economy.

Conventions have an impact on different allied industries such as tourism, hotels, handicrafts, transport, etc. Business Tourism accounts for about two percent of national output and about 13 lakh jobs in India on an annual basis. (*Source:* Tourism Satellite Account, 2002–03). Additionally the growth of this industry has a number of tertiary benefits such as upgradation of general infrastructure in urban areas, development of tourist circuits and education, and economic well being for the local populace.

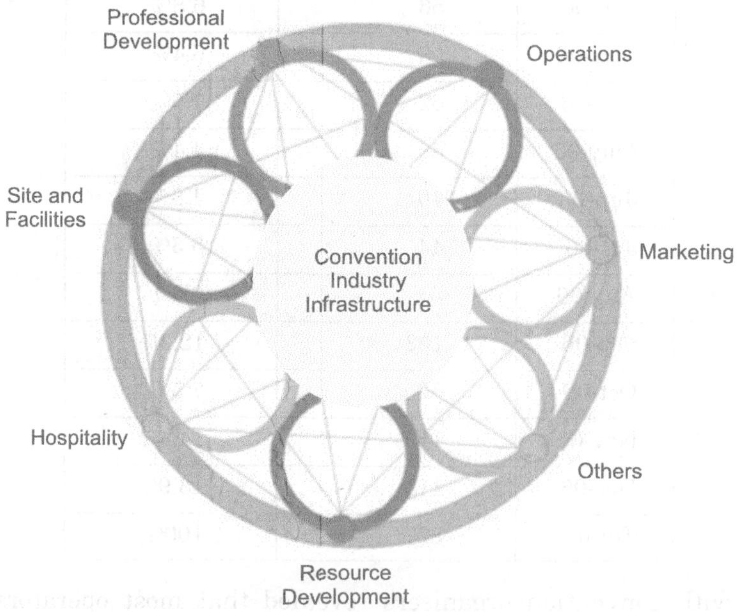

Figure 28.5: Conventions and their impact.

Economics of Conventions

Over the past decades, the growth of the worldwide convention industry has sparked an awareness of the economic significance of conventions to local and national economies. Expenditure by visitors in a convention destination sets off a complex chain of economic events, which can be described as the economic impact of convention tourism.

Three types of expenditures are generated by conventions: by delegates, by associations and by exhibitors. The true impact of conventions on the economy is difficult to calculate, as the convention industry is a composite industry with a complex amalgam of different activities in different sectors of the economy. On the expenditure side conventions result in direct and indirect contributions to the economy. Not only do they provide employment and revenue but also provide an important source of tax revenue.

Expenditure by visitors in a convention destination sets off a complex chain of economic events, which can be described as the economic impact of convention tourism. Not only do they provide employment and revenue but also provide an important source of tax revenue. The occurrence of a convention impacts many industries such as:

- Professional Congress Organizers
- Conventions and trade fair centre
- Hotels and Restaurants
- Airlines and Surface transport
- Travel Agencies
- Leisure activities
- Stand Erection companies.

Specialist suppliers: projection and audio systems, translation and simultaneous interpretation, lighting, catering, signposting, accreditations, auxiliary staff, training institutes, promotional merchandising production:

- Freight/Customs/Logistics agencies
- Handicraft and souvenirs companies
- Security and cleaning companies
- Design and printing companies.

Meetings and conventions offer high value added in terms of delegate expenditure and also serve the dual purpose of promoting international relations. It is a highly profitable type of tourism as most delegates are subsidized and tend to use costly accommodation and often travel before and after the event. The MICE sector also helps increase local government and private sector investments that result in improvements in the general hospitality environment of the destination.

Service based industries such as the convention sector have an added advantage in that they create less pollution as compared to process industries. Thus, promoting conventions generates employment and output without the disadvantages of environmental degradation. They also help in protecting and showcasing the heritage of the country by providing opportunities and venues for displaying the country's rich history in handicrafts, art forms and culture. Finally, the value chain in tourism is highly labour intensive and hence contributes significantly to employment opportunities.

- Manufacturing and Construction
- Retail and Repairs
- Hotels and catering, Restaurants
- Transport, warehousing and communications
- Financial services

- Real estate, business and rental services
- Public administration, defence and social security
- Teaching
- Community, social and personal services

Organization of conventions requires a wide range of specialists from all educational levels from university graduates to specialist technical staff and skilled manual workers. In addition ensuring that conferences happen during the off-season can make up for seasonality effects of general tourism. Thus undesirable social effects of seasonal tourism such as migration, temporary employment, and job instability are avoided. These events can also be termed as "knowledge tourism" as they promote the exchange of ideas, technology and commercial knowledge that contribute to an intangible but important source of value add to the economy of the host country.

Multiplier Effect

As seen in the previous section convention related spending has an impact on other related sectors of the economy. This impact is measured through the use of multipliers, which can be of different forms such as output, employment, income and value-added multipliers. The output multiplier measures the amount of output generated from one-unit change in spending by convention delegates or hosts. An employment multiplier estimates the number of full-time jobs generated from one unit increase in the spending by the convention delegates or hosts. The higher the labour intensity of the sector, the higher would be the employment multiplier for that sector. Typically, labour-intensive industries such as restaurants, hotels, shopping and recreational services are the sectors, which are likely to create more jobs through conventions. The income multiplier measures the effect of an extra unit of convention spending on the changes that result in the level of household incomes in the convention hosting region or country. The income multiplier is important because it most clearly demonstrates the economic impact on residents' welfare.

> **Key Characteristics of Business Tourism**
>
> Principal Characteristics of business tourism include the following:
>
> 1. It is at the high quality, high yield end of the tourism spectrum.
> 2. It is resilient, sustainable and complements the leisure tourism sector.
> 3. Investments in Business tourism facilities lead to the regeneration of urban and inner city areas.
> 4. Business Tourism stimulates future inward investment as business people see the attractions of a destination while travelling on business or to attend a conference, exhibitions or incentive, and then return to establish business operations there.
> 5. Research suggests that approximately 40% of business travellers will return with their families or colleagues as leisure visitors they have enjoyed visiting on business.

Value added multipliers used in this study include wages and salaries, operating surpluses, depreciation of fixed capital and indirect taxes less subsidies. The multiplier has been calculated at the national level using the results of the Tourism Satellite

Account of India Report prepared by NCAER for the Ministry of Tourism and the study on Tourism Employment in the Asia-Pacific Region prepared by the ISID (Pais, 2006). The methodology for calculating the direct effects of employment from the convention sector has been obtained from this paper on Tourism Employment. However, for calculation purposes, the expenditure data for conference delegates is based on the findings of the primary survey conducted among conference delegates (rather than general business travellers) and the data on expenditure for business visitors has been obtained from the IPS study conducted by NCAER.

Value Add from Tourism

According to the definitions provided by the Tourism Satellite Account (TSA), the two broad categories of expenditure are: Tourism Characteristic Goods and Services (viz.

Table 28.9: Value add from Business Tourism (detailed)

Tourism Products	Inbound Tourism Consumption (Table 4, TSA) (₹ Crores)	Domestic Tourists Consumption (Table 4, TSA) (₹ Crores)	Total Tourism Consumption (₹ Crores)
(A) Tourism Characteristic Products			
Accomodation	5,600	4,957	10,557
Food and beverages	3,854	6,709	10,563
Passenger transport services			
Railway	421	12,118	12,539
Road			0
Buses	614	69,832	70,446
Other mechanised vehicles	184	2,811	2,995
Non-mechanised road transport	20	8,257	8,277
Water	204	362	566
Air	4,932	5,686	10,618
Transport equipment rental	2,266	654	2,920
Travel Agencies and similar services	5,712	10,237	15,949
Other recreational and entertainment	2,921	226	3,147
(B) Tourism Related Products			
Clothing and garments	1,323	5,064	6,387
Processed foods		1,351	1,351
Tobacco products		790	790
Alcohol		67	67
Travel related consumer goods	2,076	3,634	5,710
Footwear		609	609
Toiletries		498	498
Gems and Jewellery	1,124	3,402	4,526
Medicines and health related items		4,037	4,037
Printing and publishing	157	145	302
Total	31,408	141,446	172,854

Source: TSA Data, Table 28.4: Total Tourism Demand by products and by forms of tourism (At Factor Cost) Total Value Added at factor cost has been taken from Table 28.6—Tourism Sattelite Account 2002–03 All expenditure in crores of INR.

Accommodation, Food and Beverage, Transport and other recreational activities) and Tourism Related Goods and services (*e.g.*, Clothing and Garments, Tobacco, Alcohol, Toiletries, Footwear, etc.). The value add to the economy from business tourism is substantial and ranges between ₹ 14,000 and ₹ 24,000 Crores/annum (2002 GDP Data). The value added at factor cost, the expenditure at market prices for tourists and business visitors has been directly obtained from the TSA report. This figure corresponds to the value added from business visitors based on the latter's contribution to the total foreign tourists' expenditure in the country.

Contribution to GDP

In order to calculate the contribution of Business Tourism to the GDP, the shares of international business tourism is assumed to be 23% (IPS) and domestic business tourism expenditure share ranging between 5–12% (an approximate international ballpark figure based on several international studies). Prorating for the two segments, the total

Table 28.10: Contribution of Business Tourism as % of GDP

	23% International + 5% of Domestic	23% International + 10% Domestic	23% International + 12% of Domestic
Business Tourism Value Added (₹ Crores)	14,296	21,368	24,197
Value Added from railway margin (₹ Crores) Value Added Transport Margin (₹ Crores) Value added from trade (₹ Crores) Total Business Tourism Value Added (₹ Crores) Gross Domestic Product (₹ Crores)	18 203 962 15,480 2,249,493	27 304 1,439 23,138 2,249,493	30 344 1,629 26,201 2,249,493
Direct contribution (%)	0.7%	1.0%	1.2%
Tourism output multiplier**	2.1	2.1	2.1
Direct and indirect contribution of business tourism to GDP	1.4%	2.2%	2.4%

Margin estimates has been taken from—Tourism Sattelite Account 2002–03.

Allocated for business tourism based on the contribution to total value added from the entire tourism business

All expenditure in crores of INR

** Tourism multiplier has been taken from Tourism Sattelite Account 2002–03

(*Source: TSA Study 2002–03*).

Value Added Business Tourism (at Factor Cost) ranges between ₹ 14,000 and 24,000 Crores. The value added from margins on the expenditure in railways, transport, and trade has been appropriated based on the share of business tourism expenditure in total tourism expenditure obtained from the IPS survey of International Tourists.

In addition to the direct effect on the economy the convention industry also adds to the multiplier effects on other related sectors. The multiplier for tourism has been obtained from the Tourism Satellite Account of India Report prepared by NCAER for the Ministry of tourism. Business tourism based on results in other countries normally has a higher multiplier than the tourism sector at large as business visitors visit on company accounts and hence spend heavily on accommodation, restaurants and commutation. Hence at 2.1 we have been conservative with the indirect effects of Business tourism on other sectors of the economy. Thus the direct and indirect contribution of business tourism to the GDP of the country is at least 1.4–2.4%.

Contribution to Employment

The methodology for estimating the contribution of business visitors in India has been based on the ISID report on Tourism employment (*Source:* Author: Pais, Jesim, ISID Working Papers, 2006/4), as it is the only study conducted in the recent past to segregate the contribution of foreign tourists to employment in India. The definition of foreign tourist for this study has been taken as "... any person normally living outside India (with an Indian or foreign nationality) and travelling to India for less than 12 months and "whose main purpose of the trip is other than the exercise of an activity remunerated from within the place visited". All other studies include the effects of domestic tourism on employment. The nature of foreign tourism is very different from that of domestic tourism and at a more specific level the nature of expenditure of foreign delegates to conventions is further different from that of local Indian delegates. The primary survey, which was conducted exclusively among Conference Delegates, revealed the expenditure patterns of this segment, the focus of this study, which was then used in conjunction with the ISID Study to derive the impact of conventions business on employment. The ISID study computes Employment coefficients for each of the sub-sectors that provide goods and services to foreign delegates such as hotels, restaurants, travel agencies, cultural and recreational services, handicrafts, textiles etc. Employment coefficients measure the ratio between employment and output/value added in a sector. In this study we define employment co-efficient for a sector as the number of workers employed in that sector for every million dollar of USD value added in that sector.

Data on value added for the years 1993–94, 1999-2000 has been obtained from the National Account Statistics of the CSO. Data on employment for 1993-94 and 1999-2000 have been obtained from the National Sample Surveys on Employment and Unemployment conducted by the NSSO. The pattern of foreign delegate expenditure has been computed from a primary survey that we had conducted on foreign participants to international conventions held in India in the last quarter of 2006.

As seen in the table given below, the value added in millions of USD has been directly obtained from the ISID study. The weights of the business visitor expenditure have been obtained from the survey that we had commissioned. Based on these estimates the employment coefficients (product of value added X respective weights) for each of the sectors have been obtained. The employment generated is then calculated by multiplying the composite employment co-efficient with the foreign exchange receipts of business visitors obtained from the RBI. Thus, based on the analysis we estimate that business tourism directly added about 13 lakh or 1.3 million jobs to the economy in 2004-05. This seems a small percentage (6%) of the number of tourism related jobs, i.e. 21.5 million (TSA, 2006) and even smaller (3.4%) when both direct and indirect jobs are considered (38.6 million, as per TSA 2006). However, the above-mentioned figure of 1.3 million indicates full-time jobs due to foreign business tourism, a sector, which is currently small, but is expected to offer greater opportunities in this sector in the coming years as far as employment (direct and indirect) is concerned. Further, organization of conventions requires a wide range of specialists from all educational levels from university graduates to specialist technical staff and skilled manual workers. Hence jobs would be added at various levels.

Table 28.11: Impact of Tourism on Employment Opportunities

	No of workers per million of value added (USD)	Weights for tourists	Weights for business tourists	Employment co-efficients	
				Foreign Tourist	Business Tourist
Accomodation	747	0.14	0.43	104.58	318.71
Food and beverages	683	0.12	0.16	81.96	110.32
Internal Transport	455	0.15	0.07	68.25	31.92
Travel services	197	0.08	0.04	15.76	7.29
Cultural and recreational services	2925	0.07	0.13	204.75	378.78
Other connected services	1075	0.09	0.10	96.75	102.48
Shopping	520	0.36	0.08	187.20	41.51
Textiles	1534	0.10	0.02	145.73	32.38
Germs and jewellery	479	0.14	0.03	65.62	14.58
Books and reading material	90	0.01	0.00	0.99	0.22
Personal goods	416	0.08	0.02	32.03	7.12
Others	558	0.04	0.01	21.76	4.84
				838.19	1008.64
Total Foreign exchange receipts in 2005 (in millions of USD) =			5731		
Foreign Exchange receipts from business tourists (millions USD) =			1318.13		
Employment co-efficient (in USD)			1008.64		
Employment generated in 2004-05(in lakhs)			13.30		

While there can be immense benefits from conventions business as highlighted above, there can be possible pitfalls as pointed out by Darling and Beato (2004) in their paper on public financing of Convention Centres. Public ownership is the dominant form of convention centre ownership accounting for a share of 85% and 64% in Europe and North America respectively. In both these continents, 67% of publicly owned convention centres make no contribution to debt service and do not cover direct operating costs. Operating losses and debt services can put significant pressure on state and municipal budgets and can force reductions in other municipal programs that have higher social priorities. According to the authors, the economic highs are often projected, neglecting the possible pitfalls of such bullish estimates. The authors warn against such enthusiastic estimates and advise on strong rationale for selection of convention sites. The authors suggest the following criteria for site selection—locations with good transport network, related recreational and tourist attractions, access to large number of good quality hotel rooms in the vicinity and an active private sector willing to invest substantially in building conventions facilities.

They suggest that the local government can act as the chief facilitator with subsidies. The government can also facilitate by bringing together a larger body of potential investors for the project. Such public-private partnerships can take different forms; however, they warn against the government getting involved in the day-to-day operations of the convention centre.

Implications for the Mice Sector in India

Business tourism contributes to at least 2.2% of India's GDP. The share of business tourism is only set to increase with the development of India as a major hub of economic activity in Asia and the world.

Based on present trends 13 lakh jobs will be directly added annually on account of business tourism without any intervention from the government. Active involvement of the government can increase opportunities manifold given the overall macro-economic conditions in both the local and global economy.

India is a large country. The impact on local economies is bound to be much higher. States like Kerala, Goa and Rajasthan, which attract a large number of foreign tourists will benefit immensely from business tourism, as the recreational tourist circuit is already better developed than the rest of the country. Their proximity to important business destinations such as Delhi, Bengaluru and Mumbai make them the ideal starting point for promoting MICE tourism in the country.

Urban centres such as Delhi, Mumbai, and Bengaluru will also substantially benefit from efforts made towards attracting business visitors. They need to shift to a service based economy to reduce the congestion and degradation caused by industrialization. The tourism sector is highly labour intensive and hence is an ideal opportunity for such centres where opportunities for business networking are already in place on account of the growth of ITES and the technology industries.

The hospitality industry is impacted by business tourism to a large extent. India's culinary traditions and cultural heritage provide an immense competitive advantage that cannot be easily replicated by competing countries in Asia and elsewhere. Additionally this industry is highly labour intensive and hence contributes to the creation of jobs while protecting and saving the country's cultural heritage.

Business visitors tend to spend more on account of the company accounts that they travel on. Hence, attracting those gives more return for money spent on developing tourism. They are well educated and well networked and hence tapping them creates word of mouth publicity that is a good way of marketing Indian destinations.

The tourism industry in India is highly seasonal (60% of events are organised between September and January). Promoting business tourism and conventions during the off-seasons will require support from the state and central governments as well as private operators in the hospitality industry. State governments like Goa and Rajasthan have slashed state taxes by half during the "off-season" to attract more visitors. Similarly, the hotels have also lowered tariffs during these months. Such initiatives can be replicated in other popular destinations to promote the lean months.

The development of any economy is related heavily to the transfer of knowledge, ideas and skills from other parts of the globe that have access to advanced technologies. Meetings and conventions are held with the explicit intention of facilitating such knowledge transfers and hence their role in the development of any economy is invaluable and is beyond the contribution that they directly make to the national or local GDP. Promoting this sector is a driver to the development of strong Indian companies and upgrading the skills of India's coveted and publicized human capital.

The tourism sector is a composite industry and hence its development helps decrease inequalities and promotes social welfare, as people with different skill sets are involved in the entire value chain. Thus the benefits of development in this sector would impact an executive in a MNC hotel chain to an artisan in a rural community, an entrepreneur running a restaurant to a driver driving a cab, a polyglot translating in French and German to a mason building roads—in short the privileged elite to the deprived rustic.

Private investments in building tourism infrastructure including convention centres should be encouraged. Public Private Partnerships is being facilitated through the provision of viability-gap funding through the Finance Ministry. Governments can facilitate the private participation by improving related infrastructure (*e.g.*, transport, communication) and speeding requisite clearances.

28.5.4. Indian Cities and Market Potential

This section of the study looks into the detailed aspects, which ideally are part customers' want lists and must have lists worldwide. This is fairly comprehensive in nature and of course in most cases, some aspects are either overlooked or considered not so important depending on the context of the conference/ convention. Data were collected through consumer survey on perceptions of India vis-à-vis other Asian destinations—which is presented in a tabular format to identify dimensions where India fares competitively or others and further summarised as part of the Importance (ranks provided by consumers for various prerequisite dimensions) and (India's) Performance (IP) matrix in the next section.

The Site Selection Process

The factors that affect the decision to locate conventions in specific centres hinges on the criteria of different association policies and requirements. However, some of the key factors those are common across different kinds of events while selecting venues are as follows:

28.5.4.1. Accessibility

Cost: the monetary expense of transportation and access

Time: the duration/distance of travel involved and the opportunity cost of that time

Frequency: the frequency of connections to the site

Convenience: the scheduling convenience of the connections

Barriers: the extent of any travel formalities, which inhibit travel such as visas, customs, etc.

28.5.4.2. Local Support

Local Chapter: the extent of assistance and backing offered by the local chapter of the Association

CVB/Convention Centre: the extent of planning, logistical and promotional support offered

Subsidies: the extent to which the destination offers to defray costs through rebates and subsidies

28.5.4.3. Other Attractions

Entertainment: Restaurants, Bars, Theatres, Nightclubs etc

Shopping: Malls, Major Department Stores, Low Prices etc

Sightseeing: Architecture, Museums, Monuments, Attractions, Parks, Historical Sites, Local Tours.

Recreation: Sports And Activities Either As Spectator Or Participant

Professional opportunities: Visiting Local Clients, Negotiations, Business Deals, Selling, Making Contacts etc.

28.5.4.4. Accommodation Facilities

Capacity: The number of rooms available and whether more than a single hotel is required

Cost: The cost of suitable accommodation at the site

Service: The perception of standards of service

Security: The extent to which the hotels provide safe and secure environment

Availability: Are the facilities available when required?

28.5.4.5. Meeting Facilities

Capacity: ability of site to provide suitable sized facilities

Layout: suitability of facility layout and floor plan

Cost: the cost of the meeting space required

Ambience: the ability of the facility to create an appropriate atmosphere and environment

Service: the perception of the standards of service

Security: the extent to which the facility provides a safe and secure meeting space

Availability: are the facilities available when required.

28.5.4.6. Information

Experience: has the site performed satisfactorily in the past

Reputation: what is the reputation of the destination among other meeting planners

Marketing: the effectiveness of the destination's marketing activities.

28.5.4.7. Site Environment

Climate: the desirability of the destination's climate

Setting: the attractiveness of the destinations surroundings

Infrastructure: the suitability and standard of local infrastructure

Hospitality: the extent to which the host organizations and community excel in welcoming visitors.

28.5.4.8. Other Criteria

Risks: the possibility of strikes, natural disasters, boycotts, and other possible adverse events

Profitability: the extent to which the site would produce a profit for the organizers

Association Promotion: would the site add credibility to the association and build membership

Novelty: the extent to which the destination represents a novel location for the association's next convention.

Table 28.12: Factors used for Considering the Venue for an International Conference (*Source: Consumer Survey*)

Rank	Factor	Score
1.	Business/Networking	7.8
2.	Total Cost	5.8
3.	Conference Facilities	5.6
4.	Miscellaneous Facilities	5.6
5.	Connectivity	5.4
6.	Accomodation	4.4
7.	Immigration	4.0
8.	Tourism	3.1
9.	Other Recreation	3.1

As seen in the table above the most important factor for conference delegates is the business/networking opportunity that is made available to them.

Benchmarking with Other Asian Destinations

In this section an attempt is made to analyse the Asian Market for conventions in terms of the overall appeal of different cities as convention venues. The attractiveness of each of the centres is compared to that of India as a conference destination. The following conclusions are based on the consumer survey conducted among conference delegates for their perception about Indian venues vis-à-vis other prominent Asian destinations. Respondents were asked to rank India against an Asian Destination, which they have already visited- and indicate whether specific facilities/ aspects were better or worse on a scale of 5 (where a score of greater than 3 would mean "better in India" or less than 3 would mean "worse in India").

Table 28.13: Comparison of Asian Destinations with India
(*Source: Primary Survey*)

	Other Locations							
Data	**Bangkok**	**Hong Kong**	**Kula Lumpur**	**Seoul**	**Shanghai**	**Singapore**	**Takyo**	**Overall**
Business/ Networking	+	+	+	–	–	+	–	+
Total Cost	+	+	+	–	+	+	+	+
Connectivity	–	–	–	–	–	–	–	–
Immigration	–	–	+	–	–	–	–	–
Acc-Quality	–	–	–	–	–	–	–	–
Acc-Prise	–	–	+	–	–	+	+	–
Food-Choice	+	+	+	–	+	–	–	+
Food-Quality	–	+	+	–	–	–	–	+
Recre-Tourism	–	+	–	–	–	+	–	+
Recrea-Other	–	+	–	–	–	–	–	–
Facilities-Conf.	–	–	–	–	–	–	–	–
Facilities-Misc.	–	–	–	–	–	–	–	–

In this Table (+) indicates "Better in India" & (–) indicates "Worse in India"

As seen in the Table above cities in India compare poorly with respect to destinations such as Seoul, Tokyo, and Shanghai. India is competitive with respect to Singapore, Hong Kong, Kuala Lumpur, and Bangkok. Overall, India compares favourably with these cities in terms of business networking opportunities, cost, culinary and tourism opportunities- however, on other attributes India fares much worse compared to these cities. As far as Seoul, Tokyo and Shanghai are concerned, India performs poorly on almost all parameters, barring attributes like Cost. These are core areas that need to be marketed as the strengths that the country has to offer. Improvement areas that have been identified include connectivity, immigration facilitation, accommodation value (both price and quality), recreational opportunities and finally the state of tourist and general infrastructure which includes local transportation, information facilitation, traffic decongestion, cleanliness and hygiene, roads, and overall quality of life.

To interpret the positioning map, one has to consider the vector of the individual variable/dimension. The position of a specific destination on the orthogonal plane determines its attractiveness on that the particular variable/dimension. Multi-dimensional maps are quite useful for interpreting relative strengths of entities when compared across various parameters/dimensions. The various dimensions are listed on the map; and the relative position of a city, compared to its peers can be ascertained by its position on the particular dimension, e.g. Tokyo is ahead of all other Asian destinations as far as "Connectivity", "Immigration", "Facilities-Conference", "Facilities-Misc." are concerned. India similarly ranks high on the dimensions of "Total Cost", "Recreation Tourism", etc.

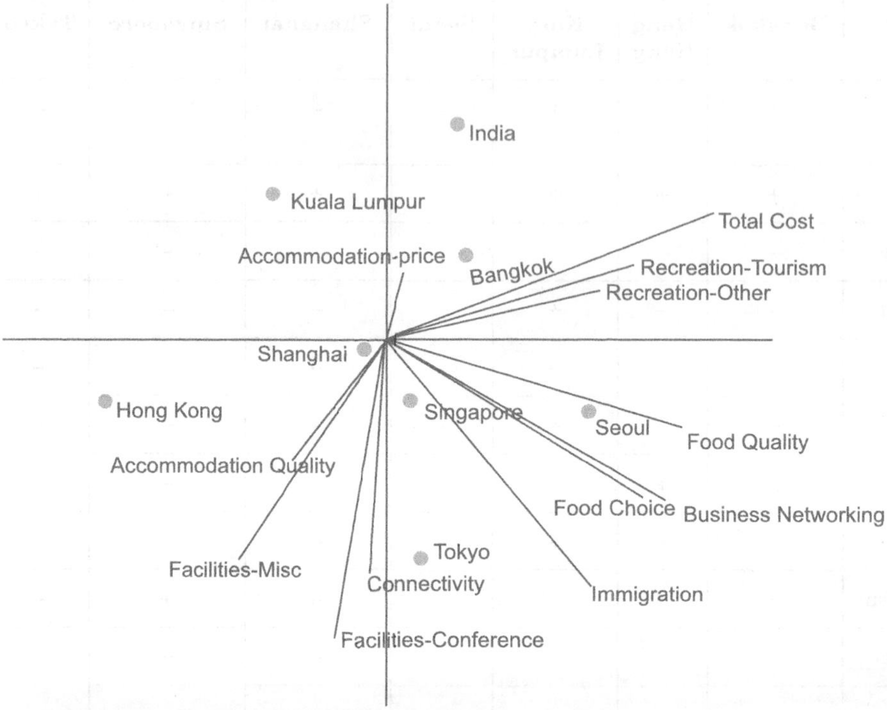

Figure 28.6: India's Position vis-à-vis other Asian Destinations.
(*Source: Primary Survey*)

In the adjoining diagram, one can see that India is perceived to be placed higher than other Asian destinations like Bangkok, Singapore, Kuala Lumpur, Singapore, etc. on the dimension of "Recreation- Tourism". This is found out by drawing an orthogonal line (dotted as shown in figure) to the vector of "Recreation– Tourism" (indicated in and pointing towards right).

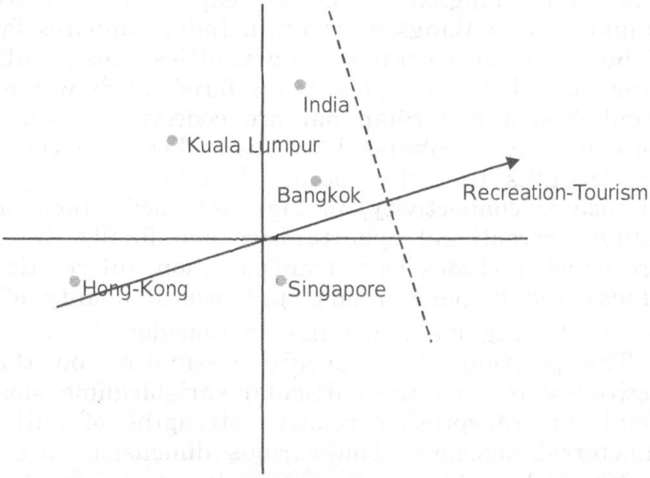

Figure 28.7: Interpretation of Positioning Map.

Convention Destinations in India

As seen in the IP matrix below, the core strengths (high importance-high performance) of India are in total cost and business/networking opportunities. The biggest weaknesses are in connectivity and facilities. Connectivity refers to the ease in accessibility of conference venues and tourism opportunities while facilities refer to conference facilities as well as the state of infrastructure in the country. Although not as important as connectivity and facilities, the other areas of improvement are recreational activities, immigration facilitation and accommodation value. Next, the perceptual map given below is a comparison of Indian cities and their suitability as a conference destination.

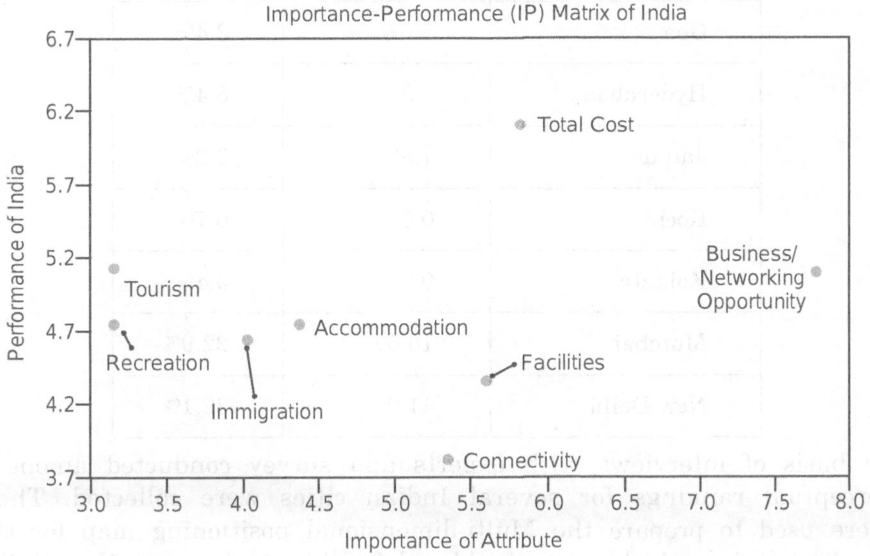

Figure 28.8: Importance-Performance Matrix-India.

Delhi and Mumbai are the most suited for staging conferences. Delhi is the city of choice as it has tourism potential, business opportunity and the general state of infrastructure is far better than in the rest of the country. Both Mumbai and Delhi have good connectivity.

Table 28.14: Preference for Indian Cities–based on Various Factors

(Source: Domestic Delegates Survey)

Location	Preferred
Bengaluru	7%
Chennai	8%
Delhi	31%
Hyderbad	7%
Mumbai	33%
Goa	3%
Others	10%
Total	100%

Table 28.15: Share of Events Across top 10 Destinations in India

(Source: Data collected on Events)

Location	Year 2005	Year 2006
Agra	0.0%	0.3%
Bengaluru	9.2%	10.6%
Chennai	12.8%	9.0%
Goa	8.6%	3.4%
Hyderabad	9.2%	8.4%
Jaipur	1.8%	2.2%
Kochi	0.0%	0.7%
Kolkata	0.9%	3.4%
Mumbai	16.5%	22.9%
New Delhi	41.0%	38.1%

On the basis of interviews with experts and survey conducted among convention visitors, perceptual rankings for several Indian cities were collected. These average rankings were used to prepare the Multi-dimensional positioning map for the different Indian cities. The Cities, which were considered for this study, were New Delhi, Mumbai, Bengaluru, Kolkata, Chennai, Kochi, Agra, Jaipur and Goa. According to this map, Mumbai ranks higher than any other city in India as far as "Business Networking" is concerned, whereas, New Delhi and Goa both rank highly on "Recreations".

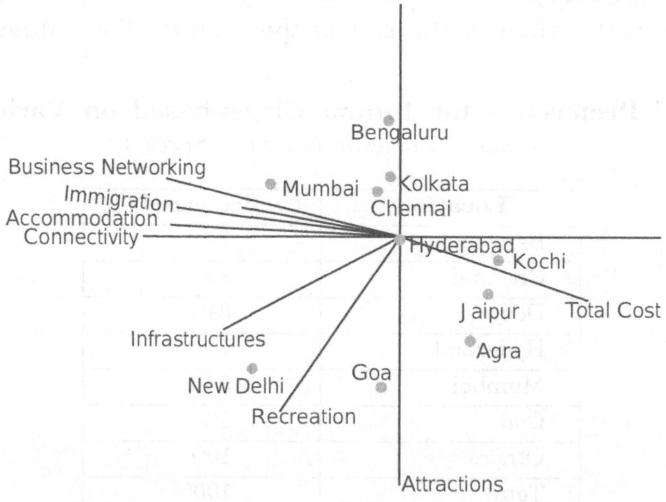

Figure 28.9: Perceptual Map for Indian Cities.

28.5.5. Key Convention Destinations in the Country

New Delhi, National Capital Region (NCR)

New Delhi is the capital city of India. It is the seventh most populous metropolis in the world. Delhi has a semi arid climate with a high variation between summer and winter temperatures. The city boasts of an impressive portfolio of industries, which include Information Technology, Telecom, Hotels, Banking, Media, Tourism, and Life Sciences. The manufacturing industry has also grown considerably. Real Estate and Tourism contribute significantly to the local economy.

The Indira Gandhi International (IGI) Airport caters to both domestic and international connections. New Delhi is well connected with over 300 flights (for details of airline connections, please refer to Appendix 9) to important destinations around the world. IGI also has a domestic airport and Safdarjung (few chartered and government flights) Airports. There are three major railway stations and it is also connected by a lot of highways. New Delhi can boast of one the best laid traffic systems in the country. Buses operated by both pubic and private enterprises ply to most locations in the city, Taxis, Auto-rickshaws and suburban railway systems also carry substantial traffic. The newly developed Delhi Metro (a combination of subway and elevated systems) has alleviated the traffic problems to a certain level in the city. The city's proactive approach in introducing Compressed Natural Gas (CNG) run buses has reduced the extent of the pollution in the city.

Delhi is one of the most historic capitals in the world and two of its monuments, the Qutb Minar and Humayun's Tomb, have been declared World Heritage Sites. It offers a multitude of interesting places and attractions to the visitor, so much so that it becomes difficult to decide where to begin exploring the city. In Old Delhi, there are attractions like mosques, forts, and other monuments that depict India's Muslim history, dating back to the Islamic invasion in the twelfth century. The important places in Old Delhi include the majestic Red Fort, the historical Chandni Chowk. In addition, Old Delhi has Raj Ghat and Shanti Vana that are modern structures constructed after India's Independence in 1947. In comparison, New Delhi is a modern city designed by Edwin Lutyens and Herbert Baker. New Delhi houses many government buildings and embassies, apart from places of historical interest. Some of the notable attractions in New Delhi include the Rashtrapati Bhawan, the one-time imperial residence of the British viceroys, the India Gate, a memorial raised in honour of the Indian soldiers martyred during the Afghan war, the Laxminarayan Temple, built by the Birlas, one of India's leading industrial families, the Akshardham Temple, the shrine of the Muslim Sufi saint, Nizam-ud-din Chishti, who died in 1325, and the lotus-shaped Bahá'í House of Worship. For the shoppers, Connaught Place offers a plethora of choices.

The City hosts the highest number of tradeshows and conventions in the country. The main convention centres are Pragati Maidan (part of India Trade Promotion Council), NSIC Complex, Vigyan Bhawan and India Expo Center, Noida. The hotels having conference facilities are Ashok Hotel, Taj Palace hotel, Taj Mahal Hotel, Le Meridien, Hyatt Regency, ITC Hotel Maurya Sheraton and Towers, The Park, and the Imperial (for details, please refer Appendix 4). In all, the city has a capacity of about 5,000 five star rooms and close to 9,000 rooms in the 3-Star and above range, along with 17 convention/banquet halls.

Pragati Maidan Exhibition Complex: Spread over 100,000 sq. metres with 17 Exhibition Halls, 3 Auditoriums and 3 Open Air Theatres The Pragati Maidan Exhibition Complex is run by the Indian Trade Promotion Organisation, a Govt. agency. Located in the heart of New Delhi, the Exhibition grounds are just 10 minutes away from the city centre - Connaught Place. The Vigyan Bhavan at New Delhi has been the host of various Heads-of-State level meets and has been witness to moments of history like the signing of the Delhi Declaration. Recent renovations have resulted in a completely new, state-of-the-art convention complex with upto date services and facilities. Befitting decor, modern projection facilities and 8-language simultaneous interpretations make for an excellent convention venue. India Habitat Centre was the first endeavour to develop an integrated convention centre in India housing convention facilities as well as peripheral facilities in the same complex. It can house close to 1,000 participants. The proposed International Convention centre at Dwarka in South Delhi, is expected to be the largest in the country. Spread over an area of 35 acres, it will have about 86,000 square metres of convention and exhibition space, with 3 halls having capacities of 2,000-12,000 delegates in theatre style seating. The site is also expected to house Commercial facilities as well Hotels with 800 rooms (300+ rooms in 5 star and above category) and a golf course.

Mumbai, Maharashtra

While New Delhi is the political capital, Mumbai is the financial capital. Mumbai contributes 10% of all factory employment, 40% of all income tax collections, 60% of all customs duty collections, 20% of all central excise tax collections, 40% of India's foreign trade and Rupees 40 billion (US$ 9 billion) in corporate taxes. A number of Indian financial institutions are headquartered in downtown Mumbai, including the Bombay Stock Exchange, the Reserve Bank of India, the National Stock Exchange of India, the Mint, and numerous conglomerates (the Tata Group, Godrej and Reliance etc). Many foreign banks and financial institutions also have branches in this area. It also has a number of Chambers of Commerce, like Maharashtra Chamber of Commerce, Industry and Agriculture (MACCIA), which was founded in the year 1927 by the great visionary and industrialist Seth Walchand Hirachand with the mission to unite and organize business class, then emerging in the pre-independent India.

Till the 1980s, Mumbai owed its prosperity largely to textile mills and the seaport, but the local economy has since diversified into engineering, diamond polishing, healthcare and information technology. Mumbai's status as the state capital means that state and federal government employees make up a large percentage of the city's workforce. Mumbai also has a large unskilled and semi-skilled labour population, who primarily earn their livelihood as hawkers, taxi drivers, mechanics and other such blue-collar professions. The port and shipping industry too employs many residents, directly or indirectly. The entertainment industry is the other major employer in Mumbai. Most of India's major television and satellite networks are headquartered in Mumbai, as well as its major publishing houses. The centre of the Hindi movie industry, Bollywood, is also located in Mumbai, along with its largest studios and movie production houses. Marathi television and film industries are based in Mumbai.

Along with the rest of India, Mumbai has witnessed an economic boom since the liberalisation of 1991. The finance boom in the mid nineties and the boom in IT exports and services in this decade has also contributed to the growth of this city. The middle class in Mumbai is the segment most impacted by this boom and is the driver behind the subsequent consumer boom. Upward mobility among 'Mumbaikars' has led to a direct increase in consumer spending. Purchasing power has grown proportionately. This growth is most apparent in the city's real estate growth as well as a rapid growth in retailing and lifestyle expenditure among its citizens. Over the past few years, the city has seen large retailing organisations set up shop, aiming to grab a chunk of the growing share of disposable incomes among the middle class. Groups like Lifestyle, Piramyds, Shoppers' Stop, Trent and Pantaloons have established chain stores across the city. International fashion labels such as Gucci and Armani are planning to set up retail stores in Mumbai by 2007/2008. The city would have over 60 malls across the downtown and suburbs, all ready to tap into the vast suburban middle class. However, on the downside, the growth in disposable incomes, a combination of low interest loans and easily available bank financing, coupled with a high demand for commercial real estate has led to property prices increasing substantially, even in some newly developed areas like the Bandra Kurla Complex, by as much as 60% in 2006. A heavy residential and commercial demand and a steady supply of state-of-the-art flats and properties in Mumbai have led to the rising land prices. Despite the rise in prices, however, property sales in Mumbai have soared in recent years.

The Chhatrapati Shivaji International Airport is the busiest in India with close to 400 flights a day, caters to cargo and international flights, while Santacruz to domestic flights. Mumbai has extensive direct connections to most destinations in Europe, Asia and North America. Mumbai has one of the best natural harbours in the world and handles passenger traffic. There are two major railway stations connecting it to rest of India. Public transport within the city is mainly BEST buses, suburban railways, metered taxis and autos. Road conditions are poor leading to traffic bottlenecks.

The convention facilities available include Bombay Exhibition Centre, Nehru Centre, World Trade Centre and The Bandra Kurla Complex. The hotels hosting conferences are The Oberoi, Leela Kempinski, Taj Mahal Palace and Tower, Taj President, Hyatt Regency, ITC Grand Maratha Sheraton and Towers, ITC Grand Central Sheraton, Grand Hyatt Mumbai and Marriott Executive apartments (for details, please refer Appendix 7.4). In all there are about 5,000 five star rooms, (with 8,000 rooms in the 3-star and above categories) and 16 convention/banquet halls in the city. Centre point in the WTC building has recently been renovated to upgrade its facilities.

Hyderabad, Andhra Pradesh

Hyderabad is known as the City of Pearls, Lakes and, lately, for its IT Companies, which earned the nickname of Cyberabad. The pearl market is situated near Charminar. Ornaments made with Rice Pearls can be bought from Char Kaman or the General Bazaar Market. Products such as silverware, saris, Nirmal and Kalamkari paintings and artefacts, unique Bidri handcrafted items, lacquer bangles studded with stones, silk-ware, cotton-ware and handloom-based clothing materials are made and traded through the city for centuries. Andhra Pradesh inherited from the erstwhile State of Hyderabad great academic institutes and research labs, both public and private institutes with very diverse areas of interest from Developmental Banking at the Institute for Development in Research and Banking Technology. The Infrastructural facilities for basic research in Hyderabad are some of the best in the country, hosting a large academic population from all over the country and beyond. Hyderabad is a major centre for pharmaceuticals with companies such as Dr. Reddy's Laboratories, Matrix Laboratories, Hetero Drugs

Limited, Divis Labs, Aurobindo Pharma Limited and Vimta Labs being housed in the city. Initiatives such as Genome Valley and the Nanotechnology park are expected to create extensive infrastructure in bio-technology.

Like many Indian cities, Hyderabad has witnessed a remarkable growth in the real estate business, thanks to a predominantly information technology-driven boom in the 1990s and the retail industry growth over the last few years which have spurred hectic commercial activity. A number of mega malls have come up or are being built in the city.

The Airport at Begumpet has both domestic and international terminals. It connects to the Middle East, South East Asia, Europe, Americas and few South Asian destinations. A new international airport at Shamsabad is expected to be operational in April 2008. There are three main railway stations connecting to locations in India. National Highways also connect to the other cities. Public transport is of the form of MMT system, Auto-rickshaws, Air Conditioned Cabs, and Public buses plying to most locations in the city.

Hyderabad is home to world-class convention centres with a perfect balance of small and big centres. The ease of accessibility of the centres makes them attractive as business visitors can mix business with pleasure. The prominent convention destinations are HICC (Hyderabad International Convention Centre- promoted by EMAAR Group of UAE), HITEX, and Shilpa Kala Vedika.

Hotels with convention facilities include the ITC Hotel Kakatiya Sheraton and Towers, Taj Group Hotels - Taj Banjara, and Taj Krishna, Fortune Katriya, Hyderabad Marriott within the city having a capacity of about 1,000 five star rooms (approximately 3,000 rooms in the 3-star and above categories) and 5 convention/banquet halls. (For details, please refer Appendix 4).

Key Attractions in the city include, The Charminar—the major landmark in Hyderabad with four graceful minarets, Faluknama Palace, which was built by Nawab Viqar al-Umra, a beautiful and stunning piece of architecture, the historic Golconda Fort, located on the outskirts of the city, it is one of the most magnificent fortress complexes in India, the Birla Mandir, and the most impressive collections of the Nizam era in the Salar Jung Museum, which houses the largest one-man collection of antiques in the world. The Hussain Sagar Lake is a man-made lake that separates the twin cities of Hyderabad and Secunderabad. It is famous also for the 18-metre tall Buddha statue on a platform in the middle of the lake, and for the Tank Bund that is the main road between the twin cities. For shoppers, Hyderabad Pearls is a must-visit item and these famous pearls and bangles sold in many quarters in the city.

Hyderabad International Convention Centre (HICC) is a world-class convention centre. This convention centre has been designed to hold conferences ranging from 50 to 5,000 delegates. The convention centre has a seating capacity of 4,000, which can expand to 6,500 seats. Event organisers have 291,000 square feet of primary meeting space equipped to handle events for about 50 to 5000 delegates. This can be increased to 6,500 delegates for special events with the help of its mobile operable walls. It has 250,000 square feet of pre-function areas supported by 32 breakout rooms. The convention centre is a pillar-free internal hall of net 6,480 sq. meters, which can be partitioned into six halls in an open capacity. This integrated complex also houses the Accor Hotels- with a capacity of 300+ rooms. Apart from this centre, HITEX is another exhibition facility designed mainly to handle exhibition and trade shows and fairs.

Chennai, Tamil Nadu

The southern city of Madras was rechristened as Chennai in the 1990s; it is the Capital city of the state of Tamil Nadu. The city has a diversified economic base. The main industries are automobile, software services, hardware manufacturing and financial services. Other important industries include petrochemicals, textiles and apparels. The Chennai Port and Ennore Port contribute greatly to its importance. The city has a fully computerised stock exchange called the Madras Stock Exchange. Chennai has the fourth largest GMP (Gross Metropolitan Product) in India.

Since the late 1990s, software development and business process outsourcing and more recently manufacturing have emerged as major areas in the city's economy. Chennai has been rated as the most attractive Indian city for off-shoring services according to A T Kearney's Indian City Services Attractiveness Index 2005. Software services giants like Infosys, TCS, Wipro, Cognizant Technology Solutions, Satyam, HCL, IBM, Accenture, have set up development centres in the city. The city is now the second largest exporter of IT and IT-Enabled Services in the country second only to Bengaluru. The city can boast of several Software Technology Parks, which houses many of these software services giants. The Mahindra World City, a Special Economic Zone (SEZ) with one of the world's largest information technology parks, is currently under construction in the outskirts of Chennai. The city has two main biotechnology parks, TICEL Biotech Park and Golden Jubilee Biotech Park at Siruseri that house biotechnology companies and laboratories. Chennai is the base for around 48 percent of India's auto components industry and 29 percent of the vehicle industry. A large number of the automotive companies in India are based in Chennai. Several global automotive companies such as Hyundai, Ford, Mitsubishi, TVS, Ashok Leyland, Caterpillar, Royal Enfield, TI Cycles, TAFE, Dunlop, MRF have manufacturing plants in and around Chennai while BMW, Mahindra and Mahindra, and Apollo Tyres have plants under construction around Chennai. The city is a major centre for the auto ancillary industry.

Chennai is also an important centre for banking and finance. At present it is home to three large national level commercial banks and many state level co-operative banks. Several large financial companies and insurance companies are headquartered in Chennai. Many Indian banks, multi-national banks and the World Bank have located their back office operations in the city. The city serves as a major back up centre for operations of many banks and financial companies in India.

The Chennai International Airport serves as the city's airport for both domestic and international flights and is the third busiest in India and is the premier international gateway in South India. The city is connected to major hubs in South Asia, South East Asia, the Middle East, Europe and North America through over thirty national and international carriers. The airport is also the second busiest cargo terminus in the country. The city is served by two major ports namely the Chennai Port, which is one of the largest artificial ports and the Ennore Port. The Chennai port is India's second busiest container hub handling general industrial cargo, automobiles etc. The Ennore port handles cargo such as coal, ore and other bulk products. Chennai Central, built 1873 and remodelled in 1900, has been the city's main railway station since 1907, taking over from Royapuram. There are two main railway terminals, the Chennai Central station, which is the city's largest railway station with trains to all the major cities like Mumbai, Kolkata, Bengaluru, Delhi, Hyderabad, Coimbatore and towns in India, and Chennai Egmore, with trains for destinations within Tamil Nadu.

Buses and trains are the most popular form of public transport. The Chennai suburban railway network consists of four rail sectors, namely Chennai Central-Arakkonam, Chennai Central- Sullurpeta, and Chennai Beach-Chengalpattu. The fourth sector is an elevated MRTS suburban train system, which is interlinked with the remaining rail network. There are plans to construct an underground Metro in the City. Hired transport facilities include metered call taxis, fixed rate tourist taxis and auto rickshaws.

Chennai is home to Chennai Trade Centre, which hosts a large number of conventions, trade shows and fairs as well as incentive meetings. Hotels having conference facilities are Taj Connemara, Taj Coromandel, Le Royal Meridien, The Park, ITC Hotel Park Sheraton and Towers, Chola Sheraton, etc. Most of the hotels have conference halls with capacities to cater to 300–600 delegates at one time. Chennai has close to 5,000 rooms in the 3-star and above category. However, there is a shortage of quality, affordable rooms in the city, which can cater to the needs of the booming business travel to this city (for details, please refer Appendix 4).

Chennai's culture reflects its diverse population. The city is known for its classical dance shows and Hindu temples. Chennai is also known for the classical Indian dance, Bharatanatyam, which is also the official dance of Tamil Nadu. An important cultural centre for Bharatanatyam is Kalakshetra (Sanskrit for "place of the arts"), located on the beach in the south of the city. Chennai is the base for the large Tamil movie industry, dubbed Kollywood after the locality of Kodambakkam where most of the movie studios are located. The industry makes about 300 Tamil movies a year, and its film soundtracks dominate the music scene in the city.

Chennai is famous for its numerous restaurants that offer light meals or Tiffin which usually include rice-based dishes like Pongal, Dosa, Idli or Vada, served with steaming hot filter coffee, a very popular beverage consumed in Chennai. This unique cuisine is replicated in many a Madras Cafe in other parts of India and the world.

Bengaluru, Karnataka

Bengaluru's ₹ 260,259 Crore (USD 51.9 billion, 2002 data) economy makes it one of the major economic centres in India. Bengaluru is India's fifth largest city. Bengaluru's per capita income of ₹2.9 lakh (US$ 6,460) is the highest for any Indian city. In the 1940s industrial visionaries such as Sir Mirza Ismail and Sir Mokshagundam Visvesvaraya played an important role in the development of Bengaluru's strong manufacturing and industrial base. Bengaluru is headquarters to several public manufacturing heavy industries such as Hindustan Aeronautics Limited (HAL), National Aerospace Laboratories (NAL), Bharat Heavy Electricals Limited (BHEL), Bharat Earth Movers Limited (BEML) and Hindustan Machine Tools (HMT). In June1972 the Indian Space Research Organisation (ISRO) was established under the Department of Space and headquartered in the city. Bangalore is called the "Silicon Valley of India" because of the large number of Information Technology companies located in the city which contribute 38% of India's ₹ 100,000 Crore (US$ 22 billion) IT and software export market. Biotechnology is a rapidly expanding field in the city. Bengaluru accounts for 47% or 127 of the approximately 265 biotechnology companies in India. Biocon, headquartered in Bangalore, is the nation's leading biotechnology company and ranks 16th in the world in revenues.

HAL Airport has both domestic and international terminals. Direct flights from Bangalore fly to destinations in Asia, Middle East and European destinations like Paris,

Frankfurt and London. However, this airport is not capable of handling the 150-odd flights it receives all through the day, as this was mainly designed for Air force operations. The increase in the number of low cost carriers has led to heavy congestion. This is one of the most congested airports in India, with very few passenger amenities. Because of this congestion problem, a new International Airport at Devanahalli is coming up which is expected to be operational by 2008. There are five railway stations connecting it to major cities in India.

Auto-rickshaws, also simply referred to, as Autos are a popular form of public transport in Bengaluru. Call Taxi service within Bengaluru is provided by several operators commonly referred to as City Taxis ply across the city and can be booked over telephone. Bengaluru Metropolitan Transport Corporation (BMTC) operates a fleet of 3,207 BMTC public buses, servicing an average of 2,800,000 commuters. An intra-city rapid rail transport system called the Namma Metro is being developed and is expected to be operational in 2008. The Metro, once ready, will encompass a 33 km (20.5 miles) elevated and underground rail network, with 32 stations. Bengaluru has earned the dubious distinction of being one of the infrastructure-deprived cities in the country, and in cases the urban infrastructure has failed dismally trying to keep up with the demand.

Bengaluru's major attractions include the Vidhana Soudha, Bull Temple, the ISKCON temple, along with the Race Course, Tipu's Palace, Ulsoor Lake, Lalbagh, Cubbon Park, Bengaluru Palace and Fort. Many view this city as a convenient transit point before moving into the sanctuary territory, backwaters and mountains in the southern states of Kerala and Tamil Nadu. The diversity of cuisine available is reflective of the social and economic diversity of Bengaluru. Roadside vendors, tea stalls, South Indian, North Indian, Chinese and Western fast food are all very popular in the city. Udupi restaurants are very popular and serve predominantly vegetarian, regional cuisine. Bengaluru has many clubs and bars, and is sometimes referred to as the Pub Capital of India.

Palace grounds hosts a number of tradeshows and exhibitions every year. Other centres are Kanteerava Indoor Stadium, Bengaluru Trade Centre (KTPO). A new centre Bengaluru International Exhibition Centre has become operational in 2006. The centre has large halls with 40,000 square metres of exhibition space in a pillar-less area providing tremendous flexibility to exhibition organisers in laying out their stalls and exhibits. Conferences can be organised in four air-conditioned halls in over 5,600 square metres of built-up space. Seating capacities of the halls range from 120 to 1,500. Another facility, the Bengaluru Convention Centre is planned near the new International Airport Devanahalli, with a capacity of 5,000 delegates and with a hotel accommodating 3,000 guests. Both these convention centres have been developed under Public Private Partnerships. Apart from that, a number of top-end hotels also host conferences. They are The Leela Palace Kempinski, The Oberoi Hotel, Taj West End, Gateway Hotel, Golden Palms Spa and Resort, ITC Hotel Windsor Sheraton and Towers, Taj Residency, and Le Meridien. Bengaluru has close to 1,700 rooms in the 3-Star and above category. This city has some of the highest room tariffs in the country due to paucity of rooms and is perceived as a very expensive destination for business travellers. As estimated by experts, a capacity extension of 10,000 rooms is urgently required for this city (for details, please refer Appendix 4).

Kolkata, West Bengal

Kolkata, formerly known as Calcutta is the capital of West Bengal. The city is the third largest urban agglomeration and the second largest city in terms of population in India. It is also referred to as the City of Joy, after the book by Dominique La Pierre. It has a tropical climate. Pollution is a lot of concern in Kolkata and the suspended particle matter (SPM) level is quite high compared to other cities leading to regular smog and haze. Kolkata is the main business, commercial and financial hub of eastern India and the north-eastern states. It is home to the Calcutta Stock Exchange – India's second-largest bourse. It is also a major commercial and military port, and the only city in the region to have an international airport. Once India's leading city and Capital, Kolkata experienced a steady economic decline in the years following India's independence due to the prevalent unstable political condition and rise in trade unionism supported by left-wing parties. Between the 1960s to the mid 1990s, flight of capital was enormous as many large factories were closed or downsized and businesses relocated. However, the city is witnessing resurgence owing to some progressive steps taken by the current Chief Minister. Kolkata's economic revival was led largely by IT services, with the IT sector growing at 70% yearly—twice that of the national average. In recent years there has been a surge of investments in real estate infrastructure sector with several new projects coming up in the city.

Kolkata is connected by all the four modes of transport; road, air, rail and water. Howrah and Sealdah are the two major railway stations, which connects to most national cities. A third station named Kolkata has also been planned. The Netaji Subhas Chandra Bose International Airport operates both domestic and international flights. However, international connections are limited to some South East Asian destinations like Singapore and Bangkok and few destinations in Europe. There are efforts to improve infrastructure at the airport to International standards to invite more and more flights out of this destination. There are passenger service through Kolkata docks to Port Blair and Andaman and Nicobar Islands.

The public transport is a mix of traditional and modern. Suburban railway, Kolkata Metro, trams, taxis, government and privately run buses, auto-rickshaws and cycle rickshaws comprise the main forms of transport. The Kolkata Metro, run by the Indian Railways, is the oldest underground system in India. It runs parallel to the Hooghly and spans the north-south length of the city covering a distance of 16.45 kilometres. It is one of the most efficient mass-transit systems for the city. Recently introduced luxury air-conditioned buses also connect parts of the city to Netaji Subhas Chandra Bose International Airport for daily travellers. The road space (matched with population density) in the city is only 6%, compared to 23% in Delhi and 17% in Mumbai, creating major traffic problems.

The chief tourist attractions are Victoria Memorial, Indian Museum, Netaji indoor Stadium, Eden Gardens, Birla Planetarium, Belur Math, Howrah Bridge, and Tagore House. However, most visitors come to this city to absorb the colonial charm, the erstwhile British architecture and the lazy, laidback lifestyle. Kolkata has long been known for its literary, artistic and revolutionary heritage. As the former capital of India, Kolkata was the birthplace of modern Indian literary and artistic thought. Kolkatans tend to have a special appreciation for art and literature; its tradition of welcoming new talent has made it a "city of furious creative energy".

The prominent convention centres are Science City and the Netaji Indoor Stadium. Apart from these, the larger hotels offering conference facilities are The Oberoi Grand, Taj Bengal, The Park, Hotel Hindustan International, ITC Hotel Sonar Bangla Sheraton and Towers, Hyatt Regency, Peerless Inn, Lytton Hotel, Fort Radisson, etc. Kolkata has a total of 2,700 rooms in the 3-Star and above categories (for details, please refer Appendix 4). This city needs another 5,000 hotel rooms in the 3-5 star categories, within the next 5 years to cater to the rising business traveller requirements.

Jaipur, Rajasthan

Jaipur also popularly known as the Pink City, historically sometimes rendered as Jeypore by the British, is the capital of Rajasthan state, India. Jaipur is the former capital of the princely state of Jaipur. Maharaja Sawai Jai Singh II, the ruler of Amber, founded the city in 1728. The population in 2003 was approximately 2.7 million. The city was built of pink stucco in imitation of sandstone, and is remarkable among pre-modern Indian cities for the width and regularity of its streets. Jaipur, with its rich and colourful past, resplendent with tales of valour and bravery is now one of the most important heritage cities in India, and is a must-see for tourists coming to India.

Jaipur Airport is situated in its satellite town of Sanganer and chartered air services are available from London, Dublin, Singapore and Dubai. The city does not have international connections till now and the available facilities are limited. The city also has limited domestic air links with few domestic destinations like Jodhpur, Udaipur, Aurangabad, Delhi, Hyderabad, Kolkata and Mumbai. Most visitors to Jaipur have to use New Delhi as the gateway. The National Highway No.8 from New Delhi connects Jaipur and after significant improvements of the highway is a pleasant journey. Options from New Delhi also include a faster Shatabdi Express, which is comfortable for visitors. Jaipur is very well connected by rail with all major cities and town in India like Agra, Delhi, Mumbai, Howrah, Chennai, Mysore, Bangalore, Lucknow, Kanpur etc. across the country and to cities like Ajmer, Sawai Madhopur, Kota, Jodhpur, Bikaner, Udaipur within Rajasthan.

The key attractions in Jaipur are Nahargarh Fort, Ambar Palace, Jaigarh Fort, Jal Mahal, Hawa Mahal, Jantar Mantar, B. M. Birla Planetarium etc. The Amber Palace complex is one of the most popular tourist sites in the city, famous for its delicate mix of Hindu and Islamic architecture. Although the structure is today known as Amber fort, the complex was initially a Palace Complex within the Fort of Amber, which is today known as Jaigarh fort. The Jaigarh Fort on the hills above the Amber Palace complex offers stunning views of the foothills of the Aravalli range, as well as attractions such as immense underground water-storage tanks, a medieval canon foundry and an impressive collection of medieval cannons including the Jaivana, which is reputed to be the world's largest cannon on wheels.

Jaipur hosts conventions in B. M. Birla Auditorium. The main auditorium has a capacity of 1300+ delegates in the theatre format; however, options are limited as far as smaller breakaway sessions are concerned.

Hotels with convention facilities include Jaimahal Palace, Le Meridien Jaipur, SMS Hotel and Welcome Hotel Rajputana Palace Sheraton. Jaipur has fairly limited accommodation options; the city currently has close to 1,600 rooms in the 3-star and above categories and close to 1,000 rooms in the 5-star range (for details, please refer Appendix 4).

Agra, Uttar Pradesh

Agra, the home to Taj Mahal, lies in the western part of the state of Uttar Pradesh. It is a tourist destination and has UNESCO World Heritage sites. Economy is agriculture based and lot of Small Scale Industries (SSI) are also there. Handicrafts, Zari Zardozi, Marvel and Stone Carving from this city are also famous.

Airport nearest to Agra town is the Kheria Airport. However, only a few options are available as far as air travel is concerned. The main railway stations are four. New Delhi and Agra are well connected and several trains ply everyday between these two cities and the primary mode of travel between the cities.

Local transportation is of the form of city bus service in which UPSRTC operates. For visitors, hired taxis as well as Tangas are available for travelling within the city.

Agra is a major tourist destination and houses the world renowned Taj Mahal, Agra Fort, Fatehpur Sikri, Aram Bagh and Sikandra, the resting place of Mughal Emperor Akbar.

There is no designated convention centre in Agra, but the hotels hosting conferences are Jaypee Palace Hotel and International Convention Centre, Welcom Hotel Mughal Sheraton, Holiday Inn, Clark's Shiraz, The Oberoi Amarvilas, Taj View Hotel, Hotel Howard Park Plaza International, Atithi, etc. Jaypee Palace Hotel has a conference space of 6,800 square metres, while Clark's Shiraz has two halls with 3,000 and 5,500 square metres areas. (for details, please refer Appendix 4).

Agra has an inventory of 2,000 3-star and above rooms and about 1,100 of them are rated in the 5-Star category.

Goa, State of Goa

Goa is India's second smallest state in terms of area and the fourth smallest in terms of population. Panaji is the state's capital. Goa is India's richest state with tourism as its primary industry.

Goa has only one airport, the Dabolim Airport, which is a controlled by the Indian Air force– most air connections to Goa are from Mumbai, New Delhi and Bengaluru. Chartered flights from European cities arrive regularly at the Dabolim Airport and bring over a 100,000 tourists every year. There is a minor port at Margao and cruise liners stop at Goa. The state has two main railway stations and two national highways connecting to the rest of India.

The public transport consists of privately operated bus, auto rickshaws, taxis and yellow-and-black two wheelers motorcycle taxi.

Goa is also known as the 'pearl of the east'. The main tourist attractions are the beaches, church, ferry rides and coconut groves. Goa is visited by hundreds and thousands of foreign and domestic tourists each year and has become one of the most popular holiday destinations for European travellers.

In Goa, a new convention centre, International Convention Centre is coming up at Panaji, which can cater to the growing need for a proper convention facility in this city/ state. This facility will have integrated meeting along with accommodation and restaurant facilities. An exhibition hall of 4,000 square metres area is also planned along with a multi-purpose Convention Hall. Currently, the Hotels having conference facilities are

Fort Aguada Beach Resort, The Leela Goa, Majorda Beach Resort, Cidade De Goa, Part Hyatt Goa Resort and Spa, Goa Marriott Resort, Taj Exotica Goa etc-most of these hotels have capacities for 300-450 delegates. According to estimates, Goa has close to 5,500 rooms in the 3-star and above categories, out of which 2,500 are under the 5-star category (for details, please refer Appendix 4).

Kochi, Kerala

Kochi, formerly known as Cochin, is a city in Kerala. While Thiruvananthapuram is the administrative capital, Kochi is the economic capital of Kerala. It is the largest urban agglomeration in the state and second largest city after Thiruvananthapuram. Due to proximity from coast, there is little seasonal variation in temperature.

It is a mix of modern and ancient. It is a rising star in the Information Technology area, while tourism and international trade contribute substantially to the state economy. It is one of the fastest growing second tier metros in India. Business sectors are gold and textile retailing, seafood and spices exports, IT, tourism, health services and banking.

The Cochin International Airport handles both domestic and international flights and is the largest Airport in Kerala-most connections are domestic although a fairly significant number of flights connect destinations in the Gulf and Middle East catering to the Kerala Diaspora. A second airport run by the Navy also operates in the city. There are two main railway stations. Kochi ranks among India's major seaports due to its being a safe harbour. It also operates passenger ships to Colombo and Lakshadweep.

Currently, Convention and Conference options in the city are quite limited, and are catered to a limited extent by the premium hotels in the City. The Le Meridien Hotel in Kochi offers moderate conference facilities, with capacities of 270-1,350 square metres (with 500 -2,000 delegates in theatre seating option) across 9 halls. It has also some smaller spaces, which can be used for smaller meetings. Taj Malabar's convention facilities include a conference hall with the capacity to cater to 300+ delegates. In 2004, the Greater Cochin Development Authority (GCDA) had proposed a state-of-the-art Convention facility at Kaloor, however, because of lack of funds and other problems, the plan has not fructified yet. Kochi has 26 hotels and 1,400 rooms under 3-star and above category, with 400 rooms in the 5-star category. Its sister town Ernakulam also provides 250 rooms and 1–5 star hotel with 110 rooms (for details, please refer Appendix 4).

28.5.6. Case Studies from India

Case1-CAAPS, New Delhi

Organising Chair: 20th Congress of Asian Association of Paediatric Surgeons (CAAPS), New Delhi; November 12–15, 2006.www.aaps2006.com

The bidding process for the conference basically entails- a proposal from an association/ individual with some standing in the professional area, along with the support the person/ organisation enjoys from the government. For a medical conference, a nomination from the concerned medical association is important, which reduces the possibility of 'conflict of interests'. The individual, before the process of bid, seeks permission from the relevant association about his candidature to bid for the conference and following the process of approval can bid for the conference. Typically, it is rare that an individual may be offered to host a conference in the very first attempt, so it may be possible that he has to bid thrice over a period of 6 years or four times in a span of 9 years. Often this can be frustrating, but the bidder has to focus as his case might be in the pipeline for the next bidding process, when it comes up in the next meeting.

Because of the very nature of the bidding process, it is important that the individual has ample amount of support from the parent Association, from conference organiser and the government. Since the conference/convention brings "name and fame" to the country, organisations like ICPB and other government agencies are expected to make concerted attempts to help the concerned group of people to showcase India in the international forums. This concerted effort needs to be there even before the actual success-when the bid is awarded to an Indian association.

The respondent suggested a proactive role for ICPB, where it can offer single-window services for a conference organiser by offering a range of services. More resources from the tourism ministry will help market the potential of convention business of India globally. He acknowledged the help received from several members of the ICPB community during the bidding process. He maintained that ICPB could play a more supportive role as a nodal agency for organisers who plan to attract international events to India.

When asked to elaborate on the various bottlenecks, he mentioned that there are large gaps as far as communication is concerned and there is no concerted effort to make the visit of the foreign delegates comfortable. Often ill-mannered personnel at the airports escort the foreign travellers, the first travel is made miserable by the avarice of local taxi and auto-rickshaw drivers and a host of other agencies. It often appears that the concerned personnel lack even the basic etiquette. Immigration is another concern, whereby delegates have to forego opportunities to attend conferences because of inordinate delays in visa processing.

According to him, ICPB should focus to improve India's competitiveness in the global conference/conventions markets by:

- Working as a real 'single-window' entity to facilitate the hosting of conference/ convention for people who need professional help.
- Adhering to strict guidelines and norms when inducting a member delegate/ organisation-focus on professionalism and proven track record before the organisation can claim to be a part of the bureau.
- Becoming the liaison entity between the individual organiser and the government. The bureau should have the access to the highest-level authorities in the government and have the capability to bring in change-through strong lobbying and making its voice heard.

Case 2-Asia Pacific Digestive Week, New Delhi

Organising Chair: http://www.apdw2008.net/ (Asia Pacific Digestive Week) 21-25 September, 2008.

The organiser of this event was interviewed about his bid for the 2008 Asia Pacific Gastro-Enterology Association Annual Conference, the efforts he is undertaking in the run up to this event, and his views on such events in India and how they compare with those held overseas.

He noted that this conference became an annual event only in 2000. Earlier it was an erratic event, which tagged along with other conferences. Since 2000, conferences have been held in Sydney, Singapore, Bangkok, Beijing, Seoul, Hong Kong, and Japan. Each time, the bid has been opened 2 to 3 years earlier. India had bid in 2005 for the 2008 event and was chosen. The event will be held in Delhi in 2008 and will be organized by the Indian Society of Gastroeneterology.

He talked at some length about India's earlier bid in 2004 to host the 2007 conference, where it lost out to Japan. He commented on the differences in approach and coordination between India and Japan for that bid. In 2004, Japan, Thailand, Sri Lanka, and Korea were the other countries competing with India for hosting the 2007 conference. A presentation was required from all bidding organizations. He said that from the presentation stage itself it was clear that India and other countries too were outclassed by Japan, which had brought a delegation of 6 or 7 people. The Japanese team made a flawless 2-minute long power point presentation along with a clear scientific proposal, a detailed budget, details on event management, tour packages, hotels for all classes of participants, etc. The steering committee from Japan even hosted a party at the Japanese Embassy and gave gifts from Japan to all guests. The Thai delegation was smaller than the Japanese one, consisting of three persons, but was also quite good. He commented that it was apparent that India stood no chance for the 2007 event, but he also learnt from this experience and persisted to bid successfully the following year.

He said that for his second bid, he used the services of an event management agency to put together a brochure, a detailed document, and a movie, in addition to a 5–10 minute long power point presentation. The agency handled travel and logistics issues. The steering committee consisted of 10–12 members, who are elected or nominated representatives from different societies. The Indian Embassy in Seoul agreed to host a dinner but ultimately this could not be worked out due to scheduling problems. He also mentioned that he had done extensive canvassing, making use of various organizational networks and his own contacts to get support for India. For bid presentation he had taken along two other doctors and a person from the event management agency. No funds were required separately for this travel; everyone, including him as the chairperson of the Indian Gastro-Enterology Association, was invited as delegate. The Delhi chapter of the organization paid for the travel costs for the agency's representative.

When questioned whether any assistance had been available at all from the government during the bid preparation and for funding travel, brochure printing, and other costs, he was categorical that he had stayed away from government. He did not seek any support form agencies such as CSIR, ICMR as he felt that there would have been too many conditions. ICPB did not play any role in the bidding process. This, he pointed out, is quite unlike the Chinese case where the Chinese government provided financial and institutional support and told its national organization to "go out and win the bid". The government support for the Thai team was also substantial. The support from the Indian Gastro-Enterology Association came in the form of an endorsement letter to him for the bid.

He said that while he had put in a lot of effort to win the bid, he did not feel that India's win was solely due to this fact. He attributed his success to other factors such as the rotation of the annual conference among countries in Asia-Pacific and the withdrawal of other competitors like Sri Lanka. Ultimately, the only country India competed with was Thailand, which had already hosted the event thus tilting the decision in India's favour. So, a combination of concerted effort by the Indian organizers, the packaging of material in a professional manner, canvassing, weak competition, and luck all helped India win the bid. He also noted that he had been strategic in his costing, by keeping the registration fee lower and had showed relatively low hotel costs (though this may not prove to be true in view of the room shortage in Delhi) to attract more participants and how that he would generate a revenue surplus from this event in India.

He then discussed about the choice of venue for this conference. He said that while Ashok Hotel is typically the choice, the parent body chose the Expo Convention Centre in Noida due to its state-of-the-art infrastructure. Its main disadvantage is that it is too far from the city and there is hardly any infrastructure around it. There are only about 100 rooms available around the centre and it is unlikely that the promised 250 or so rooms will materialize by 2008. This will require arrangements for travel to and from the hotels in Delhi. He expressed his concerns about the reliability of the transport arrangements.

He was asked about the requirements for winning an international bid based on his own experience. He mentioned four points in order of importance.

- It is essential to have good infrastructure both within the premises where the event is held and around it. Sufficient capacity, good seating, good audiovisual facilities, and hotel infrastructure are a must. Investments should be directed towards building up these facilities in India.
- The bidding group must show that there will be a profit from hosting the event. In his case, 50% of the profits will accrue to the Indian Society of Gastro-Enterology and the rest will go to the International Body.
- It is important to make a professional presentation.
- Networking, lobbying, use of contacts is required well ahead of time. Also, one needs to gauge one's competitors well ahead of time.

He also talked at length about his experiences in other countries and gave a comparative perspective of where India does not score well in hosting such international events. The main issue was infrastructure, starting from arrival at the airport itself and journey to the hotel from the airport to logistics and convention facilities for the event. He noted that overseas, they are sincere and better organized even in receiving guests. Our conference staff, from drivers to reception desk persons, all lack professionalism. They lack a sense of time and do not go all out to ensure that things go well. Road and transport infrastructure is another big drawback in India. He compared the case of Seoul, where the conference was held a few years ago. Although the conference venue was far from the accommodation, the event was well organized and the staff and drivers ferrying people from the hotel to the shuttle were well trained and punctual, the buses were good, and there were no delays. The roads and traffic conditions make it difficult to achieve these standards in most Indian cities. In his view, the Seoul Convention Centre is the best centre he has seen so far in Asia and comparable to those in the West. It has hotels on one side which are well connected to the centre, a basement where there is lot of scope for recreation, including cinema, food courts, pubs, and even a supermarket. Bus connectivity is good between the centre and the city. While the Sydney Convention Centre is good, the hotels are a bit far. He also pointed out that it lacks the warmth and hospitality that many of the Asian convention centres have. In his view, there is also a cultural dimension in hosting events where Asian centres score over their Western counterparts. He also talked a bit about his experience in Austria where at some international conference that he had attended, each delegate was issued a pass and unlimited travel on public transport (subway and bus) along with map. Such an option is not possible in India given our poor public transport infrastructure. While the conference in Beijing in 2007 is expected to be attended by 3000 or so people, it is expected that some 5000 persons will attend the event in India in 2008. The convention centre at Noida will be able to accommodate this number, but transport to and from the centre will be a problem and will increase the costs of his society significantly. Regulatory clearances are not a major problem in India or in most countries, though it is not easy to get clearance in the case of China, he noted. Pre-conference logistics, he said, are good at most places although different societies go about organizing events quite differently.

He was also asked about the benefits that would accrue from hosting this particular conference and more generally from hosting conventions and conferences. He said that as regards such events generally, there are economic benefits derived due to the people who visit the country and spend as tourists and delegates, visits that may be repeated in future. India gains visibility, tourism is promoted, and such events provide a good opportunity to showcase the country. For this particular event, there would be benefits to the Indian medical community. Local scientists are always more likely to participate in such meets and present their work. More moderators, presenters, chairs, etc., are likely to be Indian than if the event were held elsewhere and the latter would get a better opportunity to project their views. Foreigners would get to know about the expertise available in India. Thus, there are research and networking benefits to the medical community in this field in India.

The discussion also touched upon the required measures to build India's conventions industry. He noted that first and foremost, one should build good and convenient convention centres in all major cities in India, namely in Delhi, Mumbai, Chennai, Bengaluru, Kolkata, and Hyderabad. These centres should be connected with public transport. There should be surrounding entertainment and leisure related infrastructure, such as food courts, shops, and hotels in the vicinity, pubs, and other recreational facilities, along with safety measures. He noted that there is a tendency in India to think that the convention starts and ends with the centre but it is just as important to create the ambience around the centre so that people can enjoy their stay and have avenues for spending. Only such a holistic approach can maximize the benefits for the country.

When questioned specifically about the role ICPB can play, He stated that he would prefer its role to be limited to providing some financial assistance for making the bid as societies typically hesitate to put in money at the proposal stage itself. This assistance would cover printing and documentation expenses for the bid and any travel costs for the presenting team. He had incurred ₹ 60,000 for printing a simple document for the bid. He would have like the bureau to do it or at least subsidize it. Some corpus could also be made available by the bureau to throw a small party at the venue at the time of bidding, with the help of the embassy in the host country. He also noted that there is no marketing at all by India while others like Singapore do an excellent job marketing their country as a destination for conventions and conferences. They provide tour packages not only for delegates but for accompanying persons along with special offers at stores. India needs to think through a comprehensive way of organizing such events, from the bid through the hosting process. While government interference is not welcome, government's role is required in terms of preliminary financial and marketing support and development of infrastructure in and around convention centres.

Specifically, from the point of view of his society and probably most Indian professional societies, he said that although Indian professionals are ahead in many areas, India's representation is not good in international meets. It is costly to attend such meets and institutional money and government fellowships are limited. India's representation does not match its contributions and there are few Indians in steering committees which decide such bids, all of which work against India in bidding for international events. The Thai medical professionals get a lot of grants from their government if their paper is accepted (US$2,500 to be specific) while Indian professionals are unable to go due to lack of funds. All this feeds back into low visibility and poor marketing of India in international events.

He felt that India's chances of being a major global convention destination depends on a major improvement in its infrastructure.

Case 3-IPMA 2005, New Delhi

Organising Chair: International Project Management Association 19th World Congress 2005, organized at Ashok Hotel, New Delhi, Nov. 13-16, 2005.

He started by noting that convention related infrastructure comes in the way of building up India's conventions industry. The other problem he highlighted was that people who organize such events typically lack project management and integrated planning skills. One needs a sincere approach to detail in organizing such big events. In the absence of training for project management, the organisers face difficulties in creating and managing detailed plans.

He talked a bit about his own event, which he said he had hosted successfully. He bid for the event in November 2004. This was on high-level project management, with lot of ministers and policy makers attending. He coordinated the staff as the programme director and in his capacity as President of the Association of 42 countries. He said that no other congress had been so well organized in Delhi to the best of his knowledge. Everything happened like clockwork. Thirteen parallel streams organised in tandem went off without problems. There was no delay in any part of the programme. Around 300 foreigners and over 150 speakers attended the event. All publishing of documents was done locally in Noida. By Indian standards, this was a mega event with some 1300 delegates in all.

He was, however, not happy with several things in the run up to the event. He said the event management company did not handle the registration process well prior to the event by them and his organization had to put in a lot of effort to get the large number of participants that they eventually did. The event management partner fell short of his expectations. The company was selected based on a bidding procedure but this gave him no advantage as they were unable to get a single delegate over a long period. This indicated how little we have in event management support resources. He had considered 4 or 5 other competitors for this bid but he went by reputation and not pricing and still found the management unsatisfactory. He also outsourced some other parts of the event, such as hall management. He said he believed in trust and partnership with other organizations in hosting such events with sharing of profits so that there are adequate incentives to partners.

He expressed dissatisfaction on some regulatory issues, such as traffic police approval requirements for some events that he had organized in certain venues, like the Bharatiya Kendra which led him to change the venue to Shri Ram Kendra. He thought some of these regulatory clearances were unnecessary. He mentioned lack of transparency and documentation on the part of regulatory authorities, which made it difficult to know in advance what is allowed and the checklist that has to be followed. Traffic jams were another problem he faced, which made it difficult to keep things on time, but he managed to get the event going on time and to maintain schedule. He also said that the tolerance for poor quality is high in India resulting in poorly organized events. The bar needs to be raised on standards.

This event, which is held annually, will take place this year in Shanghai. Earlier it had always been in Europe. After Shanghai, it will again go back to Europe for the next 20 years. So, there is not much of an issue of getting a bid as it happens more or less by rotation.

In general, he stressed the need for training courses on project management skills for key personnel in the conventions business. He said that certified project managers and scientific ways for getting such skills (knowing the typology, methodology, etc. of executing projects) needs to be emphasised if we plan to attract and host large events.

Case 4-World Treenut Convention 2008

Organiser of Kaju India 2006-The Golden Meet, Kovalam, Kerala. September 15-17, 2006. (Discussions focussed on World Treenut Convention).

The Cashew Export Promotion Council (CEPC) plays an important part in promoting Indian Cashew Exports by participating in specialised International Food Fairs/ Exhibitions/ Fairs abroad. India recently lost the bid for World Treenut Congress (WNC) to Chile for hosting the 2008 Convention. However, this was primarily because of the fact that the Spain-based International Nut Council (INC) was renamed as the International Nut and Dry Fruits Council, and as Chile is the largest player in Dry Fruits, Chile was offered to host the Convention. There are benefits for bringing the congress to India. INC has a budget of € 1600 per delegate and the total number of attendees is usually close to 600-700, which translates into a revenue flow of a Euros 1 million for the local body-to be used to spend on dinner, lunch and delegate kits to participants. India as a venue can offer an extensive range, being the largest player in Cashew in the world. With good infrastructure and entertainment options, golf courses and spouse tours, it can be made attractive. Hosting a conference in the country can be very cost effective and there is a huge potential for tourism too, which can be capitalised.

Recently, Kaju India 2006 hosted in Kochi was a success. A total of 245 delegates participated in the event. This included 118 Cashew Export Promotion Council (CEPC) members, 84 non-members (Domestic-Brokers, Traders, Service Providers, etc.) and 43 foreign delegates - comprising of Buyers from markets around the world. These buyers account for 80–85% the global trade in cashew. This kind of a conference serves as an effective buyer-seller meet. The World Cashew Congress was held earlier (2002) at Kochi, Kerala. These meets can have potentially huge benefits; quality up gradation, knowledge updating and face-to-face interactions with potential buyers help improve understanding of the market needs.

Help from the government is provided through the Market Access Initiative (MAI) Scheme through the Ministry of Commerce. Government funds 2/3rd of the expenses for the event to the tune of ₹ 2 million. This fund helps cover venue costs, publicity, cost of catalogues, hiring charges for translator/interpreters, etc. The government is also promoting similar marketing initiatives through the Market Development Assistance Scheme.

The impact of events like Kaju India 2006 can be summarised as follows:

- Firstly, the awareness about technology and its usage can be spread among the exporters; an exhibit was arranged by the Agricultural University for educating exporters about processing of cashew-that was useful.
- Secondly, exporters can gain because of the greater access to world markets.
- Thirdly, the local economy also benefits from the hosting of the conferences, as there is tourism expenditure, employment opportunities, which are generated.
- The respondent was not aware of India Convention Promotion Bureau (ICPB) and its activities. However, on being apprised of the activities, had the view that ICPB has a role to play in preparation of bids and marketing of the conferences.

28.5.7. Summary Highlights from Case Studies and Interviews

Almost all the organisers have expressed their concerns over infrastructure; lack of roads, adequate capacities at airports as well as quality accommodation facilities at reasonable prices. Overall, the current infrastructure is not capable of handling very large conferences even at major destinations.

Visa regime needs to be simplified.

Most organisers felt that high hotel rates during the tourist season are a dampener for attracting events to India.

Support from the government to bid for conferences can bring tourism revenues to India. Governments of Thailand, China and Taiwan and other Asian countries send impressive delegations, which strengthen their cases. Delegations from these countries arrive with aggressive backing and clear mandate from the government to bid and win conventions, which can be adopted by our Indian government.

A professional body to track international meetings market and support Indian associations will help tilt the decision for location in favour of India. ICPB's potential role is enormous in terms of providing guidance for organisers.

Most agreed that the benefits of organising international conferences cannot be measured only in expenditure terms- they open up far greater opportunities- access to markets, boosting entrepreneurial ventures, giving young professionals opportunities to interact with the best of the minds in the world.

28.5.8. Identifying Gaps-Infrastructure + Institutional + Regulations

In this section, we have summarised the key gaps in attracting international conventions to India. These observations were arrived through an analysis of the consumer survey (identifying key dimensions), study of prominent international destinations, interviews with professionals which are described under the section on case studies.

Most prominent convention destinations have succeeded because of a conscious effort to develop infrastructure for convention business. Although most European and North American convention centres have been largely funded by public investment, experiences from Singapore. Bangkok and Jakarta indicate that Public-Private Partnerships (PPP) can work equally well.

The critical aspect is to understand the Eco-System for convention business, which thrives on availability of good quality and affordable hotel rooms, excellent connectivity, well developed public transport network and ancillary facilities around the convention venue.

Top destinations in the world have retained their position due to support provided by their governments. Most cities have invested heavily in local transport network—an integrated mass transit network to enable travellers seamlessly transfer between different transport facilities within the city. In India, these investments have been patchy. ICPB, as a nodal agency, is uniquely placed to lobby with the governments at the central and state level for improving convention and allied infrastructure.

Almost all conference organising associations and individual organisers agreed on the need for a nodal body, which can facilitate the entire process of convention management. They reiterated the need for a single-window clearance mechanism through ICPB. However, awareness of ICPB is limited outside Delhi.

Most Asian destinations are now aggressively marketing their convention facilities. Their diplomatic missions actively support delegations while bidding for conventions. India's diplomatic missions abroad will have to play a greater supportive role especially during the bidding process for conventions. ICPB and the India Tourism offices will have to exhibit visible support from the government during the bid presentation.

Convention Boards around the world including Vienna, Singapore, Brussels and Bangkok have been lauded for their pro-active role in promoting conventions in the city/ country. ICPB is currently perceived as a 'liaison' body, which informs potential opportunities to its member fraternity. Thus there is scope for enhancing ICPB's role.

Although inbound tourism has grown significantly in recent years, tourism policies need to evolve to catch up with more tourist friendly countries. The immigration process deters many from travelling to the country. Many organisers felt that the Conference visa requirement should be done away with as this acts as a deterrent to travellers planning to visit India.

The shortage of hotel rooms and multiplicity of taxes lead to high prices in major tourist destinations in India making these centres less competitive as compared to places like Singapore and Bangkok. One of ICPB's roles will be to lobby with the central and state governments to rationalise the taxes applicable for tourists.

28.6. ICPB-FUTURE DIRECTION

Article 28.6 outlines possible steps that can be taken to develop the Indian conventions industry. One possible direction is to take a bottom-up approach whereby central and state governments can help develop basic tourism infrastructure, such as setting up more accommodation facilities, improving transport infrastructure, developing airports, and providing regulatory and institutional support to facilitate the hosting of conferences and meeting, rather than investing large sums for building free standing convention centres in the short term. Thus, under this approach, promotion of the conventions industry would be part and parcel of the overall development of the tourism industry and other infrastructural development and the focus would be on the small and medium segment, which can be more readily handled with India's prevailing convention and related infrastructure. The alternate approach that is outlined is the top down approach wherein the government engages in the development of convention centres, usually in conjunction with private parties. This approach would require the development of a "convention ecosystem" as done by the other Asian countries, where convention facilities are complemented by accommodation, recreational, shopping, culinary, and other facilities. Such an approach is recommended for the top ten convention destinations in the country where the scope for multiplier effects is greater.

Article 28.6 also outlines the role of organizations such as ICPB and other process related improvements that would be required to support either a top down or bottom up approach. Under either approach, there would be a need to develop infrastructure, specifically for setting up convention centres or for allied facilities to enable the convention business. Given the Finance Ministry provisions for 'viability gap financing' of infrastructure projects, recently announced tax incentives for setting up convention centres in the NCR region and the Tourism Ministry's assistance for Large Revenue Generating Projects, the study suggests that ICPB can take a more proactive approach to encourage private investment in this business through public-private partnerships. In addition to attracting greater private sector participation, the study notes the need for greater involvement of professionals in the bidding process, possible changes in the organizational structure of ICPB, greater facilitation by ICPB as a nodal agency with other government ministries, and more focused marketing and lobbying efforts by ICPB to promote the conventions industry. The study also points out the need for human resource development, where ICPB can take the lead in organizing training and certification courses along with institutions and professional bodies by utilizing the scheme for Capacity Building for Service Providers as provided by the Tourism Ministry. Other areas to be examined include tax regulations and administrative issues such as immigration and clearances from various line ministries and local bodies for hosting events. ICPB and the Tourism Ministry should coordinate with the state governments of key convention destinations to reduce the taxes during the off-season and the hotels to reduce tariffs to attract events during the lean summer months.

The focus of this Article is to look into the Indian Market context and suggest some strategies for positioning as well exploring emerging opportunities in the worldwide conventions market. The analysis of this article comes as a culmination of the analysis of the domestic and international market and emerging trends. Organisational changes and prescriptive guidelines are also suggested for leveraging emerging opportunities in the market.

28.6.1. Review of Market

The South Asian economies are expected to contribute significantly to the global travel and tourism market in the next decade (2007–16). Based on an analysis of direct and indirect impacts of the tourism sector, WTTC has estimated that Travel and Tourism

(T and T) will contribute about 7% to India's GDP. Currently, tourism contributes to 2.4% of the GDP and rough estimates indicate that the conventions contribute to about 0.1–0.16% of GDP or 5% of total tourism revenues as shown in the figure below.

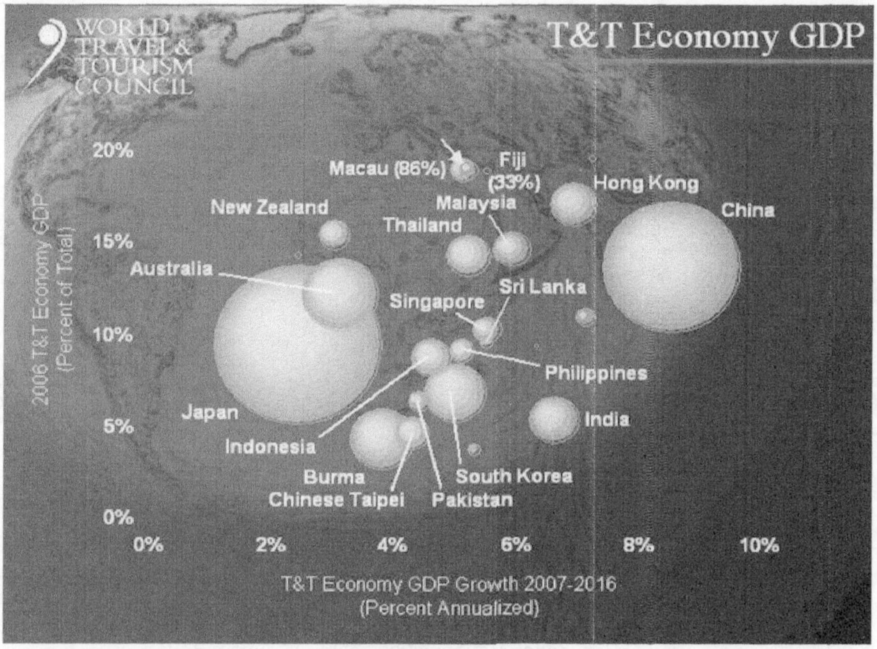

Figure 28.10: Travel and Tourism Economy is Asia Oceania Region (growth vs. Share). (*Source: WTTC*)

While the share of the conventions market is small compared to the total tourism market, India fares as well as other important convention destinations like Austria, China and the Middle East in terms of the size of this segment, which is close to the world average of 5-7%. However, the total tourism market for India is currently small as compared to the huge potential for growth. India's share of 0.1-0.16% (conventions market) of GDP is much less than the world average of 0.4-0.5% of GDP for larger well-developed economies, and an average of around 1-1.5% for smaller countries. There have been efforts from the state governments to set up convention centres in various destinations with public funds as well as private-public partnerships to promote convention tourism. These investments are expected to have a positive impact on the convention market in the country. In the following section, we assess two models for developing convention centres and related infrastructure.

Currently, India's Tourism share is close to 2.4% of GDP, whereas the share of conventions business as a percentage of Total tourism revenues is comparable with other key destinations. Singapore stands out because of its large share of conventions business in total tourism revenues with close to 30% of total tourism revenues. India is expected to increase its tourism shares (as % of GDP) in the coming years, with more tourism friendly policies and it is expected that conventions as a percentage of tourism expenditure would also grow.

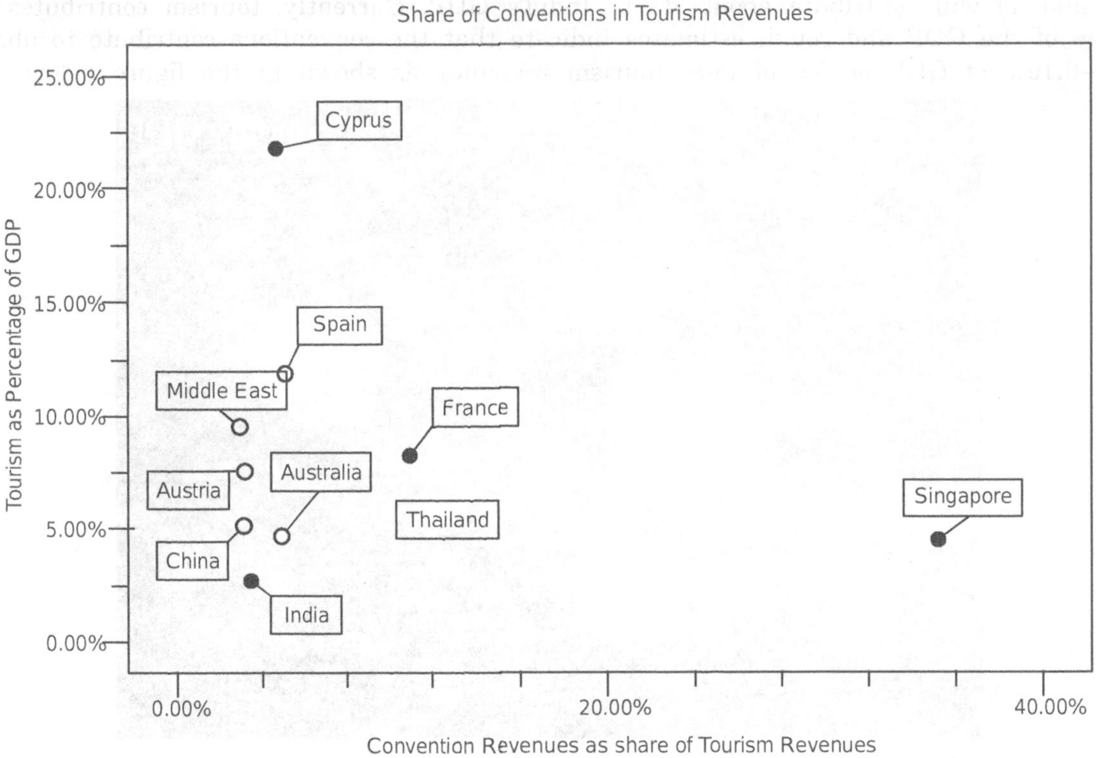

Figure 28.11: India-Tourism share in GDP as well as Conventions' share in tourism revenues. *(Source: National Account Statistics of various countries)*

28.6.2. Developing Convention Infrastructure

Global Models

Two different models have been adopted for setting up infrastructure for conventions and meetings business around the world. Cities in North America and Europe have depended on public investments for setting up conventions infrastructure. These two regions had dominated the market for conventions worldwide since the seventies. In recent years, the emergence of conventions' destinations in the Asia-Oceania region has paralleled the emergence of strong economies. The Asian model for growth in conventions business has been fuelled by mostly private enterprises; Singapore, Bangkok, Kuala Lumpur and Jakarta are good examples of private investments driving growth in conventions markets. In India, the Hyderabad International Convention Centre (HICC) is an example of such a facility. This ₹ 300 Crore centre was set up as a joint venture between Dubai-based Emaar Properties and the Andhra Pradesh Industrial Infrastructure Corporation Limited in a 76–24 percent partnership.

The following sections delve into the two options that can be explored at different levels, the Central and the various State Governments, ICPB and the Ministry of Tourism.

Government Initiatives-Opinion 1(Bottom Up Approach)

Tourism in India is poised to grow, buoyed by recent initiatives from the Ministry of Tourism. Business Tourism is also growing because of the rising economic importance of the region. India's sterling performance in areas of IT, Biotechnology, Medicine as well as manufacturing have made it an economic hotspot. However, amidst this growth, concerns remain regarding the various infrastructure requirements, viz. airports, quality roads and most importantly adequate number of hotel rooms across all price ranges. The current boom has witnessed the steep rise in room tariffs across cities in India, especially for properties in New Delhi, Mumbai, Chennai, Hyderabad and Bengaluru.

From the point of view of the hotels, it can be mentioned that along with this economic boom, the cost of real estate has soared in these cities, which make it prohibitively expensive for these hotels to opt for ambitious expansion plans, which are needed to bridge the demand-supply gap and stem the rise in room tariffs. The State governments can step in to encourage the capacity building activities of various hotels, by offering tax sops and aiding land procurement. Most top-end hotels can be extended further incentives for developing larger capacity (800–1000 delegates) convention facilities, which can cater to the medium sized conferences and conventions.

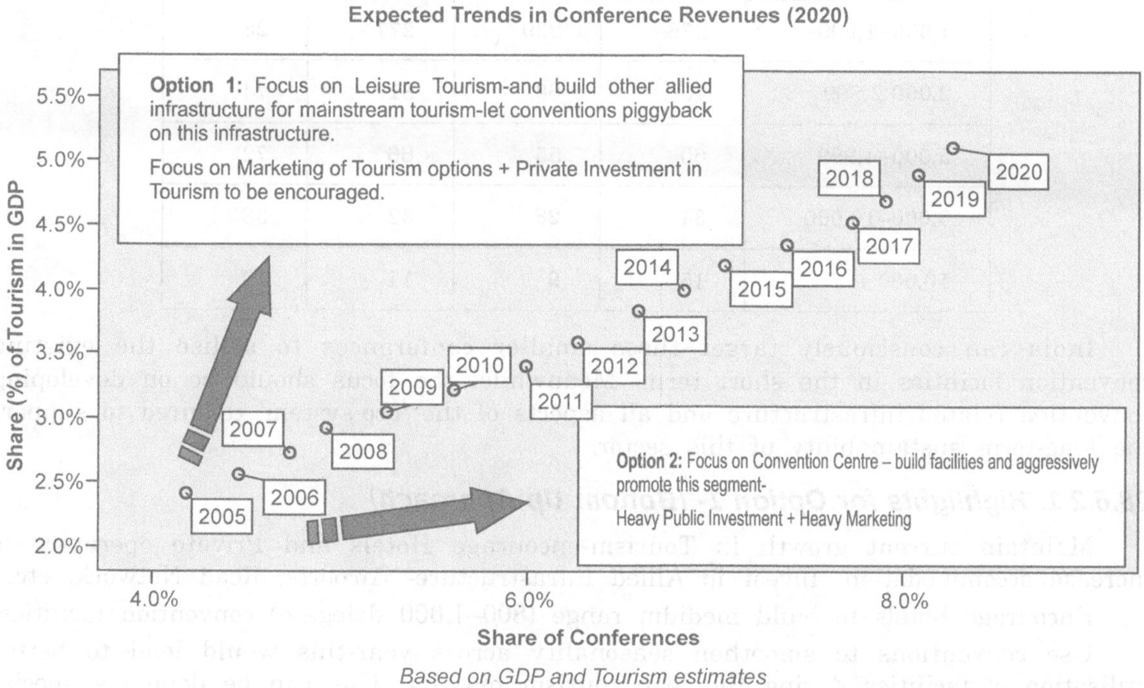

Figure 28.12: Future Directions-Growth Projections in the Conventions Business-Options.

The share of smaller meetings with fewer delegates (50 to 499) is increasing as a percentage as shown in the table below. These are mostly the conference/conventions handled by various professional associations, who tend to meet annually across different destinations in the world.

Studies have indicated that free-standing Convention Centres may not be financially viable. The existing inventory of convention facilities may be adequate to meet the demand in the short term if there is careful planning and conscious effort to market existing convention facilities and hotel rooms during the lean seasons. At present, most conferences are organised during the peak tourism months, stretching the already overloaded tourism infrastructure.

Table 28.16: Average Number of Participants at International Meetings Per Year

Category	Number of Meeting (2000–2005)			
	2000	2003	2004	2005
50–149	259	505	576	750
150–249	333	454	533	573
250–499	558	583	744	766
500–999	455	426	550	535
1,000–1,999	276	239	277	284
2,000-2,999	78	60	81	74
3,000–4,999	60	55	66	72
5,000–10,000	34	28	32	38
10,000 +	15	9	11	12

India can consciously target these smaller conferences to utilise the existing convention facilities in the short term. Meanwhile, the focus should be on developing convention related infrastructure and all aspects of the 'eco-system' required to support the long-term sustainability of this sector.

28.6.2.1. Highlights for Option 1- (Bottom Up Approach)

Maintain current growth in Tourism-encourage Hotels and Private operators to increase accommodation. Invest in Allied Infrastructure- Airports, Road Network, etc.

Encourage hotels to build medium range (800–1,000 delegate) convention facilities

Use conventions to smoothen seasonality across year-this would lead to better utilisation of facilities during the lean tourism months. This can be done via special promotional tariffs during "off-season" and reduced tax rates to encourage more visitors.

Focus on smaller conferences segments-promoting Indian destinations to International Associations. Key benefits from catering to these segments are:

- Smaller delegation– can be managed much easier in view of the infrastructure bottlenecks that are present in the country- so even in short term this market can be approached.

- Premium segment– average revenues per delegate much higher, however, positioning and attracting such a premium segment would mean that infrastructure backup has to be of top quality. Extremely discerning segment- possible negative word of mouth in case of failure to deliver on promises.

28.6.2.2. Government Initiatives-Option-2(Top Down Approach)

The other option for the government, involves a replication of the North American/ European model, investing in building Convention infrastructure. Currently, these efforts are going on in New Delhi for the development of the Dwaraka Convention Centre, in Goa, and in Bengaluru (near the new International Airport at Devanahalli). However, in some cases the government has entered into negotiations with private parties and convention/exhibition centres have been developed through the public-private partnership (PPP) route.

The finance and the tourism ministries have initiatives for developing convention infrastructure through the (1) Viability Gap Funding and (2) Assistance for Large Revenue Generating Projects (LRGPs) respectively. The Finance Ministry is providing financial support to bridge the 'viability gap' of infrastructure projects undertaken through Public Private Partnership (PPP) for developing international convention centres and tourism related infrastructure. Viability gap funding will normally be in the form of a capital grant at the stage of project construction. Other forms of financial assistance (*e.g.*, subordinated loans, operation and maintenance support grant or interest subsidy) require sanction on a case-to-case basis. The viability gap funding is limited to twenty percent of the total project cost. Funding can range from below ₹100 Crores to over ₹200 Crores with defined sanctioning authorities ranging from an Empowered Institution to the Empowered Committee, chaired by the Additional Secretary (Department of Economic Affairs, Ministry of Finance) and the Finance Minister. (*Source:* http://finmin.nic.in/the_ministry/dept_eco_affairs/uuu/PPPGuidelines.pdf). The LRGP scheme of the Ministry of Tourism provides assistance/subsidy to the tune of ₹50 Crores for setting up convention centres. In addition, the Finance Ministry has also announced tax incentives for developing convention centres in the national capital region (NCR).

Such aggressive plans for development of infrastructure are expected to attract some business immediately. However, the long-term viability of such a model would come from building an integrated system or the 'Convention Eco-System'. A stand-alone Convention Centre does not automatically generate business tourism revenues. Most Asian countries have followed a model, where Golf Courses, 5-Star rooms, Clubs, Theatres and other sources of entertainment and other tourist attractions complement the convention facilities in most locations. Examples include the Suntec Convention Centre in Singapore and Putrajaya in Kuala Lumpur.

The top down development of convention infrastructure can be taken up in a phased manner; focussing on already well-developed centres/ clusters and then moving onto the less-developed clusters. Currently, the six (6) leading conventions destinations, or broadly two (2) regional clusters can be focussed in Phase 1- Cluster 1- New Delhi, Agra and Jaipur and Cluster 2 would be Mumbai, Pune, Goa and Bengaluru. The choice of these two (2) major convention clusters is because of the wide range of opportunities and attractions they can offer visitors. In the subsequent phases, the development of conventions infrastructure can be extended to other cities and towns in the country.

Cluster 1: Visitors to any city in this cluster have access to any of these cities, quite easily as the connectivity is good, New Delhi offers excellent ambience for business, Jaipur offers Rajasthan's grandeur, and Agra is of course famous in its own right as a tourist destination. For conference visitors, it would be an ideal mix of business and pleasure.

Cluster 2: Bengaluru, with its emergent economy is a hot destination for business travellers, however, it offers less in terms of leisure tourism options (apart from its pubs!), which can be supplemented by a visit to Goa, with easy connectivity with Goa, and people can touch down at Mumbai-as the exit point. Alternatively Mumbai can be marketed as the convention destination, with a short trip to Goa to supplement that.

These two clusters can have huge potential for convention tourism if marketed in an integrated manner, where leisure tourism (Goa, Agra and Jaipur) can be used to complement business interests (Mumbai, New Delhi and Bengaluru). In the subsequent phases, convention infrastructure in cities like Hyderabad, Kolkata, Chennai and Kochi, can be further developed to create the "Eco-Systems". There are possibilities for Chennai too, by developing a complementary location for leisure at Puducherry or Mahabalipuram. Kochi similarly could be positioned along with backwaters of Kerala.

A key aspect of this model is that individual state governments need to develop regional models of cooperation to facilitate the smooth flow of conventions visitors/ delegates traffic between states to facilitate the growth of these "Clusters" as effective "Eco-systems".

28.6.2.3. Highlights for Option 2- (Top Down Approach)

Public Investment complemented by private participation in Convention Infrastructure can jumpstart the convention business. Focus should also be to develop other complementary infrastructure—airports, hotel rooms and road networks to ensure sustainable business growth.

Focus should be to develop and utilise the conventions 'Eco-System'.

This infrastructure can be planned in two distinct clusters-covering six (6) cities as part of the Phase I of development. In Phase II, the other 4 cities may be covered under subsequent plans.

New and upcoming convention and exhibition centres in Goa, Bengaluru and Hyderabad have been set up through the Public-Private-Partnership (PPP) model.

Goa Convention Centre

A new Convention Centre is coming up at Dona Paula, near Panaji. It is being developed as a Public-Private-Partnership project with the government providing 25 acres of land to the developer, the DLF Group, which was selected through a competitive bidding process. The project cost is estimated at ₹400 Crores. It will operate on the Build-Operate-Transfer (BOT) model. DLF will pay the Government of Goa a sum of ₹161 Crores during the signing of the contract and a 5% share of the revenue from the fifth year onwards. The convention centre will cater to 2,000–4,000 delegates. The integrated complex will house a gymnasium, shopping mall, various recreational facilities and two hotels. DLF plans to invite the Hilton Group, its existing joint venture partner for hotels, to participate in the development of the hotels. This project is expected to be completed in 18 months, i.e., September 2008. Goa Tourism is trying to tap the growing MICE segment to manage the demand in off-peak seasons, and there is also a plan to position Goa for "Golf-Tourism", with a golf course being planned at Betul, in South Goa.

Bengaluru International Exhibition Centre (BIEC)

The Indian Machine Tool Manufacturers' Association (IMTMA) has set up the international exhibition centre at a cost of over ₹120 Crores on a private-public partnership basis. The funds for this project were shared by the Government of India (a grant of ₹35 Crores), IMTMA (₹40 Crores) and the EXIM Bank, which provided ₹40 Crores for the project and ₹10 Crore as bridge loan. The convention centre is built on 40-acres purchased from Nandi Infrastructure Corridor Enterprise (NICE) at concessional rates. The centre has facilities for exhibitions, product demonstrations, international seminars and skill development training and support facilities. It houses a design institute, the country's first such private institution for training young engineers on the latest in design skills, apart from having a productivity training centre. It will host the Association's highly acclaimed International Machine Tool Exhibition (IMTEX) and other IMTMA- organised events. IMTEX 2007 and ToolTech 2007 were organised at the BIEC during January 2007. The centre is also available to the Indian industry for scheduling international events. The association has also tied up with Deutsche Messe AG - owners of world's largest exhibition facility in Hanover, Germany for organising exhibitions at the BIEC and for promoting BIEC worldwide. Deutsche Messe will also conduct training for personnel managing the BIEC.

Bengaluru International Convention Centre (BICC)

The Karnataka government has presented a plan for developing a Convention Centre near the upcoming international airport at Devanahalli. This centre, with a seating capacity of 5,000 and hotel accommodation for 3,000 tourists, has been planned to attract the MICE sector and international business visitors. The centre will be built through the public-private partnership route. Karnataka State Industrial Investment and Development Corporation Limited (KSIIDC) has already allotted 35 acres of land near the airport complex to Karnataka State Tourism Department for developing the convention centre. Competitive bids have been invited from interested parties. It is expected that work will begin in the next financial year (2007–08).

Hyderabad International Convention Centre (HICC)

This world-class convention centre was completed in just 11 months, at an expense of $39 million (₹180 Crores) near Hitec City, in the outskirts of Hyderabad. HICC has been built by Cyberabad Convention Centre Pvt Ltd, a joint venture between UAE-based Emaar Properties and the Andhra Pradesh Industrial Infrastructure Corporation Ltd (APIIC), a government-owned company. Emaar Properties holds 74 percent stake in the joint venture while 26 percent is held by APIIC. The government supported the project by allotting 15 acres of land. A five-star 300-room Novotel Hotel, an 18-hole Golf course and plush villas have been developed near the Convention Centre. The Emaar group has invested $35 million for the convention centre and another $30 million to develop the hotel.

Dwarka Convention Centre (Proposed)

The Delhi Development Authority (DDA) has recently invited proposals from developers and private investors for construction of the upcoming International Convention and Exhibition Centre at Dwarka in South Delhi on BOM (Build Operate Maintain) basis. This facility is expected to house Convention and Exhibition space, along with hotels and allied commercial facilities. DDA has earmarked 35 acres for this project and the total built up area is estimated at 183,000 square metres, and 86,000 square metres would be part of the Convention and exhibition centre. Hotels would have at least 800 rooms, out of which 300 should be in the five-star and above categories.

Proposed Path of Development

It is evident from the discussions that India needs to focus on developing allied infrastructure to attract conference visitors. For a developing nation like India, the bottom up approach entailing investment in Roads, Airports and Hotel rooms is the logical direction ahead, rather than heavy public investments in building stand-alone convention centres. However, it should be borne in mind, that at least one world-class convention centre needs to be developed in each of the top 10 destinations in the country to demonstrate the capacity to host large international conventions. Although, the current market trends indicate a steady shift towards smaller sized (delegate-wise) conventions, it is also true that all the major convention destinations have invested in building impressive convention facilities to signal their capabilities of hosting large conventions.

Therefore focus should be to:

- Build allied infrastructure, *e.g.*, Roads, Airports and Urban transport facilities
- Encourage private investment in increasing Room capacities
- Facilitate P-P-P to set up integrated world-class convention facilities in the top 10 destinations to signal capabilities

Viability Gap Funding—The "End All" Solution?

The Finance Ministry's plan to consider viability gap funding for infrastructure sectors is a welcome initiative. However, it should be noted that viability gap funding by itself cannot help in encouraging private partnerships in building convention infrastructure as has been observed till now. The lack of modern convention infrastructure in the country has been because of the limited development of allied infrastructure in the country. Most private investors realise that the long-term viability of any investment in modern convention infrastructure would only stem from the growth in allied infrastructure, adequate roads, efficient and integrated urban transport, airports and rail infrastructure, etc. Similarly, adequate investments in education and subsequent manpower development are also required to make the convention industry grow. While most tourism analysts have expressed optimism about the growth of leisure and business tourism in the country, they are concerned about the slow growth in supporting infrastructure.

India could miss out potential opportunities during the travel and tourism boom due to infrastructure inadequacies.

28.6.3. Marketing Process and Organisation Structure-Action Plans

Prospecting for New Business

At present, ICPB's role in promoting conventions in the country is limited due to resource constraints. The marketing activities have been confined to presence at stalls during the EIBTM, IMEX and other major international travel and tourism related events.

The study of the annual budget indicates that funds available for marketing activities and promoting convention business in the country is quite limited. Therefore, the efforts must be to make ICPB into a self-financed entity in the coming years. At the same time, efforts should be put in place to infuse professional management into the organisation to run the various marketing related functions.

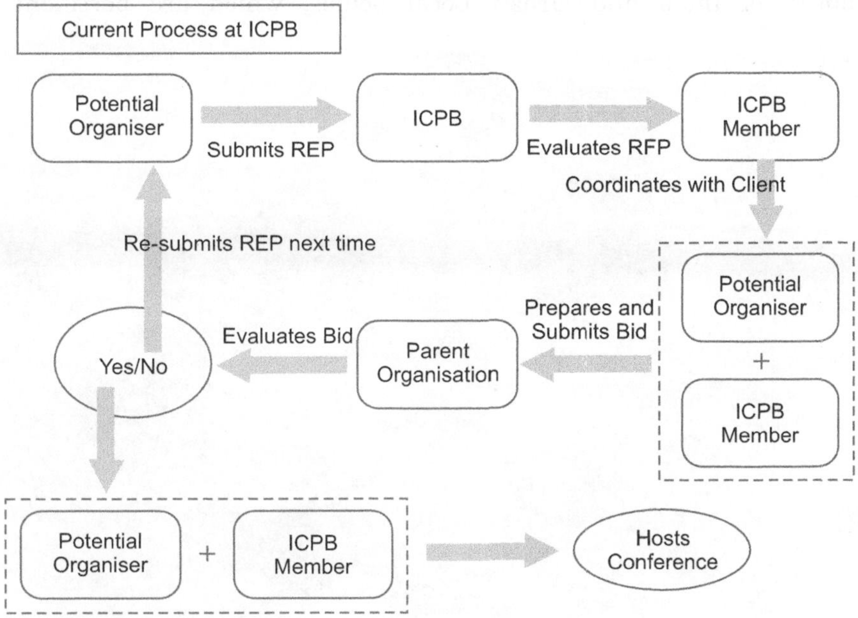

Figure 28.13: The current process of handling new requests.

6.1.3.1. The Way Ahead

ICPB can play a greater role in promoting the conventions business. However, this would require several changes in the way the bureau's organisational structure. ICPB can take up a much more proactive role by generating leads from information available in conference databases to which it subscribes. It can use this information to encourage professionals in respective areas (*e.g.*, medicine, biotech, etc) to bid for upcoming events. Being a nodal agency, it can further facilitate by working with the Ministry of Home Affairs (MHA) for faster clearance of conference visas for these events. As the risk of managing the bidding process is quite high, ICPB can be an important part of the entire bidding process lending credibility to the bid. It can also create provisions in its budget to fund bids for larger conferences.

Building the Eco-System

The long-term sustainability of conference business can be ensured through building an extensive network of allied infrastructure, which ranges from availability of hotel rooms, excellent connectivity to the venue, a well-developed transport network and other tourist attractions. Currently, this understanding of dependence is low, and conventions are regarded as a stand-alone phenomenon. As the nodal agency, ICPB too has a similar role to play, bridging other members in this network. The following figure summarises this view.

ICPB, by virtue of its position, is well connected to the Ministry of Tourism, Professional Convention organisers, various Convention Centres and other Hotels and Restaurants (marked in continuous lines). However, it is imperative that the organisation develops effective networks with entities like the Home Ministry (as well as MEA), Airport Authority of India and Urban Local bodies, which are pertinent for holding

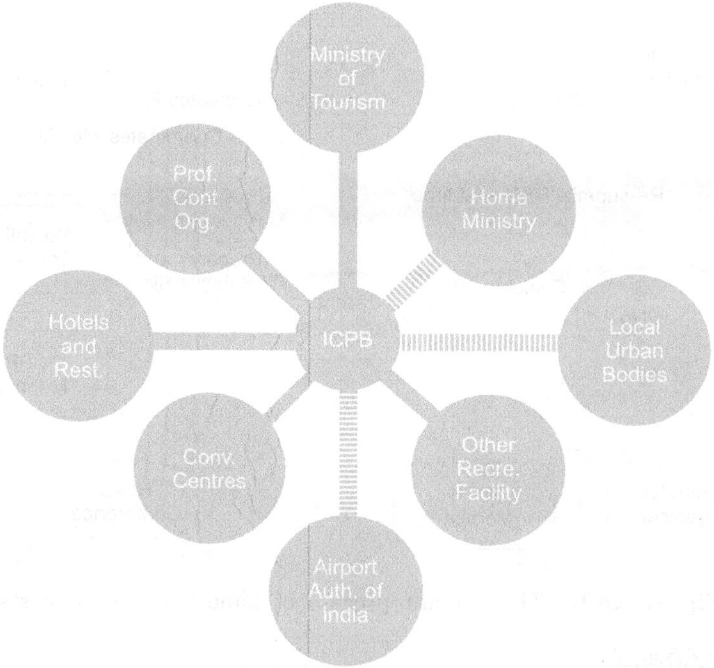

Figure 28.14: ICPB and other members in the Network.

conventions/events in any destination. Several world destinations have established procedures for facilitating the conference/convention visitors' entry to the country by setting up separate, dedicated kiosk for arrivals at airports, access to places of interest in the destination, by working closely with these respective entities.

Availability of Funds for ICPB

Convention Promotion boards/bureaus in major convention destinations have large budgets earmarked for promotional activities. The city-state of Singapore has an annual budget of US $100 million for the Singapore Tourism Board. Similarly, popular city promotion bureaus in Europe have budgets in the range of € 1 to € 5 million for running respective bureaus. In the USA, even a smaller city (e.g. Albuquerque in the State of New Mexico) boasts of a budget of over US $ 5 million for running its operations. Compared to these figures, the ICPB's fund availability of ₹ 5 million for promoting convention destinations countrywide is too small. As far as expenses are concerned, ICPB spends a large share of its funds on promotional expenses; however, in terms of absolute numbers the amount is quite small. A marketing budget of at least ₹ 1 Crore is required to promote individual destinations in the country.

Table 28.17: Sources and Use of Funds (Percent Wise) for Popular International Destinations vis-à-vis ICPB

Revenue Head	ICPB (%)	Singapore (%)	Barcelona (%)
Share of Public funds through Cess/ Tax sharing with State/Central Govt.	0	23	0
Government Funds	41	77	16.5
Membership Fees	29	0	35
Marketing Activities generating funds	30	0	48.5

Expense Head	ICPB (%)	Singapore (%)	Barcelona (%)
Promotional Activities	75	90	48
Personnel Costs	12.5	5	33
Surveys & Research Publications	10	5	19

A significant share of the revenues of major convention bureaus comes from a share of the city, state and central government taxes. Visitors to Vienna, Warsaw as well as other European destinations are charged a bed-tax equivalent of € 1, which is used by the city promotion bureaus to further promote the city and market its key events. Others have opted for a percentage share in revenues from taxes, where the city promotion bureaus get tax funds from city councils. A similar mode can be opted for ICPB. As an alternative to the fixed tax and percentage share mechanisms, the hotels, restaurants and other recreational establishments can charge a slabbed tax based on the "star" ratings, as shown in the table below.

However, tourists/visitors in India are heavily taxed—so these additional taxes may become a burden. Rationalisation of taxes applicable taxes for tourists/visitors need to be carried out and the cess should be part of the rationalised framework, and not merely added to the existing taxes

Table 28.18: Slabbed "tax" or Cess for Hotels/Restaurants/Recreational Centres (Suggestive figures)

Categories of Establishment	Tax Or Cess (₹)
Hotels Less than 3 star	50
Hotels with 3 & 4 star ratings	75
Hotels with 5 Star Ratings	150
Hotels with 5 Star Deluxe and higher ratings	200
Restaurants with bills greater than ₹ 1000	50
Requirements with bills greater than ₹ 5000	100
Recreational Facilities (Spa, Bowling alleys etc) for services over ₹ 1000	25
Recreational Facilities (Spa, Bowling alleys, etc) for services over ₹ 5000	50

ICPB has two distinct roles, which is promoting individual destinations as well as India as a whole. The regional offices would manage the promotion of individual destinations, while the central office of ICPB can engage in promoting India as a convention destination. Funds to the order of ₹ 5 Crores need to be earmarked for each of the 4 regional offices, while ₹ 10 Crores would be needed at the central office.

Other sources of funding include the Market Access Initiative (MAI) Scheme proposed by the Ministry of Commerce, under which the ministry can fund various marketing projects abroad. This would allow holding an event abroad to promote India as a unique convention destination (funds upto ₹ 5 Crores) or Brand Promotion Activities (upto ₹ 1 Crore).

Organisational Structure

Any public private partnership has to be run by professionals to manage conflicts of interest that arise on account of differences in objectives in the functioning of any council. Hence it is proposed that ICPB immediately appoint professional managers who report to the board comprising of members from the government and the industry. Further, most established convention bureaus have a large staff base of at least 8–10 Full Time Equivalent (FTE) comprising of market development officers and market analysts.

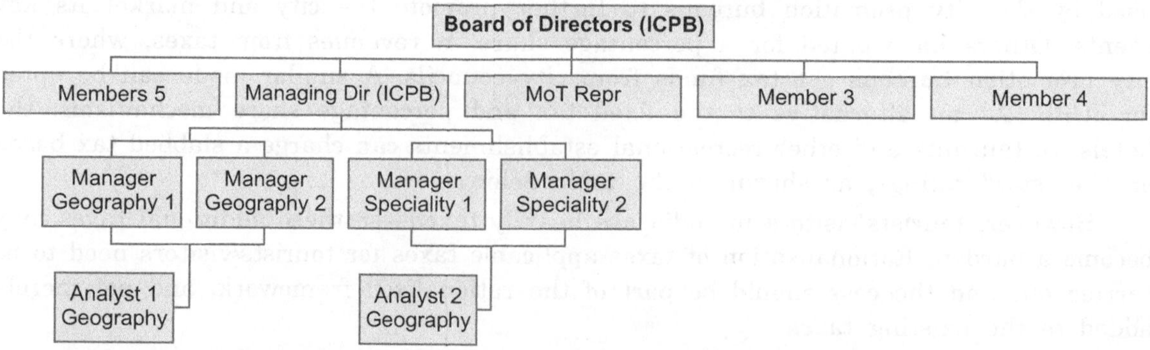

Figure 28.15: Proposed Organisation at ICPB- exploring competence and expertise areas.

With the setting up of regional offices, these offices need to replicate the process/systems of the central offices and need to be staffed by marketing professionals, engaged in analysis and market development activities at the zone/state levels.

Most of the world destinations have developed some "competence areas". For India to develop such niches, extensive research and services marketing capabilities need to be promoted. In order to address this need, professional managers can be hired from the travel and tourism industry with specific training and inputs on convention business. In the short-term horizon, professional managers can be hired with focus on geographical segments, or according to target customers' specialities (Medical Conventions, IT and ITeS or Education focus) and then subsequently aligned according to the specific geography and speciality combinations. Vienna Convention Bureau has a set of managers who have responsibilities shared across geographies including domain specialities (e.g. Medical, Physics and Technology, IT, etc.) The managers and analysts can be trained periodically in various marketing tools and techniques- *e.g.*, Barcelona City convention bureau hosts regular training modules for its managers with its partnership programmes across 7 top European business schools. Similar training modules can be developed for ICPB in marketing, communication and project management tools through reputed educational institutes and corporate entities.

Manpower Development

According to the Federation of Hotels, Restaurants Association of India (FHRAI) the country suffers from a shortage of personnel. The current ratio of supervisors to number of rooms is low, and with the increase in numbers of hotel rooms, this situation is expected to become worse. The Convention Industry is currently facing a dearth of trained manpower, and very few institutes train candidates for the specific requirements of this segment. Government as well as private institutions need to introduce vocational courses and specific training modules in the curriculum to cater to this industry. ICPB can further work with leading business schools in the country to train personnel in marketing and communication tools. Currently, none of the Hospitality management training institutes focus on Conventions Management as a speciality. Courses are offered by reputed universities in the US, UK, Canada as well as New Zealand. ICPB should work closely with educational institutions to develop modules on Conventions Management.

The Ministry of Tourism (MoT) has launched the Capability Building for Service Providers (CBSP) scheme to tourism service providers. Traditionally, the training facilities offered through institutions like Food Craft Institutes (FCI), Institutes of Hotel Management (IHM) and others have catered to the organised sector, and the unorganised sector, which contributes large number of jobs in the tourism sector, had been left out. Through this scheme, the MoT would arrange for a wide range of areas, *e.g.*, awareness programmes, skill development, language training for guides, etc. These training would be imparted through India Tourism Offices, IHM, FCI, Indian Institute of Tourism and Travel Management, NCHMCT, of State/UT Tourism Departments, State Tourism Development Corporations, India Tourism Development Corporation (ITDC), State/Center Training/academic Institutions, etc.

Attractiveness Matrix

As already depicted the conferences around the world are moving towards meetings that are small in size and hence the most attractive segments are below 500 delegates. Additionally the medical sector accounts for about 40% of both the worldwide and Indian convention market. Hence it the most attractive segment to begin the targeting exercises. India has earned a name for itself in the IT and ITES sectors and hence they provide a natural niche that the country can target to host conventions. Finally India has an extensive academic network amongst NRIs and within the country and it is a sector that has immense prospects for the transfer and accumulation of knowledge assets.

Table 28.19: Attractiveness Matrix for India

Industry Segment	Medical	IT & ITES	Academics
50-149	Attractive	Attractive	Attractive
150-249	Very Attractive	Very Attractive	Very Attractive
250-499	Very Attractive	Very Attractive	Very Attractive
500-999	Somewhat Attractive	Somewhat Attractive	Somewhat Attractive
1,000- 1,500	Somewhat Attractive	Somewhat Attractive	Somewhat Attractive

Building A Green Image

One of the interesting trends in the recent years has been the move towards developing a "green" convention infrastructure. Climate change and global warming have been flagged as high priority areas in the MICE area and many destinations are positioning themselves as "green" destinations, offering environment friendly measures to reduce CO_2 emissions, and setting low energy requirements for such set ups. Since the available convention infrastructure is minimal, India can straightaway position itself as a "green" location by developing large number of "green" centres, since they are found to be more cost effective as well as creating a niche for itself with a headstart in this area. The recently developed BIEC is a "green" facility.

Partnerships

Some of the major convention destinations have entered into interesting partnerships, which allow them to position their destinations uniquely. Barcelona has partnered with the leading universities and business schools in the city and district to offer "Corporate and Outdoor Training" to incentive customers, where visitors can undergo managerial training in a natural and relaxed setting. India can also offer similar differentiated offerings, as most of its important destinations are also centres of higher education, which combine modern management techniques with traditional ethos and spirituality.

28.6.4. Recommendations

This section consolidates the suggestions made in the preceding sections. It summarises these recommendations in terms of roles that various stakeholders like Central and State Governments, and ICPB can play.

Role of ICPB

ICPB needs to take up a more proactive role for marketing India as a conventions destination. It can collect and collate information on upcoming events all over the world-and identify partners, who can host such conferences in the country. This would keep ICPB abreast of the latest trends in the world conventions market and enable it to position India better among the peers.

It needs to reorganise its structure, and focus on Geographical and sectoral specialisations by hiring professional managers.

The larger share of conventions business takes place in the two cities, New Delhi and Mumbai. There is a growing need to spread the business in other major centres. Therefore, the organisation needs to reach out to PCOs and other stakeholders around the country by setting up at least 4 regional centres.

In the short-term, the need is to utilise the available Convention Infrastructure efficiently. Careful planning and marketing is required to target specific conventions (please refer the Attractiveness Matrix) as well as manage off-peak demands well. Conferences with fewer delegates (<500 delegates) can be organised during the off-peak months of April-August, using existing inventory of convention facilities.

The sector suffers due to shortage of professionally qualified resources; ICPB should actively work with Government and Private institutions to develop curriculum for Conference and Conventions Management. In this regard, partnerships can be developed with leading domestic and international schools.

Role of State and Central Governments

ICPB would need to have access to greater funds for implementing its marketing plans and to develop its professional management team. The current funds are inadequate to run an effective marketing plan for the promoting the conventions business in this country. The Ministry of Tourism needs to supplement the funds made available to ICPB for implementing these changes. Leading conventions destinations, in Europe and North America, like Vienna, Warsaw, Prague, Toronto, charge a "Bed Tax" or a Tourism Tax in the order of \$1–\$2, which is used to supplement the membership fees that City Councils and Convention Bureaus generate. This tax is again ploughed back in the different promotional activities, showcasing the cities. Similarly, a slabbed cess/tax can be collected by Hotels, Restaurants and Other recreational centres to create such a fund for ICPB.

Support from various government departments and local bodies are required to successfully organise any convention. ICPB can play the role of a 'single window' agency to facilitate this process.

The Ministry of External Affairs (MEA) and the Ministry of Home Affairs (MHA) can simplify the immigration for business and convention tourists. One of the areas of contention is the "conference visa", which entails a cumbersome process of application, which deters many visitors to India. Further, there have been concerns about the inordinate delays in issuance of visa- (ref. Appendix 7 for Visa schedules), which can be sped up to facilitate more conference participants to visit India.

Studies have indicated that current levels as well as the multiplicity of taxes (Luxury Tax, Service Tax) make hotel prices prohibitively high - adding upto 27–31% on the charges as compared to 10–12% in destinations like Singapore and Thailand. The government should also review the existing taxes and levies affecting the convention industry directly or indirectly—and simplify the process of taxation for tourists, as it makes the industry less competitive vis-à-vis other destinations. (Please refer Appendix 6 for Luxury Tax rates in top ten destinations). State governments like Goa and Rajasthan have already reduced their off-season tax rates to promote tourism. Other state governments can be motivated to lower taxes during lean months to increase visitor traffic and events.

28.6.5. Conclusion

The study indicates that there is a huge potential in the country for conventions business to take off in the coming future. A booming economy and a resurgent tourism sector augur well for the future of convention tourism in this country. However, there are substantial challenges faced by the Ministries and various stakeholders in terms of infrastructure development and policy reforms. Recent initiatives from the Finance Ministry to propose the Viability Gap funding is an acknowledgement of the fact that investment is required in this sector and this has been lauded as a positive step, which can contribute to the growth of conventions in the country. It is heartening to see that similar measures are taken up by other key ministries Ministry of External Affairs to issue Multiple Entry Business Visas as well as the Ministry of Tourism proposing the setting up Bed and Breakfast (B and B) centres in the national capital. Such forward-looking initiatives, along with a proactive market focussed ICPB and effective Public Private Partnerships can work together to make India a global conventions destination.

CROSS CULTURAL COMMUNICATION

CHAPTER 29

CROSS CULTURAL COMMUNICATION

Learning Objectives:

• What is Cross Cultural Communication? • Background to Cross Cultural Communication • Basic Terms • Cultural Barriers to Effective Communication • Other Cultures are not Like Yours • Overcoming Language Barriers in Communication• Misinterpretation of Communication • Six Fundamental Patterns of Cultural Differences Aspects of Cross Cultural Communication • Respecting our Differences and Working Together • Cross Cultural Communication Consultants • Multicultural Communication Tips • Basic Steps to Cultural Competence • Successful Cross Cultural Communication • Effective Cross Cultural Communication Skills—Developing Awareness of Individual Cultures • Cross Cultural Communication Strategies • Importance of Cross Cultural Communication in Business • Cross Cultural Solutions for International Business • Cross Cultural Advertising • Language in Cross Cultural Advertising Communication Style in Cross Cultural Advertising • Colors, Numbers and Images in Cross Cultural Advertising • Cultural Values in Cross Cultural Advertising • Cross Cultural Analysis in Public Relations Language and Culture • Communication Channels • PR Materials • Cross Cultural Communication across Languages • Ten Strategies for Success Abroad.

29.1. WHAT IS CROSS CULTURAL COMMUNICATION?

The term cross-cultural "implies interaction with persons of different cultural, ethnic, racial, gender, sexual orientation, religious, age and class backgrounds. Cross cultural communication" is a process of exchanging, negotiating, and mediating one's cultural differences through language, non-verbal gestures, and space relationships. It is also the process by which people express their openness to an intercultural experience.

Cross cultural communication is defined by Gotland University as "a process of exchanging, negotiating, and mediating one's cultural differences through language, non-verbal gestures, and space relationships." Business communication is the exchange of messages related to companies through symbols, action and verbal words.

In the literature on cross cultural communication, the terms 'cross cultural communication', 'intercultural communication' and 'cross national communication' are frequently used interchangeably. Although 'cross cultural communication' and 'intercultural communication' can be treated synonymously, an important distinction needs to be made between 'cross cultural communication' and 'cross national communication'.

Cross-national communication' takes place across political or national borders while 'cross cultural communication' takes place across cultures. Both terms have their usefulness. If one is talking about communications between a multinational organization and its subsidiaries located in other countries, either 'cross-national communication' or 'cross cultural communication' can be used. However, if one is speaking of communications between colleagues working in a multicultural organization located in a certain country, the term 'cross cultural communication' is obviously more appropriate. In this study, the term 'cross cultural communication' is used.

Two words need to be defined: 'culture' and 'communication'. As both have various meanings, depending on the intention of the writer or speaker, for present purposes their definitions are as follows.

Culture can be defined as a community's shared values, attitudes, behaviour and acts of communicating that are passed from one generation to the next. Communication means a goal-directed and context-bound exchange of meaning between two or more parties. In other words, communication takes place between people for a specific reason by a particular medium and in a particular environment. An American meets a Japanese to negotiate a business deal. This context in which the communication takes place can be either within the same culture or across different cultures. In the example given, the business negotiation obviously takes place across different cultures. The communication involved is therefore a culture-bound activity. To communicate means expressing the uniqueness of one's cultural heritage, and this includes not only the verbal and non-verbal peculiarities but also the preferred medium and context of communication.

The scope for cross-cultural communication is extremely wide. It is a multidisciplinary field of study with roots in anthropology, sociology, psychology, and linguistics, among other disciplines.

Intercultural communication in its most basic form refers to an academic field of study and research. It seeks to understand how people from different countries and cultures behave, communicate and perceive the world around them. The findings of such academic research are then applied to 'real life' situations such as how to create cultural synergy between people from different cultures within a business or how psychologists understand their patients.

The definition of intercultural communication must also include strands of the field that contribute to it such as anthropology, cultural studies, psychology and communication.

There are many researchers and academics of note within the intercultural field, who naturally all have different definitions of 'intercultural communication'. For example Karlfried Knapp defines it as "Intercultural communication, can...be defined as the interpersonal interaction between members of different groups, which differ from each other in respect of the knowledge shared by their members and in respect of their linguistic forms of symbolic behaviour." The theories developed by the researchers and academics can and has been applied to many fields such as business, management, marketing, advertising and website design.

29.1.1. Background to Cross-cultural Communication

The first cross-cultural studies were carried out by Abū Rayhān Bīrūnī, who wrote detailed comparative studies on the anthropology of religions, peoples and cultures in the Middle East, Mediterranean and especially the Indian subcontinent. He presented his findings with objectivity and neutrality using cross-cultural comparisons.

Extensive cross-cultural studies were later carried out by 19th century anthroplogists such as Tylor and Morgan. One of Tylor's first studies gave rise to the central statistical issue of cross-cultural studies: Galton's problem.

The modern era of cross-cultural studies began with George Murdock (1949). Murdock set up a number of foundational data sets, including the Human Relations Area Files, and the Ethnographic Atlas. Together with Douglas R. White, he developed the widely used Standard Cross-Cultural Sample, currently maintained by the open access electronic journal World Cultures.

In the past decade, there has become an increasing pressure for universities across the world to incorporate intercultural and international understanding and knowledge into the education of their students. International literacy and cross-cultural understanding have become critical to a country's cultural, technological, economic, and political health. It has become essential for universities to educate, or more importantly, "transform", to function effectively and comfortably in a world characterized by close; multi-faceted relationships and permeable borders. Students must possess a certain level of global competence to understand the world they live in and how they fit into this world. This level of global competence starts at ground level—the university and its faculty—with how they generate and transmit cross-cultural knowledge and information to students.

Cross cultural communication endeavours to bring together such relatively unrelated areas as cultural anthropology and established areas of communication. Its core is to establish and understand how people from different cultures communicate with each other. Its charge is to also produce some guidelines with which people from different cultures can better communicate with each other.

Cross cultural communication, as in many scholarly fields, is a combination of many other fields. These fields include anthropology, cultural studies, psychology and communication. The field has also moved both toward the treatment of interethnic relations, and toward the study of communication strategies used by co-cultural populations, *i.e.*, communication strategies used to deal with majority or mainstream populations.

The study of languages other than one's own can not only serve to help us understand what we as human beings have in common, but also assist us in understanding the diversity which underlies not only our languages, but also our ways of constructing and organizing knowledge, and the many different realities in which we all live and interact. Such understanding has profound implications with respect to developing a critical awareness of social relationships. Understanding social relationships and the way other cultures work is the groundwork of successful globalization business efforts.

(For those eager to dig deeper it may be a good idea to look into the works by Edward T. Hall, Geert Hofstede, Harry C. Triandis, Fons Trompenaars, Clifford Geertz and Shalom Schwartz).

During the past decades the growth of globalisation, immigration and international tourism has involved large numbers of people in cross-cultural interaction (also referred to as inter-cultural interaction or international relations) whether they have liked it or not.

This has led to an increased desire and need for knowledge regarding cross cultural communication on many levels. There is the theoretical field of cross cultural communication and the applied field of cross-cultural training.

29.1.2. Basic Terms

Reading the literature, websites or promotional material many ask 'what is the difference between 'intercultural' and 'cross cultural'? What is 'cross cultural awareness' as opposed to 'cross cultural knowledge' or, are 'cultural sensitivity' and 'cultural competence' the same thing?

With a view to clarifying some of the above mentioned terminology, this article will examine terms used in relation to building cross cultural understanding within the business world.

Cross cultural understanding simply refers to the basic ability of people within business to recognise, interpret and correctly react to people, incidences or situations that are open to misunderstanding due to cultural differences. The fundamental intention of cross cultural training is to equip the learner(s) with the appropriate skills to attain cross cultural understanding.

Once the foundations of cross cultural understanding have been laid, the learner(s), either through continued training or experiences within the workplace, gradually attains a more acute appreciation of cultural differences. The different types of appreciation are cross cultural knowledge, cross cultural awareness, cross cultural sensitivity and cross cultural competence. Although all the terms may appear similar in meaning, subtle differences exist between them.

Cross Cultural Knowledge is critical to basic cross cultural understanding. Without it cross cultural appreciation cannot take place. It refers to a surface level familiarization with cultural characteristics, values, beliefs and behaviours.

Cross Cultural Awareness develops from cross cultural knowledge as the learner understands and appreciates a culture internally. This may also be accompanied by changes within the learner's behaviour and attitudes such as a greater flexibility and openness.

Cross Cultural Sensitivity is a natural by-product of awareness and refers to an ability to read into situations, contexts and behaviours that are culturally rooted and be able to react to them appropriately. An suitable response necessitates that the actor no longer carries his/her own culturally determined interpretations of the situation or behaviour (*i.e.*, good/bad, right/wrong) which can only be nurtured through both cross cultural knowledge and awareness.

Cross Cultural Competence is and should be the aim of all those dealing with multicultural clients, customers or colleagues. 'Competence' is the final stage of cross cultural understanding and signifies the actor's ability to work effectively across cultures. Cross cultural competency is beyond knowledge, awareness and sensitivity in that it is the digestion, integration and transformation of all the skills and information acquired through them, applied to create cultural synergy within the workplace.

Cultural competency is a term used to describe the ability to work, communicate and live across cultures and cultural boundaries. One achieves this through an instilled understanding of cultures on a general level as well as an informed one about specific cultures on a more detailed level. As well as knowledge it has to work in tandem with behavioural and attitudinal changes.

Cultural competency is important in this day and age for exactly the reasons cited in this article. We, as citizens of planet earth, are no longer confined to our national and cultural borders. We mix with people from different cultures, ethnicities, religions and colours on a daily basis. In order to make this intercultural experience work on all levels from education to business to government, people have to develop basic skills in intercultural communication and understanding.

29.2. CULTURAL BARRIERS TO EFFECTIVE COMMUNICATION

Effective communication with people of different cultures is especially challenging. Cultures provide people with ways of thinking—ways of seeing, hearing, and interpreting the world. Thus the same words can mean different things to people from different cultures, even when they talk the "same" language. When the languages are different, and translation has to be used to communicate, the potential for misunderstandings increases.

Stella Ting-Toomey describes three ways in which culture interferes with effective cross-cultural understanding. First is what she calls "**cognitive constraints**." These are the frames of reference or world views that provide a backdrop that all new information is compared to or inserted into.

Second are "**behaviour constraints**." Each culture has its own rules about proper behaviour which affect verbal and non-verbal communication. Whether one looks the other person in the eye-or not; whether one says what one means overtly or talks around the issue; how close the people stand to each other when they are talking—all of these and many more are rules of politeness which differ from culture to culture.

Ting-Toomey's third factor is "**emotional constraints**." Different cultures regulate the display of emotion differently. Some cultures get very emotional when they are debating an issue. They yell, they cry, they exhibit their anger, fear, frustration, and other feelings openly. Other cultures try to keep their emotions hidden, exhibiting or sharing only the "rational" or factual aspects of the situation.

All of these differences tend to lead to communication problems. If the people involved are not aware of the potential for such problems, they are even more likely to fall victim to them, although it takes more than awareness to overcome these problems and communicate effectively across cultures.

29.2.1. Other Cultures are not Like Yours

No matter who you are or where you live, no matter what nation or culture you come from, you will need to recognize one very important truth when you do business with colleagues in other countries. Other people-although they may dress like you, speak your language, or even work for the same company-are not "just like you".

You'll do business with people that have very different histories, languages, and ways of doing business. They will have a different sense of time, and a different sense of humor. They will have different ways of negotiating, and different perceptions of when a deal has truly been made. They will also have different expectations of what it means to follow through on commitments and agreements. In a word, they will have different cultures!

You need to know the rules.

Are you a sales manager setting up new distribution channels? A service representative working with overseas colleagues to set up new systems? A manager helping to run an overseas subsidiary or open a new manufacturing plant? Whoever you are, whatever you are doing, if you are interacting with people from other cultures, you need to know something about them.

A Cross-Culture Awareness course can be an essential first step in that process. When you do business with companies in other countries, you are not just staying in a different hotel, eating a different meal, and meeting in different offices. You are entering someone else's world, and you need to understand the history of its people, the rules, the culture runs by, and the way they view the business process.

Inter-cultural understanding does not come overnight. It will only come with preparation, effort, and an open mind.

Every business traveler should know something about the country they are visiting-its history, its people, its heritage. It helps you make conversation, helps you learn more from the experience, and is a sign of respect for those you are meeting.

Once you understand the basic facts about a culture, and something about its social rules, you are ready to do business. When does yes mean yes? When does may be mean no? When should you raise the issue of payment? How are commitments followed through? —In order to get the best results, you need to know how business is done in your partner's culture.

Social issues form the backbone of any culture. People in different countries conduct their lives in different ways: Which colour flowers to bring? Which hand to shake? How to address your colleagues? Who speaks first? It is far better to know the rules than to risk offending anyone and losing a deal.

Knowing the rules is one thing. Being prepared for the little things that can go wrong, is quite another. And little things can always go wrong!

Companies worldwide are actively training their staff in Inter-Cultural awareness, sensitization and communications in order to help their sales, service and management employees prepare for interacting and doing business, successfully, with other cultures.

They include manufacturers, service companies and consultants from electronics, telecommunications, pharmaceutical, construction, government, training and education, tourism, automotive, consumer electronics, marine engineering, and many other organizations.

How do we prepare for a different culture? An environment that, for all its outwardly similarities, is completely different from the one we are accustomed to? For instance:

How do you manage a team of culturally diverse employees?

You must negotiate contracts, but does your counterpart share your cultural preconceptions just because he is dressed like you?

You must hire and train new staff, but how is time and education viewed in another culture? You must host a foreign delegation, but what are their goals and cultural needs?

How do you respond to an ambiguous command from your manager if he/she is from a different culture?

However, with the process of globalization, especially the increasing of global trade, it is unavoidable that different cultures will meet, conflict, and blend together. People from different culture find it is hard to communicate not only due to language barrier but also affected by culture styles. For instance, in independent cultures, such as in the United States, Canada, and Western Europe, an independent figure of self is dominant. This independent figure is characterized by a sense of self relatively distinct from others and the environment. In interdependent cultures, usually identified as Asian as well as many Latin American, African, and Southern European cultures, an interdependent figure of self is dominant. There is a much greater emphasis on the interrelatedness of the individual to others and the environment, the self is meaningful only (or primarily) in the context of social relationships, duties, and roles. In some degree, the effect brought by cultural difference override the language gap. And this culture style difference contributes to one of the biggest challenge for cross-culture communication. Effective communication with people of different cultures is especially challenging. Cultures provide people with ways of thinking—ways of seeing, hearing, and interpreting the world. Thus the same words can mean different things to people from different cultures, even when they talk the "same" language. When the languages are different, and translation has to be used to communicate, the potential for misunderstandings increases. The study of cross cultural communication is fast becoming a global research area. As a result, cultural differences in the study of cross-cultural communication can already be found. For example, cross cultural communication is generally considered to fall within the larger field of communication studies in the US, but it is emerging as a sub-field of applied linguistics in the UK.

As the application of cross cultural communication theory to foreign language education is increasingly appreciated around the world, cross cultural communication classes can be found within foreign language departments of some universities, while other schools are placing cross cultural communication programs in their departments of education.

29.3. OVERCOMING LANGUAGE BARRIERS IN COMMUNICATION

As business becomes more global, we have more opportunities to speak to an ever-wider range of nationalities and people. Increasingly, the world is using English, and this APPEARS to give us, as native speakers, great advantages. However, communication between people of different cultural backgrounds involves much more than them overcoming the language barrier by speaking our language!

To effectively communicate across cultures, the first thing is to identify how our use of English can cause intercultural misunderstandings by creating a language barrier in communication...

Issues of Language. Language differences are hugely significant. Language isn't just how people speak—it is who they are. Knowing the language gives you an insight into the people. When you learn the language of another people, you notice differences in structure, vocabulary and shades of meaning, and that helps you to understand *their* outlook. I can't teach you another language but I can help you transform your English into an international language, by helping you understand the deeper meanings of 'their' English.

The English language, for example, has sayings that reflect an efficient, activist driven society: "Actions speak louder than words" and "Time is money". The language itself is structured efficiently too: subject - verb - object. Japanese leaves the verb till the end to modify or do away with, depending on the reaction of the listener; the quest being for harmony. Thailand has 12 words for "you", denoting the importance of seniority. An East African tribe has numerous words for green, reflecting the importance to them of Nature's many shades. Nepal has different words for "uncle", according to whether he is the brother of your mother or father, and whether he is older or younger than your parent. French and Hindi both have "familiar" terms for you/thou, which are used either for intimates such as your family or when speaking down to someone. In French it's "tu/toi", in Hindi it's "toom". In both cases, your tone of voice makes the distinction. Arabs will tend to use the passive voice, e.g. "It was observed ..." instead of "I observed ..." because they are more fatalistic than active in approach to life.

In each case, the national characteristics are revealed in the structure of their language. Those attitudes are carried over into the way they use English, even if they do not translate directly from their language into English. The significance, however, isn't just the linguistic differences, but rather the attitudes that lie behind them, and the cultural values that give rise to those attitudes.

The cultural differences in linguistics described above are only a few of the challenges in international communications. In order to overcome them, you need to first see them clearly and objectively; this skill can be learned. Secondly, you must understand how you are being perceived by counterparts from other cultures; this is a challenge of self-awareness. Finally, you need to use effective cross-cultural communications, which means developing skills such as communicating in English with non-native English speakers, using language, gestures and body language understood across cultures.

29.3.1. Misinterpretation of Communication

Social conflicts often involve some misunderstanding. Conflict parties communicate by what they say (or do not say) and how they behave toward one another. Even normal interaction may involve faulty communication, but conflict seems to worsen the problem. The higher the level of conflict, the more costly misunderstandings may be. During the Cold War, miscommunication between U.S. and Soviet leaders could have been catastrophic in its consequences. At every stage and level of conflict, clear communication among parties usually works to reduce unwise decisions by and costs for the participants.

All communication has two parts: a sender and a receiver. The sender has a message he or she intends to transmit, and she puts it in words which, to her, best reflect what she is thinking. But many things can intervene to prevent the intended message from being received.

If the communication is verbal, tone of voice can influence interpretation. The bosses' words "hey, I noticed you were taking an especially long break this morning," could be interpreted as an attack if he said that in a disapproving tone; while the comment might be seen as a minor reminder about office rules, if it was said in a friendly way. If the employee had a problem requiring the long break, the comment might have even been a friendly inquiry about what has happening and whether the employee needed any help. Here, tone of voice as well as situational and relationship factors would influence the interpretation of the message.

Nonverbal cues also are important. Is the sender's posture open and friendly, or closed and cold? Is her facial expression friendly or accusatory? All of these factors influence how the same words will be received.

In addition to how the message is sent, many additional factors determine how the message is interpreted by the receiver. All new information we learn is compared with the knowledge we already have. If it confirms what we already know, we will likely receive the new information accurately, though we may pay little attention to it. If it disputes our previous assumptions or interpretation of the situation, we may distort it in our mind so that it is made to fit our world view, or we may dismiss the information as deceptive, misguided, or simply wrong.

If the message is ambiguous, the receiver is especially likely to clarify it for herself in a way which corresponds with her expectations. For example, if two people are involved in an escalated conflict, and they each assume that the other is going to be aggressive and hostile, then any ambiguous message will be interpreted as aggressive and hostile, even if it was not intended to be that way at all. Our expectations work as blinders or filters that distort what we see so that it fits our preconceived images of the world.

An analogy can be made to the science experiment done to test people's interpretation of visual cues. When people were given eye-glasses which turned the world upside down, they had to suffer through with upside down images for a week or two. But after that, their brains learned to turn the images back over again, so they were seeing things right side up. The same thing happens when we hear something we "know" is wrong. Our brain "fixes" it.

Given our tendency to hear what we expect to hear, it is very easy for people in conflict to misunderstand each other. Communication is already likely to be strained, and people will, most likely, want to hide the truth to some extent. Thus the potential for misperceptions and misunderstandings is high, which can make conflict management or resolution more difficult.

29.3.2. Six Fundamental Patterns of Cultural Differences

We all communicate with others all the time—in our homes, in our workplaces, in the groups we belong to, and in the community. No matter how well we think we understand each other, communication is hard. Just think, for example, how often we hear things like, "He doesn't get it," or "She didn't really hear what I meant to say." "Culture" is often at the root of communication challenges. Our culture influences how we approach problems, and how we participate in groups and in communities. When we participate in groups we are often surprised at how differently people approach their work together.

Culture is a complex concept, with many different definitions. But, simply put, "culture" refers to a group or community with which we share common experiences that shape the way we understand the world. It includes groups that we are born into, such as gender, race, or national origin. It also includes groups we join or become part of.

For example, we can acquire a new culture by moving to a new region, by a change in our economic status, or by becoming disabled. When we think of culture this broadly, we realize we all belong to many cultures at once.

Our histories are a critical piece of our cultures. Historical experiences—whether of five years ago or of ten generations back—shape who we are. Knowledge of our history can help us understand ourselves and one another better. Exploring the ways in which various groups within our society have related to each other is key to opening channels for cross-cultural communication.

In a world as complex as ours, each of us is shaped by many factors, and culture is one of the powerful forces that acts on us. Anthropologists Kevin Avruch and Peter Black explain the importance of culture this way: One's own culture provides the "lens" through which we view the world; the "logic"... by which we order it; the "grammar" ... by which it makes sense. In other words, culture is central to what we see, how we make sense of what we see, and how we express ourselves.

As people from different cultural groups take on the exciting challenge of working together, cultural values sometimes conflict. We can misunderstand each other, and react in ways that can hinder what are otherwise promising partnerships. Oftentimes, we aren't aware that culture is acting upon us. Sometimes, we are not even aware that we have cultural values or assumptions that are different from others'.

Six fundamental patterns of cultural differences—ways in which cultures, as a whole, tend to vary from one another—are described below. The descriptions point out some of the recurring causes of cross cultural communication difficulties. As you enter into multicultural dialogue or collaboration, keep these generalized differences in mind. Next time you find yourself in a confusing situation, and you suspect that cross-cultural differences are at play, try reviewing this list. Ask yourself how culture may be shaping your own reactions, and try to see the world from others' points of view.

The way people communicate varies widely between, and even within, cultures. One aspect of communication style is language usage. Across cultures, some words and phrases are used in different ways. For example, even in countries that share the English language, the meaning of "yes" varies from "maybe, I'll consider it" to "definitely so," with many shades in between.

Another major aspect of communication style is the degree of importance given to non-verbal communication. Non-verbal communication includes not only facial expressions and gestures; it also involves seating arrangements, personal distance, and sense of time. In addition, different norms regarding the appropriate degree of assertiveness in communicating can add to cultural misunderstandings. For instance, some white Americans typically consider raised voices to be a sign that a fight has begun, while some black, Jewish and Italian Americans often feel that an increase in volume is a sign of an exciting conversation among friends. Thus, some white Americans may react with greater alarm to a loud discussion than would members of some American ethnic or non-white racial groups.

29.3.3. Different Attitudes Toward Conflict

Some cultures view conflict as a positive thing, while others view it as something to be avoided. In the U.S., conflict is not usually desirable; but people often are encouraged to deal directly with conflicts that do arise. In fact, face-to-face meetings customarily are recommended as the way to work through whatever problems exist. In contrast, in many Eastern countries, open conflict is experienced as embarrassing or demeaning; as a rule, differences are best worked out quietly. A written exchange might be the favoured means to address the conflict.

29.3.4. Different Approaches to Completing Tasks

From culture to culture, there are different ways that people move toward completing tasks. Some reasons include different access to resources, different judgments of the rewards associated with task completion, different notions of time, and varied ideas about how relationship-building and task-oriented work should go together.

When it comes to working together effectively on a task, cultures differ with respect to the importance placed on establishing relationships early on in the collaboration. A case in point, Asian and Hispanic cultures tend to attach more value to developing relationships at the beginning of a shared project and more emphasis on task completion toward the end as compared with European-Americans. European-Americans tend to focus immediately on the task at hand, and let relationships develop as they work on the task. This does not mean that people from any one of these cultural backgrounds are more or less committed to accomplishing the task, or value relationships more or less; it means they may pursue them differently.

29.3.5. Different Decision-Making Styles

The roles individuals play in decision-making vary widely from culture to culture. For example, in the U.S., decisions are frequently delegated—that is, an official assigns responsibility for a particular matter to a subordinate. In many Southern European and Latin American countries, there is a strong value placed on holding decision-making responsibilities oneself. When decisions are made by groups of people, majority rule is a common approach in the U.S.; in Japan consensus is the preferred mode. Be aware that individuals' expectations about their own roles in shaping a decision may be influenced by their cultural frame of reference.

29.3.6. Different Attitudes Toward Disclosure

In some cultures, it is not appropriate to be frank about emotions, about the reasons behind a conflict or a misunderstanding, or about personal information. Keep this in mind when you are in a dialogue or when you are working with others. When you are dealing with a conflict, be mindful that people may differ in what they feel comfortable revealing. Questions that may seem natural to you—What was the conflict about? What was your role in the conflict? What was the sequence of events?—may seem intrusive to others. The variation among cultures in attitudes toward disclosure is also something to consider before you conclude that you have an accurate reading of the views, experiences, and goals of the people with whom you are working.

29.3.7. Different Approaches to Knowing

Notable differences occur among cultural groups when it comes to epistemologies—that is, the ways people come to know things. European cultures tend to consider information acquired through cognitive means, such as counting and measuring, more valid than other ways of coming to know things. Compare that to African cultures' preference for affective ways of knowing, including symbolic imagery and rhythm. Asian cultures' epistemologies tend to emphasize the validity of knowledge gained through striving toward transcendence.

Recent popular works demonstrate that our own society is paying more attention to previously overlooked ways of knowing. Indeed, these different approaches to knowing could affect ways of analyzing a community problem or finding ways to resolve it. Some members of your group may want to do library research to understand a shared problem better and identify possible solutions. Others may prefer to visit places and people who have experienced challenges like the ones you are facing, and get a feeling for what has worked elsewhere.

29.4. ASPECTS OF CROSS CULTURAL COMMUNICATION

There are several parameters that may be perceived differently by people of different cultures. These may include:

High and low context cultures: Context is the most important cultural dimension and also immensely difficult to define. The idea of context in culture was an idea put forth by an anthropologist by the name of Edward T Hall. Hall breaks up culture into two main groups: High and Low context cultures. He refers to context as the stimuli, environment or ambiance surrounding the environment. Depending on how a culture relies on the three points to communicate their meaning, will place them in either High or Low context cultures. For example, Hall goes on to explain that low-context cultures assume that the individuals know very little about what they are being told, and therefore must be given a lot of background information. High-Context cultures assume the individual is knowledgeable about the subject and has to be given very little background information.

Non-verbal, oral and written: The main goal behind improving intercultural audiences is to pay special attention to specific areas of communication to enhance the effectiveness of the intercultural messages. These specific areas are broken down into three sub categories; Non-Verbal, Oral and Written messages.

Non-verbal contact involves everything from something as obvious as eye contact and facial expressions to more discrete forms of expression such as the use of space. Experts have label the term Kinesics to mean communicating through body movement. Huseman, author of Business Communication, explains that the two most prominent ways of communication through Kinesics is eye contact and facial expressions.

Eye contact, Huseman goes on to explain, is the key factor in setting the tone between two individuals and greatly differs in meaning between cultures. In the Americas and Western Europe eye contact is interpreted the same way, conveying interest and honesty. People who avoid eye contact when speaking are viewed in a negative light, withholding information and lacking in general confidence. However, in the Middle East, Africa, and especially Asia eye contact is seen as disrespectful and even challenging of one's authority. People who make eye contact, but only briefly, are seen as respectful and courteous.

Facial expressions are their own language by comparison, and universal throughout all cultures. Dale Leathers, for example, states that facial expression can communicate ten basic classes of meaning.

The final part to Non-Verbal communication lies in our ***gestures***, and can be broken down into five subcategories; Emblems, Illustrators, Regulators, Affect Displays, and Adaptors. Emblems and Illustrators are the easiest to communicate since Emblems refer to sign language (such as the "Thumbs Up" which is one of the most recognized symbols in the world) and Illustrators mimic what we speak (such as gesturing how much time is left by holding up a certain amount of fingers. Regulators act as a way of conveying meaning through gestures (raising up one's hand for instance indicates that one has a certain question about what was just said) and become more complicated since the same regulator can have different meanings across different cultures (making a circle with ones hand for instance in the Americas means O.K but in Japan the gesture is symbolic for money, and in France conveys the notion of worthlessness). The last two, Affect Displays and Adaptors, are the two the individual has very little to no control over. Affect Displays reveal emotions such as happiness (through a smile) or sadness (mouth trembling, tears) where Adaptors are more subtle such as a yawn or clenching fists in anger.

The last Non-verbal type of communication deals with communication through the space around us, or ***Proxemics.*** Huseman goes on to explain that Hall identifies three types of space; Feature-Fixed Space, Semifixed Feature Space and Informal Space. Feature-Fixed space deals with how cultures arrange their space on a large scale, such as buildings and parks. Semifixed Feature Space deals with how we arrange our space inside said buildings, such as the placement of our desks, chairs and plants. Informal space is the space that we place importance on. Talking distance, how close people sit to one another and office space are all examples. A production line worker will often have to make an appointment to see his supervisor however the supervisor is free to visit the production line workers at will.

Oral and written communication is generally easier to learn, adapt and deal with in the business world for the simple fact that each language is unique. The one difficulty that comes into play is Paralanguage, "Language refers to what is said, Paralanguage refers to how it is said. Even though, logically, the same words should convey the same meaning the volume, rate, and emphasis placed on those words can change the meaning of the phrase. The example given by Huseman took the sentence "I would like to help you" and simply by placing the emphases on the words I, Like, Help, You in four different sentences changes the meaning of the phrase.

29.5. RESPECTING OUR DIFFERENCES AND WORKING TOGETHER

In addition to helping us to understand ourselves and our own cultural frames of reference, knowledge of these six patterns of cultural difference can help us to understand the people who are different from us. An appreciation of patterns of cultural difference can assist us in processing what it means to be different in ways that are respectful of others, not faultfinding or damaging.

Anthropologists Avruch and Black have noted that, when faced by an interaction that we do not understand, people tend to interpret the others involved as "abnormal," "weird," or "wrong." This tendency, if indulged, gives rise on the individual level to prejudice. If this propensity is either consciously or unconsciously integrated into organizational structures, then prejudice takes root in our institutions—in the structures, laws, policies, and procedures that shape our lives. Consequently, it is vital that we learn to control the human tendency to translate "different from me" into "less than me." We can learn to do this.

We can also learn to collaborate across cultural lines as individuals and as a society. Awareness of cultural differences doesn't have to divide us from each other. It doesn't have to paralyze us either, for fear of not saying the "right thing." In fact, becoming more aware of our cultural differences, as well as exploring our similarities, can help us communicate with each other more effectively. Recognizing where cultural differences are at work is the first step toward understanding and respecting each other.

Learning about different ways that people communicate can enrich our lives. People's different communication styles reflect deeper philosophies and world views which are the foundation of their culture. Understanding these deeper philosophies gives us a broader picture of what the world has to offer us.

Learning about people's cultures has the potential to give us a mirror image of our own. We have the opportunity to challenge our assumptions about the "right" way of doing things, and consider a variety of approaches. We have a chance to learn new ways to solve problems that we had previously given up on, accepting the difficulties as "just the way things are."

Lastly, if we are open to learning about people from other cultures, we become less lonely. Prejudice and stereotypes separate us from whole groups of people who could be friends and partners in working for change. Many of us long for real contact. Talking with people different from ourselves gives us hope and energizes us to take on the challenge of improving our communities and worlds.

29.5.1. Guidelines for Multicultural Collaboration

Cultural questions—about who we are and how we identify ourselves – are at the heart of *Toward a More Perfect Union in an Age of Diversity*, and will be at the heart of your discussions. As you set to work on multicultural collaboration in your community, keep in mind these additional guidelines:

Learn from generalizations about other cultures, but don't use those generalizations to stereotype, "write off," or oversimplify your ideas about another person. The best use of a generalization is to add it to your storehouse of knowledge so that you better understand and appreciate other interesting, multi-faceted human beings.

Practice, practice, practice. That's the first rule, because it's in the doing that we actually get better at cross cultural communication.

Don't assume that there is one right way (yours!) to communicate. Keep questioning your assumptions about the "right way" to communicate. For example, think about your body language; postures that indicate receptivity in one culture might indicate aggressiveness in another.

Don't assume that breakdowns in communication occur because other people are on the wrong track. Search for ways to make the communication work, rather than searching for who should receive the blame for the breakdown.

Listen actively and empathetically. Try to put yourself in the other person's shoes. Especially when another person's perceptions or ideas are very different from your own, you might need to operate at the edge of your own comfort zone.

Respect others' choices about whether to engage in communication with you. Honor their opinions about what is going on.

Stop, suspend judgment, and try to look at the situation as an outsider.

Be prepared for a discussion of the past. Use this as an opportunity to develop an understanding from "the other's" point of view, rather than getting defensive or impatient. Acknowledge historical events that have taken place. Be open to learning more about them. Honest acknowledgment of the mistreatment and oppression that have taken place on the basis of cultural difference is vital for effective communication.

Awareness of current power imbalances—and an openness to hearing each other's perceptions of those imbalances—is also necessary for understanding each other and working together.

Remember that cultural norms may not apply to the behaviour of any particular individual. We are all shaped by many, many factors—our ethnic background, our family, our education, our personalities—and are more complicated than any cultural norm could suggest. Check your interpretations if you are uncertain what is meant.

29.5.2. Cross Cultural Communication Consultants

During the past decades the growth of globalisation, immigration and international tourism has involved large numbers of people in cross-cultural interaction (also referred to as inter-cultural interaction or international relations) whether they have liked it or not.

This has led to an increased desire and need for knowledge regarding cross-cultural communication on many levels. There is the theoretical field of cross-cultural communication and the applied field of cross-cultural training.

Cross cultural communication consultants have come a long way in the short period of time such specialists have been in demand. No longer are they expatriates with a few years overseas experience and the capability to impart their knowledge onto others. Cross cultural consultants now bring expertise that is founded upon a number of key factors.

Cross cultural consultants generally have a broad knowledge and experience of two or more different cultures. This knowledge is then employed to assist companies and individuals overcome challenges brought about through cross cultural differences in business. Areas in which assistance is needed may range from relocation briefings to company mergers or management techniques. The ability to diagnose and treat cross cultural problems is developed through their experience in a number of different fields.

Cross cultural consultants will generally have an academic background either in specific courses such as 'Cross Cultural Communication and Trade' or 'Cross Cultural Psychology' or in related courses such as 'International Relations' or 'Business Studies'. Their studies will equip them with the academic skills and knowledge of the field that will later be applied in the business context.

It is critical for cross cultural consultants to have considerable business experience. If this is lacking then academic knowledge is not usually sufficient to understand the mechanics of business operations. In order to understand how things work and the different challenges facing managers and staff it is critical to have experienced it first hand.

Through courses and practical experience a cross cultural consultant will have knowledge of training techniques. This will include communication skills, presentation methods, the use of activities and utilization of different technology and media.

Experience of living abroad, mixing with different cultures, speaking different languages and working in foreign offices is vital for any cross cultural consultant. Without having been exposed to a different culture how can one advise on working effectively with that culture? It is important that this emersion in the target culture has been to the extent that the cross cultural consultant can totally empathise with the culture and understand its dynamics.

Language carries with it cultural coding. All experts, commentators and linguists are unanimous that without knowledge of the language the culture can never be appreciated. A cross cultural consultant will therefore have this insider knowledge not only through living and working in a country but also by using and understanding the language.

The complexity and diversity of cross cultural challenges in the international business world is reflected in the broad knowledge and skills of cross cultural consultants. Drawing on expertise gained through a variety of interrelated fields, the cross cultural consultant is now truly a specialist of great importance.

29.5.3. Multicultural Communication Tips

Here are some language and communication tips from AMA's new seminar Managing Multicultural Teams for Peak Performance, that are of particular benefit to managers of culturally diverse teams:

- Simplify your message by using less complex sentence structures and vocabulary.
- Never shout to be understood.
- Define the meaning of critical technical words and acronyms.
- Avoid non-standard abbreviations, such as "U R" for "you are."
- Be patient and try to follow team members' ideas and logic, which may be different from yours.
- Ask people to repeat once, maybe twice, if you do not understand them. If that does not work, ask them to say it in a different manner.
- Remain cool and composed, even when you have made a mistake that results in embarrassment for you or when you feel embarrassed by others (in most cases, they did not mean to embarrass you).
- When you feel strong emotions about something said or done by someone who comes from a culturally different background than you do, clarify their meanings and intentions before you express your emotions.
- If you cannot think of any positive interpretation of someone else's actions or words, chances are you are missing something. Clarify with the person or with someone who has experience in dealing with similar cultural groups.
- Adapt your space requirements to those of your counterparts whenever possible. You can judge someone's comfort zone by the distance to which they extend their hand when shaking hands.
- When someone does or says something that seems weird and/or wrong, give him/her the benefit of the doubt. Ask yourself: "How else could I interpret these words or actions?"

- Communicate important messages via several different media to ensure that they are received. Make sure that all the messages are consistent.

29.5.4. Tips for Native English Speakers

- Avoid "isn't it?" questions. Because this way of formulating questions does not exist in many other languages, it can be confusing for non-native English speakers. For example, to the question, "You are coming, aren't you?" they may answer, "Yes" (I am coming) or "No" (I am coming), depending on how they interpret the question.
- Ask the person if he/she wants help with finding words that might convey their meaning.
- If you do not understand a word, ask the person to spell it, write it down, use a synonym or say the word in his/her native language and have someone else translate, if possible.
- Try to involve non-native English speakers, particularly during brainstorming sessions, by asking explicitly for their input.
- If you receive a voice mail message that you do not understand, ask another non-native English speaker from the same linguistic background to listen to it and "translate" for you.
- In continuous meetings, provide some break time so that non-native English speakers can take a rest from the concentration required to follow the conversation.
- Avoid scheduling presentations by non-native English speakers at the end of the day, when fatigue may affect their English speaking skills.
- Consider providing ESL courses to the non-native English speakers on your staff or team.
- Offer to proofread non-native English speakers' documents or presentations.
- Slow down your delivery and clearly articulate each word. Avoid contractions that are difficult for non-native English speakers to understand (i.e., "gonna," "wanna").

In face-to-face meetings, face the people to whom you speak.

29.5.5. Tips for Non-native English Speakers

- If you do not mind people suggesting words so that you can communicate more quickly, say so.
- Try to participate in discussions, especially brainstorming sessions, even if you feel uncomfortable.
- If your organization offers ESL courses, take them, even if your English is already functional. Courses designed to help you modify your accent to make it more understandable by native English speakers can be particularly beneficial.
- Keep a dictionary handy and make sure the words you use mean what you think they mean.

- Ask a native English speaker for help with your documents, presentations and even sensitive e-mails or phone calls, if necessary.
- Before calling someone, think of what you want to say and look up any words that you are unsure of. If you must leave a voice mail message, compose the message on paper, then read it into the phone.
- Make sure you know and use appropriately the technical words that people in your field use. Find a native English speaker who will take the time to discuss this with you; use sketches, diagrams and pictures to ensure that you understand correctly. Use the terms repeatedly until they become second nature.
- Do not attempt to use slang and idiomatic expressions until you are quite comfortable with the language. Using these incorrectly or in the wrong situation can backfire.

29.6. BASIC STEPS TO CULTURAL COMPETENCE

As more or more people from different backgrounds, countries, cultures and religions immigrate to foreign lands, those countries become an intercultural melting pot. In order for the native people and the immigrant population to blend and create a thriving and successful atmosphere both sides need to develop some sort of intercultural tolerance and understanding of the differences that may exist between them. An example of poor intercultural understanding, or one based simply on stereotypes, is offered by the town of Herouxville in Quebec, Canada.

A declaration issued by the town in January 2007, which was designed to inform immigrants, "that the way of life which they abandoned when they left their countries of origin cannot be recreated here [*i.e.*, Herouxville]". It then went on to state that the immigrant population would therefore have to refrain from their cultural norms and activities such as to "kill women by stoning them in public, burning them alive, burning them with acid, circumcising them, etc."

The declaration paints a rather sad picture of the officials that administer the town and highlights not only their rather insular outlook but a world view of "others" based on crass and frankly incorrect stereotypes. To simply consider that anyone from another country (in this case more than likely a Middle Eastern or Asian one) regards the stoning of women and burning them alive as part of daily life derives from crude, and media led, stereotypes of other peoples.

Stereotypes are at their most basic level a set of assumed characteristics about a certain group of people whose actual beliefs, habits and realities more often than not disagree with the imposed assumptions. Stereotypes are usually based on factors such as exaggeration, distortion, ignorance, racism, cultural factors or even historical experiences. Stereotyping is therefore rightly seen as a negative way of seeing people. This is even true of what are called "positive stereotypes". A positive stereotype is where we use a blanket expression for a whole people, *i.e.*, all the Chinese are great at maths, all Germans are well organised or all English people are well mannered. Although the intent behind the statement is positive, it still does not reflect the truth.

What we have witnessed in Herouxville should not be seen as an isolated incident. Such assumptions about foreigners exist all over the planet. However, this does not make it right or excusable. The message it does give is that there is a lot of work to be done in order to educate people to become more culturally competent.

Cultural competency is important in this day and age for exactly the reasons cited in this article. We, as citizens of planet earth, are no longer confined to our national and cultural borders. We mix with people from different cultures, ethnicities, religions and colours on a daily basis. In order to make this intercultural experience work on all levels from education to business to government, people have to develop basic skills in intercultural communication and understanding. In order to assist the officials at Herouxville, five basic steps to cultural competence are presented below:

1. ***Break Assumptions.*** Everyone makes or has assumptions about others. Assumptions are beliefs rather than objective truth and are usually influenced by a number of subjective factors. People need to assess their assumptions and ask themselves why they hold those ideas or beliefs.
2. ***Empathise.*** In order to come to appreciate and understand people from different cultures, empathy is vital. Through putting yourself in someone else's shoes you come to see or appreciate their point of view.
3. ***Involve.*** Involving others in your world and involving yourself in other's empowers and educates. Don't build walls between people but learn from one another.
4. ***Avoid Herd Mentality.*** Herd mentality refers to a closed and one dimensional approach. Such a way of thinking curbs creativity, innovation and advancement as people are restricted in how to think, approach and engage with people or challenges. Cultural competency can only develop if people are encouraged to think as individuals, bring their cultural influences to the table and share ideas that may be outside the box.
5. ***Shun Insensitivity.*** People can and do behave in culturally insensitive ways. By attacking someone's person, you attack their culture and therefore their dignity. This can only be divisive. Cultural competency is based upon people thinking through words and actions to ensure they do not act inappropriately. When insensitive behaviour is witnessed it is the responsibility of all to shun it and ensure it remains unacceptable.
6. ***Be Wise.*** Wisdom is not called wisdom for nothing. People need to be aware how to interact with people with respect and knowledge. Cultural competency is essentially founded upon wisdom, *i.e.*, showing maturity of thought and action in dealing with people. Through thinking things out and have background knowledge to intercultural differences much of the communication problems witnessed within business could be avoided.

29.7. SUCCESSFUL CROSS CULTURAL COMMUNICATION

In today's global business environment, more and more of us are required to understand people who comes from countries and cultures different from our own. While there is no short and easy way to learn about a given culture in any depth, there are some general principles that lead to success in communicating and conducting business with people of backgrounds unlike our own.

Here are some important points to understand:

Direct experience is the best way to begin to learn any culture. Just as the best way to learn a new language is to become immersed in that language, so too is it most helpful to learn another culture by jumping right in. This may not always be practical, but radio stations, music, trips to religious organizations or other clubs that cater to members of a specific group—all of these things can be helpful ways to begin.

Differences can feel like a threat at first. No one likes to feel like a stranger, and feeling unable to communicate or to decipher aspects of behaviour that don't fit with our own habitual experiences can make any of us feel alone. This is a natural part of human experience, but even so, it is important to keep these feelings in perspective and remember that differences are less important than commonalities.

We tend to overlook similarities and notice just the differences when we first begin to interact with members of another culture. And then, when we apply the standards of interpretation that we would use in our own cultures to the behaviour of those in the unfamiliar culture, we will draw mistaken conclusions. We all share 98% of the same DNA, and we are all far more alike than we are different, but that's easy to forget in the beginning.

Stereotyping due to overgeneralization is a common occurrence, especially among those who only interact with another culture infrequently. When we are faced with uncertainty, the human mind naturally seeks to create some order or system from what we observe. This is especially true when we may feel vulnerable due to uncertainty. So the mind creates its own set of rules or generalizations – which may be based on some surface realities and patterns—but which fail to account for real experience and individual variation. What's more, since we may feel threatened, the human mind can presume negative motives or draw negative inferences from the generalizations we create/observe, which forms then forms the basis of prejudice.

There is always more variation within groups than there is between them. What does that mean? That means that no matter how much we may perceive groups A and B as different, the amount of difference between those groups is dwarfed by the amount of variation within each group. In other words, both groups have shy people and daring people, honest and dishonest, bellicose and accommodating types, etc. There each group is much more of mixed stew of types of people, and the patterns within each group are more alike than different. It's just that culture and history shape the customs and rituals though which those various aspects of human nature are expressed. Think of it this way: both Apple and Microsoft operating systems allow you to accomplish work with a word processing system. The work is the same, but the language, the coding, though which that basic work is accomplished or expressed is different. This is why cross cultural communication takes work – we have to go back and examine aspects of our own "operating systems" and understand the "systems" of others to be able to communicate between the two "platforms."

For precisely the reason described above, our own cultural identities are not apparent to us until we begin to interact with others from different backgrounds.

Finally, cultures are always changing, especially as they interact with each other. Even from within, cultures move and flow and change through time, even when they think they don't. But the pace of change is accelerated when cultures that reinforce different styles of communication, and which accent different binding customs and values, interact with each other. The result is often disorienting (to say the least), but the result is inevitably that both cultures change in the process. Individuals who begin to bridge these gaps are like pioneers, blazing paths and creating plausible options for hybrid identities for others to copy and test in the future.

29.7.1. Effective Cross Cultural Communication Skills

Culture is about human expression. It involves the behaviour, beliefs and practices of individuals and their communities. Culture takes many forms and can be expressed in many different ways such as art, music, sport, entertainment, religion, ceremonies, and of course through our verbal and non-verbal communication.

Cross Cultural communication requires some understanding of every Culture in the world and if you don't have an understanding of the different cultures than how do you communicate to someone who understands and relates to the world differently to you. This is what I am getting to, so keep reading please.

The main and most prominent key to effective cross-cultural communication is knowledge. It is absolutely essential that people understand the potential problems of cross cultural communication, and make a huge conscious effort to overcome these problems. It is also very important to know that your efforts will not always be successful, and to be prepared to adjust your behaviour accordingly.

A lot of people always assume that there is a significant possibility that cultural differences are the cause of communication problems. And to some extent they are correct. Effective communication with people of different cultures is especially challenging. Cultures provide people with ways of thinking—ways of seeing, hearing, and interpreting the world. Thus the same words can mean different things to people from different cultures, even when they talk the "same" language. When the languages are different, and translation has to be used to communicate, the potential for misunderstandings increases.

Please, you need to remember, that even in your own culture, the verbal and non-verbal communications have different meanings to different people. And just like in your own culture there are misunderstandings happening all the time, and just over simple things where both of you speak the same language. So it is fairly safe to assume that there are going to be misunderstandings in cross cultural communications as well due to verbal and non-verbal communication having different meanings to different people.

Always be willing to be patient and forgiving, rather than hostile and aggressive, if problems develop. One should respond slowly and carefully in cross-cultural exchanges, not jumping to the conclusion that you know what is being thought and said.

William Ury's suggestion for heated conflicts is to stop, listen, and think, or as he puts it "go to the balcony" when the situation gets tense. By this he means withdraw from the situation, step back, and reflect on what is going on before you act. This helps in cross cultural communication as well. When things seem to be going badly, stop or slow down and think. What could be going on here? Is it possible I miss-understood what they said, or they have miss-understood me? Often misinterpretation or misunderstanding is the source of the problem.

Reflective Listening is one of the key ingredients in cross cultural communication. Reflective Listening is used a lot to check out the meaning of what someone says—by repeating back what you think you have heard. You are then able to confirm that you understand what has been said accurately. This is so helpful as many times words and even gestures are used differently between languages or cultural groups.

Stella Ting-Toomey describes three ways in which culture interferes with effective cross-cultural understanding. First is what she calls "cognitive constraints." These are the frames of reference or world views that provide a backdrop that all new information is compared to or inserted into.

Second are "behaviour constraints." Each culture has its own rules about proper behaviour which affect verbal and non-verbal communication. Whether one looks the other person in the eye-or not; whether one says what one means overtly or talks around the issue; how close the people stand to each other when they are talking—all of these and many more are rules of politeness which differ from culture to culture.

Ting-Toomey's third factor is "emotional constraints." Different cultures regulate the display of emotion differently. Some cultures get very emotional when they are debating an issue. They yell, they cry, they exhibit their anger, fear, frustration, and other feelings openly. Other cultures try to keep their emotions hidden, exhibiting or sharing only the "rational" or factual aspects of the situation.

All of these differences tend to lead to communication problems. If the people involved are not aware of the potential for such problems, they are even more likely to fall victim to them, although it takes more than awareness to overcome these problems and communicate effectively across cultures.

Often a mediator or intermediary who is familiar with both cultures can be helpful in cross cultural communication situations, and diffuse any conflicts before they arise. They can translate both the substance and the manner of what is being said. For instance, they can tone down strong statements that would be considered appropriate in one culture but not in another, before they are given to people from a culture that does not talk together in such a strong way. They can also adjust the timing of what is said and done. Some cultures move quickly to the point; others talk about other things long enough to establish rapport or a relationship with the other person. If discussion on the primary topic begins too soon, the group that needs a "warm up" first will feel uncomfortable. A mediator or intermediary who understands this can explain the problem, and make appropriate procedural adjustments.

In these cases, engaging in extra discussions about the process and the manner of carrying out the discussions is appropriate, as is extra time for confirming and re-confirming understandings at every step in the dialogue or negotiating process.

29.8. DEVELOPING AWARENESS OF INDIVIDUAL CULTURES

The Internet and modern technology have opened up new marketplaces, and allow us to promote our businesses to new geographic locations and cultures. And given that it can now be as easy to work with people remotely as it is to work face-to-face, cross-cultural communication is increasingly the new norm.

After all, if communication is electronic, it's as easy to work with someone in another country as it is to work with someone in the next town.

And why limit yourself to working with people within convenient driving distance when, just as conveniently, you can work with the most knowledgeable people in the entire world?

For those of us who are native English-speakers, it is fortunate that English seems to be the language that people use if they want to reach the widest possible audience.

However, even for native English speakers, cross cultural communication can be an issue: Just witness the mutual incomprehension that can sometimes arise between people from different English-speaking countries.

In this new world, good cross cultural communication is a must.

However, some learning the basics about culture and at least something about the language of communication in different countries is important. This is necessary even for the basic level of understanding required to engage in appropriate greetings and physical contact, which can be a tricky area inter-culturally. For instance, kissing a business associate is not considered an appropriate business practice in the U.S., but in Paris, one peck on each cheek is an acceptable greeting. And, the handshake that is widely accepted in the U.S. is not recognized in all other cultures.

While many companies now offer training in the different cultures where the company conducts business, it is important that employees communicating across cultures practice patience and work to increase their knowledge and understanding of these cultures. This requires the ability to see that a person's own behaviours and reactions are oftentimes culturally driven and that while they may not match are own, they are culturally appropriate.

If a leader or manager of a team that is working across cultures or incorporates individuals who speak different languages, practice different religions, or are members of a society that requires a new understanding, he or she needs to work to convey this.

Consider any special needs the individuals on your team may have. For instance, they may observe different holidays, or even have different hours of operation. Be mindful of time zone differences and work to keep everyone involved aware and respectful of such differences.

Generally speaking, patience, courtesy and a bit of curiosity go a long way. And, if you are unsure of any differences that may exist, simply ask team members. Again, this may best be done in a one-on-one setting so that no one feels "put on the spot" or self-conscious, perhaps even embarrassed, about discussing their own needs or differences or needs.

29.9. CROSS CULTURAL COMMUNICATION STRATEGIES

The key to effective cross cultural communication is knowledge. First, it is essential that people understand the potential problems of cross cultural communication, and make a conscious effort to overcome these problems. Second, it is important to assume that one's efforts will not always be successful, and adjust one's behaviour appropriately.

For example, one should always assume that there is a significant possibility that cultural differences are causing communication problems, and be willing to be patient and forgiving, rather than hostile and aggressive, if problems develop. One should respond slowly and carefully in cross-cultural exchanges, not jumping to the conclusion that you know what is being thought and said.

William Ury's suggestion for heated conflicts is to stop, listen, and think, or as he puts it "go to the balcony" when the situation gets tense. By this he means withdraw from the situation, step back, and reflect on what is going on before you act. This helps in cross cultural communication as well. When things seem to be going badly, stop or slow down and think. What could be going on here? Is it possible I misinterpreted what they said, or they misinterpreted me? Often misinterpretation is the source of the problem.

Active listening can sometimes be used to check this out–by repeating what one thinks he or she heard, one can confirm that one understands the communication accurately. If words are used differently between languages or cultural groups, however, even active listening can overlook misunderstandings.

Often intermediaries who are familiar with both cultures can be helpful in cross cultural communication situations. They can translate both the substance and the manner of what is said. For instance, they can tone down strong statements that would be considered appropriate in one culture but not in another, before they are given to people from a culture that does not talk together in such a strong way. They can also adjust the timing of what is said and done. Some cultures move quickly to the point; others talk about other things long enough to establish rapport or a relationship with the other person. If discussion on the primary topic begins too soon, the group that needs a "warm up" first will feel uncomfortable. A mediator or intermediary who understands this can explain the problem, and make appropriate procedural adjustments.

Yet sometimes intermediaries can make communication even more difficult. If a mediator is the same culture or nationality as one of the disputants, but not the other, this gives the appearance of bias, even when none exists. Even when bias is not intended, it is common for mediators to be more supportive or more understanding of the person who is of his or her own culture, simply because they understand them better. Yet when the mediator is of a third cultural group, the potential for cross-cultural misunderstandings increases further. In this case engaging in extra discussions about the process and the manner of carrying out the discussions is appropriate, as is extra time for confirming and re-confirming understandings at every step in the dialogue or negotiating process.

29.10. IMPORTANCE OF CROSS CULTURAL COMMUNICATION IN BUSINESS

As the business world becomes increasingly global, the need for effective cross cultural communication is essential. Cross cultural communication in business plays a vital role in building international customers, employee relations and business partnerships. Cross cultural communication in business requires effort, technique and the addressing of different hurdles that commonly prevent communication from being effective.

Importance. Cross cultural communication in business plays a vital role in successfully establishing the product or service in a different area of the globe. When the communication is effective, the product or service is appropriately tailored to the cultural norms and expectations resulting in the use or purchase of the product. Ineffective communication cross culturally can offend, confuse or send a misunderstood message which could lead to broken relations with investors or employees.

Barriers–Language. A common cross cultural barrier in business communication is the use of language. Not every business globally does business in English. Even if they do, there can be different meanings for the same English word. According to the website of business communication group Kwintessential, language barriers come in the form of either the use of inappropriate language or the use of foreign languages.

Barriers–Culture. Each culture has a different set of values, business ethics, languages, behaviour, expected etiquette and expression. Not knowing the differences in the country that the company is doing business in can lead to communication barriers that prohibit the messages from being effective.

Barriers–Company culture. A company culture is the norms and expectations within a company. This can be the organizational structure, policies and specific procedures that create a unique culture within the company. Expanding business communication cross culturally requires the business to assess its current culture and identify any possible hindrances that the company culture may present in a different country.

Intercultural communication is of importance to international businesses as it examines how people from different cultures, beliefs and religions come together to work and communicate with each other.

Demands for intercultural communication skills are increasing as more and more businesses go global or international. They realize that there are barriers and limitations when entering a foreign territory. Without the help of intercultural communication they can unknowingly cause confusion and misunderstandings. For these intercultural businesses to breach the cultural barriers encountered when stepping into foreign grounds it is vital for them to fully understand the cultural differences that exist so as to prevent damaging business relations due to intercultural communication gaps.

There are many theories that set principles to help interpret the basis of intercultural communication. These theories help to iron out possible ripples of misunderstanding by giving a basic guideline on how to address situations. These guidelines help prevent clashes between different cultures groups caused by misperceptions.

The basic skills of intercultural communication are fundamentally general communication skills that can be used universally by all cultures and races. These skills are simply tweaked in a direction that takes the cultural limitation into consideration. An example of such communication skills in the intercultural environment is to listen without judging, repeat what you understand, confirm meanings, give suggestions and acknowledge a mutual understanding.

In a nutshell the main purpose of following such theories is to earn respect from others. Respect in all cultures in the world is a common language and by earning it through respecting other peoples culture and religion; the favour is returned.

According to the University of Colorado, knowledge is the key to effective cross cultural business communication. Knowledge takes a step back and observes the differences between the two cultures and makes adjustments based on the observation. One approach to ensuring the cross cultural communication is being effective is to implement active listening that uses questions to clarify the message.

Few successful businesses are now mono-cultural in their make-up. Even if a business or organization is not dealing internationally the chances are that they employ people from foreign countries. At a higher level globalisation has meant companies are having to look further a field for new revenue streams, products, services, etc. This requires working and dealing with people from different cultures.

The leaders of today's organisations and businesses need to be adept at managing people of different cultures. They need to be able to grasp the essence of each culture quickly, because culture is so important in shaping customer or employee behaviour. Leaders must also learn to shape culture (at least that in their own organisations) so that it is positive, and aligned with the direction the organization is taking.

For those looking to the subject and wanting some quick tips on how to improve their intercultural leadership qualities, the following simple tips can get you on your way.

1. Learn about the cultures of people that you work and interact with. Start from scratch and forget your assumptions and stereotypes. There are many free online resources.
2. Get a book about intercultural communication and learn about the subject from an academic level. Noted academics such as Geert Hofstede, Fons Trompenaars and David Hall have all published books that will go a long way in unravelling the intricacies of cultural differences.
3. Take some formal training from intercultural experts. For very little outlay a day course can go a long way in helping you understand how culture impacts you and your work.
4. Try and attend events or occasions where you can submerge yourself in another culture. Use the opportunity to observe how people communicate and interact with one another. If you get the chance to travel abroad do the same when there.
5. Start listening and paying more attention when dealing with someone from another culture. You will be surprised how much you pick up by slowing down. Don't jump to conclusions and think actions and behaviours through.
6. Temper your own communication style. Pay attention to the rate at which you speak, what non-verbal messages you may be sending, ask for confirmation of understanding, avoid using slang and idioms.
7. Learn to tolerate uncertainty. There will be a great deal of unknowns when doing business across cultures. Definitive, concrete answers may not always be given. Focus on what you can determine and try to let go of minor details that are unclear.
8. Be patient with others and yourself. Don't give-up. A proper intercultural library of knowledge only comes with time.
9. Keep on top of your own development. Continually assess your advancement and make adjustments.
10. Ask for help and don't be afraid to apologise for mistakes. People generally are appreciative that you are trying to understand them.

The path to effective intercultural leadership is long but not hard. Essentially it is about opening your mind with which comes greater flexibility and creativity. You will soon see results in your new leadership approach as you become able to communicate naturally with all manner of cultures in your sphere of work.

The theories developed by the researchers and academics can and has been applied to many fields such as business, management, marketing, advertising and website design. As business becomes more and more international, many companies need to know how best to structure their companies, manage staff and communicate with customers. Intercultural communication gives them an insight into the areas they need to address or understand. Intercultural communication theories are now also used within the education, health care and other public services due to growing multicultural populations.

29.11. CROSS-CULTURAL SOLUTIONS FOR INTERNATIONAL BUSINESS

Globalisation, the expansion of intercontinental trade, technological advances and the increase in the number of companies dealing on the international stage have brought about a dramatic change in the frequency, context and means by which people from different cultural backgrounds interact.

Cross cultural solutions to international business demands are increasingly being viewed as a valid and necessary method in enhancing communication and interaction in between companies and customers and between colleagues.

Cross cultural consultancies are involved in aiding companies to find solutions to the challenges cross cultural differences carry.

International and national businesses are ultimately the result of people. As with incompatible software, if people are running on different cultural coding, problems can occur. Cross cultural consultancies therefore concentrate their efforts on interpersonal communication.

Different cultures and cultural backgrounds between a highly diverse staff base brings with it obstacles, challenges and difficulties. Cross cultural differences manifest in general areas such as in behaviour, etiquette, norms, values, expressions, group mechanics and non-verbal communication. These cross cultural differences then follow on through to high level areas such as management styles, corporate culture, marketing, HR and PR.

In order to overcome potential pitfalls, specialist attention is required in the form of a cross cultural consultant. As one would approach a doctor for a medical diagnosis or an accountant to examine finances, cross cultural consultants offer the expertise, experience and know-how to diagnose problems and provide solutions to interpersonal cultural differences.

Within companies there are many facets in which cultural differences manifest. Some key areas which cross cultural consultants deal with include, but are not exclusive to, the following:

Cross Cultural HR: HR covers a wide range of business critical areas that need cross cultural analysis. Consultants may offer advice on a number of areas including recruitment, relocation, international assignments, staff retention and training programmes.

Cross Cultural Team-Building: In order to have a well functioning business unit within a company, communication is critical. Cross cultural consultants will provide tools and methods to promote staff integration, reduce cross cultural conflicts and build team spirit. This is essentially done through highlighting differences and building on strengths to ensure they are used positively.

Cross Cultural Synergy: International mergers, acquisitions and joint-ventures require people from different cultural backgrounds to harmonise in order to succeed. Cross cultural consultants counsel on group mechanics, communication styles, norms, values and integration processes.

Cross Cultural Awareness Training: Working with colleagues, customers or clients from different cultural backgrounds, with different religions, values and etiquettes can occasionally lead to problems. Cross cultural awareness training is usually a generic introduction into a culture, country, region or religion. The aim is to equip the trainee with the adequate knowledge to deal comfortably with people from different cultures, avoiding misunderstandings and mistakes.

Cross Cultural Training for Expatriate Relocation: Staff that travel overseas need to understand the cultural basics of the host country or region. Knowledge of the country's history, culture, laws, traditions, business practices and social etiquettes all help to minimise the impact of culture shock and hence smooth their transition overseas.

Cross Cultural Negotiations: Equipped with their knowledge of the two or more cultures that can be meeting around the negotiation table, a cross cultural consultant advises on areas such as negotiation strategies, styles, planning, closure and etiquette in order to increase the chance of a successful outcome, free from misunderstandings, suspicions and general cross cultural communication breakdown.

Cross Cultural PR Consultancy: Brand image, public relations and advertising are all areas companies must be careful of when moving out of the national context. Tastes and values change dramatically from continent to continent. It is crucial to understand whether the brand name, image or advertising campaign is culturally applicable in the target country. Cross cultural consultants examine words, images, pictures, colours and symbols to ensure they fit well with the target culture.

Cross Cultural Language Training: Language training is an area where little investment is made by companies, but where the business advantages are great. Linguistic knowledge goes a long way in bridging cultural gaps and smoothing lines of communication. Cross cultural consultancies provide language training to business staff, moulding their learning to the business environment in which they work.

In conclusion, clearly the role and expertise of cross cultural communication consultants is important for today's international business. The potential pitfalls cross cultural differences present to companies are extensive. In essence a cross cultural consultant's primary objective is integration. This integration, between colleagues, clients and customers is crucial for business success. Equipped with experience, knowledge and above all objectivity, a cross cultural consultant creates bridges of understanding and opens lines of communication.

29.12. CROSS CULTURAL ADVERTISING

Culture affects everything we do. This applies to all areas of human life from personal relationships to conducting business abroad. When interacting within our native cultures, culture acts as a framework of understanding. However, when interacting with different cultures this framework no longer applies due to cross cultural differences.

Cross cultural communication aims to help minimise the negative impact of cross cultural differences through building common frameworks for people of different cultures to interact within. In business, cross cultural solutions are applied in areas such as HR, team building, foreign trade, negotiations and website design.

Cross cultural communication solutions are also critical to effective cross cultural advertising. Services and products are usually designed and marketed at a domestic audience. When a product is then marketed at an international audience the same domestic advertising campaign abroad will in most cases be ineffective.

The essence of successful advertising is convincing people that a product is meant for them. By purchasing it, they will receive some benefit, whether it be lifestyle, status, convenience or financial. However, when an advertising campaign is taken abroad different values and perceptions as to what enhances status or gives convenience exist. These differences make the original advertising campaign defunct.

It is therefore critical to any cross cultural advertising campaign that an understanding of a particular culture is acquired. By way of highlighting areas of cross cultural differences in advertising a few examples shall be examined.

29.12.1. Language in Cross Cultural Advertising

It may seem somewhat obvious to state that language is key to effective cross cultural advertising. However, the fact that companies persistently fail to check linguistic implications of company or product names and slogans demonstrates that such issues are not being properly addressed.

The advertising world is littered with examples of linguistic cross cultural blunders. Of the more comical was Ford's introduction of the 'Pinto' in Brazil. After seeing sales fail, they soon realised that this was due to the fact that Brazilians did not want to be seen driving a car meaning 'tiny male genitals'.

Language must also be analysed for its cultural suitability. For example, the slogan employed by the computer games manufacturer, EA Sports, "Challenge Everything" raises grumbles of disapproval in religious or hierarchical societies where harmonious relationships are maintained through the values of respect and non-confrontation.

It is imperative therefore that language be examined carefully in any cross cultural advertising campaign.

29.12.2. Communication Style in Cross Cultural Advertising

Understanding the way in which other cultures communicate allows the advertising campaign to speak to the potential customer in a way they understand and appreciate. For example, communication styles can be explicit or implicit. An explicit communicator (*e.g.*, USA) assumes the listener is unaware of background information or related issues to the topic of discussion and therefore provides it themselves. Implicit communicators (*e.g.*, Japan) assume the listener is well informed on the subject and minimises information relayed on the premise that the listener will understand from implication. An explicit communicator would find an implicit communication style vague, whereas an implicit communicator would find an explicit communication style exaggerated.

29.12.3. Colours, Numbers and Images in Cross Cultural Advertising

Even the simplest and most taken for granted aspects of advertising need to be inspected under a cross cultural microscope. Colours, numbers, symbols and images do not all translate well across cultures.

In some cultures there are lucky colours, such as red in China and unlucky colours, such as black in Japan. Some colours have certain significance; green is considered a special colour in Islam and some colours have tribal associations in parts of Africa.

Many hotels in the USA or UK do not have a room 13 or a 13th floor. Similarly, Nippon Airways in Japan do not have the seat numbers 4 or 9. If there are numbers with negative connotations abroad, presenting or packaging products in those numbers when advertising should be avoided.

Images are also culturally sensitive. Whereas it is common to see pictures of women in bikinis on advertising posters on the streets of London, such images would cause outrage in the Middle East.

29.12.4. Cultural Values in Cross Cultural Advertising

When advertising abroad, the cultural values underpinning the society must be analysed carefully. Is there a religion that is practised by the majority of the people? Is the society collectivist or individualist? Is it family orientated? Is it hierarchical? Is there a dominant political or economic ideology? All of these will impact an advertising campaign if left unexamined.

For example, advertising that focuses on individual success, independence and stressing the word "I" would be received negatively in countries where teamwork is considered a positive quality. Rebelliousness or lack of respect for authority should always be avoided in family orientated or hierarchical societies.

By way of conclusion, we can see that the principles of advertising run through to cross cultural advertising too. That is know your market, what is attractive to them and what their aspirations are. Cross cultural advertising is simply about using common sense and analysing how the different elements of an advertising campaign are impacted by culture and modifying them to best speak to the target audience.

29.13. CROSS CULTURAL ANALYSIS IN PUBLIC RELATIONS

The Public Relations (PR) industry is responsible for creating and maintaining relationships between clients and customers. Through areas such as brand management, advertising, media relations and crisis management, PR practitioners seek to foster interest, trust and belief in a product or company.

PR practitioners are aware of how best to carry this out when dealing within their own nations and cultures, however, when dealing with a foreign audience it is critical that cross cultural differences are recognised.

By way of illustrating the impact cross cultural awareness can have on the success or failure of a PR campaign a brief example can be cited:

Pepsodent tried to sell its toothpaste in Southeast Asia by emphasizing that it "whitens your teeth." They found out that the local natives chew betel nuts to blacken their teeth because they found it attractive. Had the PR company behind this campaign analysed the cross cultural issues related to Pepsodent's product, the failure of this PR campaign could have been avoided.

Cross cultural differences can make or break a PR campaign. It is therefore crucial that PR practitioners dealing with PR campaigns that incorporate a cross cultural element analyse likely cross cultural differences. A few key areas shall be highlighted in order to help PR practitioners begin to consider how culture may affect future projects.

29.13.1. Language and Culture

In order for a PR campaign to be successful abroad, an appreciation of the target language and its cultural nuances is necessary. The PR and advertising industries are littered with examples of poor translations and a lack of cross cultural understanding leading to PR failure. For example, when Ford launched the 'Pinto' in Brazil they were puzzled as to why sales were dead. Fortunately they found out that Brazilians did not want to be seen driving a car meaning 'small male genitals' and promptly changed the name.

Translation of documents, slogans and literature must be checked and double checked for meanings and cross cultural nuances. This should not only take place between languages but also within languages. Even in English there are cross cultural differences in meanings. For example, the airline UAL headlined an article about Paul Hogan, star of Crocodile Dundee, with, "Paul Hogan Camps it up" which unfortunately in the UK and Australia is slang for "flaunting homosexuality".

Areas where the spoken word is used in PR, such as press conferences or interviews, should be prepared for within a cross cultural framework. In short, speaking styles and the content used differs across cultures.

British and American communication styles are described as 'explicit', meaning messages are conveyed solely through words. Correlating background information is deemed necessary and divulged, ambiguity is avoided and spoken words have literal meaning. In many other cultures, communication is 'implicit'. The message listeners are likely to interpret is based on factors such as who is speaking, the context and non-verbal cues. Spoken words do not fully convey the whole story as listeners are expected to read between the lines.

With relation to content, speakers must be aware of the cross cultural differences in humour, metaphors, aphorisms and anecdotes. In addition, references to topics such as politics and/or religion can be a very sensitive issue in other cultures.

When the spoken word is used the cross cultural distinctions of the target culture must be incorporated in order to help the speaker appeal to and identify with the audience.

Press releases, features and copywriting all require a certain amount of cross cultural sensitivity when being applied abroad. Journalistic traditions, writing styles, news worthiness, delivery systems and whether a 'free press' exists are all areas that will affect how the written word is tailored.

In addition, the most important point, from a cross cultural perspective, is how to write in a way that engages the readers in that society or culture. Some cultures may prefer colourful and inspirational writing, others factual and objective. Some may be motivated by language that incorporates a religious or moral tone, others by a money-orientated or materialistic one.

When writing, the first step should always be to look at and integrate the cross cultural particulars of the target audience.

29.13.2. Communication Channels

PR practitioners employ many different communication channels when trying to circulate information relating to their campaign. The main channels of communication in the UK or America are the radio, the press, TV, internet and public spaces. However, these channels may not always be applicable abroad.

In many countries the radio, TV or newspapers may not be the primary source of information. Literacy rates may be poor and/or radios may be expensive. In Africa, only 1.4% of the population have access to the internet. Even where such channels of communication do exist, such as TV, some methods used by PR practitioners, namely guerrilla marketing, would be interpreted differently in foreign countries. For example, interrupting live TV may be laughed at in the UK but in other countries it would be seen as irresponsible and rebellious.

The usual channels of communication in some countries would simply have no effect in terms of PR. In such countries, local alternatives need to be sought such as religious leaders, tribal chiefs, school teachers or NGO's. Information coming from such figures will not only reach the audience but be perceived as more credible than if it were from foreigners.

29.13.3. PR Materials

The use of publicity materials in PR campaigns such as logos, slogans, pictures, colours and designs must all be cross culturally examined. Pictures of seemingly innocuous things in one culture could mean something different in another. For example, a company advertised eyeglasses in Thailand by featuring a variety of cute animals wearing glasses. The ad failed as animals are considered to be a low form of life in Thailand and no self respecting Thai would wear anything worn by animals. Similarly, logos or symbols are culturally sensitive. A soft drink was introduced into Arab countries with an attractive label that had a six-pointed star on it. The Arabs interpreted this as pro-Israeli and refused to buy it.

The above cited areas are but a few of those that require decent cross cultural assessment by PR practitioners if they wish their international and cross cultural campaigns to succeed. The aim of implementing a cross cultural analysis in PR is to build campaigns that target the audience as best as possible, meaning appealing to their world view while avoiding offense.

29.14. CROSS-CULTURAL COMMUNICATION ACROSS LANGUAGES

Cross cultural communication is not the sole reserve of the business world. In fact, all of us in one form or another come across situations that require some kind of cross cultural communication and understanding.

One such situation is when communicating with foreigners. We all encounter people at work, on holiday or elsewhere who do not share the same language as us. Although we consider language the main means of communicating, language only represents 7% of what we communicate. There are many ways of overcoming the language barrier to allow for some cross cultural communication.

When faced with a situation in which there is no common language these points may help you to get your message across:

Say it without words: Use hands, arms, legs, gestures, facial expressions and everything else your charades experience has taught you.

Use emotions: Even in our own language and culture we do not always use language to express fright, frustration, anger or joy. Emotions transcend linguistic barriers.

Try out words: Sometimes we share common words and we do not know it. Additionally people from different cultures will have a passive knowledge of English gained through the media. Try saying the word slowly or with a different pronunciation.

Draw it: If you really cannot explain 'milk' to the Greek shop owner draw the cow, the udders and the milk. Pictures speak louder than words. Most cultures will be able to spot what you are getting at straight away.

Ask for help: If there are others around you do not be shy to ask for their assistance. It is often possible to find a willing translator.

Confirm meanings: If you are unsure whether the message has been understood confirm meanings. When doing so do not ask, 'Do you understand?' as the answer will often be 'yes' even if it is 'no'. Try re-phrasing what you have agreed or discussed.

Be patient: The key to overcoming the language barrier is to exercise patience. It is not your fault or the other person's that you cannot speak each others language.

The above points will help you to overcome cross cultural communication problems and ensure you manage to get your message across in one form or another.

29.15. TEN STRATEGIES FOR SUCCESS ABROAD

Working across cultures requires a diverse skill set and a different approach from business in general. When bridging cultures both similar and foreign to your own, certain strategies are crucial to international business success. Here are ten strategies for interacting with people from different cultures.

Learn about the business beforehand. This general business strategy becomes increasingly important when dealing with businesses across cultures. Get on their website, check out their promotional material. Get a feel for the atmosphere, attitude, and angle that the business has. Many cultural factors are passed down from the societal level to businesses. However, each organization will have its own culture, personality, and way of doing things.

Observe. Because your mind is processing a lot of information in new environments, your observation skills when working across cultures may be flooded or unfocused. Keep your observation skills engaged and alert to elements that will help you do business. Notice how people act, dress, and treat each other. Especially if you come from a culture that emphasizes verbal communication, make a point of looking for messages that are conveyed without being said. Being able to read a situation will greatly improve your ability to have a successful meeting.

Ask questions. Many people don't want to reveal how little they know about other cultures, so they don't ask questions. Ultimately, they limit their ability to work in other cultures. Questions show you are interested in your colleague's culture. This interest and consideration helps build your relationship, which is especially important if your culture has a reputation for trying to culturally dominate others (*e.g.*, the U.S.). Demonstrate that you are working to create synergy between your cultures with questions. In doing so, you create room for the mistakes you may make; people are more willing to look past cultural blunders if they know you are trying to learn about the culture you are working with.

Stay aware of yourself. Some people feel like they have somewhat of an out-of-body experience when in cross-cultural situations because they are focused on everything new outside of themselves. There can be so much going on around you that you forget to focus on yourself as well. Take advantage of down time (and make time for it) so you can get in touch with your body and feelings. What's your gut feeling? Where is it coming from? This process can help you feel more grounded and secure in your experience abroad.

Allow for more time. Working across cultures takes more time. Communication may be slowed and logistics may be different. You may be working with a culture with a different concept of time altogether. Expect most things to take longer than they would when dealing with a business from your same culture or country. Also give yourself more time to process all the information before making decisions.

Look for individual differences. Overviews of cultures are meant to be guidelines only. Individuals may have values and behaviours that vary greatly from those of their native culture. Many people make the mistake of trying to fit people they are working with into cultural molds, when often they don't fit. People's values and behaviours are influenced in part by their culture, but also by their background, experiences, and personality. Be careful not to attribute too much of what you observe to a cultural difference.

Find the humor. Humor heals and helps you through difficult situations. Travel can be stressful, as can new environments and change in general. This stress can limit both your flexibility and your ability to handle cross-cultural situations. Combat stress with humor. Be able to step away (at least mentally) from situations and find the humor in them.

Learn to tolerate uncertainty. This is an essential skill, and one that can be extremely difficult for people from some cultures where directness and exactness are valued (*e.g.*, Germany, the US). There will be a great deal of unknowns when doing business across cultures. Definitive, concrete answers may not always be given, especially if you are working with a culture with a high tolerance for uncertainty. Focus on what you can determine and try to let go of minor details that are unclear. (Similarly, if you come from a culture that doesn't place a high value on exactness and are working with someone from a culture that does, try to provide clarification and details when possible.)

Go early. If your meeting is face-to-face and you'll be traveling abroad, go a few days before your scheduled meeting. Give yourself time to adjust; you will have to deal with physical adjustments (jet lag, different foods) as well as a number of cultural adjustments as well. These changes can be overwhelming and should be spread out to make them manageable. Give yourself time to adjust physically and then your mind will be better able to make cultural adjustments that are essential for success.

Build your intercultural skills. When working with people from different cultures, you need a solid understanding of the norms of that culture. You also need communication skills and business strategies that can be applied across cultures. The items listed above reflect some of the necessary skills for intercultural work in general. However, individuals need to further their intercultural competence based on their own situations and needs.

To determine what skills you need to develop, reflect on past intercultural experiences (for people with limited experience abroad, think of experiences working and interacting with people and groups different from you). When do you become uncomfortable, rigid, or shut down? What mistakes have you made in the past? Commit yourself to continually developing the skills that will help you in similar situations in the future.

View your experiences with different cultures as a trajectory, rather than a string of individual experiences. Link the different experiences you have and you can link the personal development and learning that comes with them.

29.16. RESULTS OF POOR CROSS CULTURAL AWARENESS

Having a poor understanding of the influence of cross cultural differences in areas such as management, PR, advertising and negotiations can eventually lead to blunders that can have damaging consequences.

It is crucial for today's business personnel to understand the impact of cross cultural differences on business, trade and internal company organisation. The success or failure of a company, venture, merger or acquisition is essentially in the hands of people. If these people are not cross culturally aware then misunderstandings, offence and a break down in communication can occur.

The need for greater cross cultural awareness is heightened in our global economies. Cross cultural differences in matters such as language, etiquette, non-verbal communication, norms and values can, do and will lead to cross cultural blunders.

To illustrate this we have provided a few examples of cross cultural blunders that could have been avoided with appropriate cross cultural awareness training:

- An American oil rig supervisor in Indonesia shouted at an employee to take a boat to shore. Since it is no-one berates an Indonesian in public, a mob of outraged workers chased the supervisor with axes.
- Pepsodent tried to sell its toothpaste in Southeast Asia by emphasizing that it "whitens your teeth." They found out that the local natives chew betel nuts to blacken their teeth which they find attractive.
- A company advertised eyeglasses in Thailand by featuring a variety of cute animals wearing glasses. The ad was a poor choice since animals are considered to be a form of low life and no self respecting Thai would wear anything worn by animals.
- The soft drink Fresca was being promoted by a saleswoman in Mexico. She was surprised that her sales pitch was greeted with laughter, and later embarrassed when she learned that fresca is slang for "lesbian."
- When President George Bush went to Japan with Lee Iacocca and other American business magnates, and directly made explicit and direct demands on Japanese leaders, they violated Japanese etiquette. To the Japanese (who use high context language) it is considered rude and a sign of ignorance or desperation to lower oneself to make direct demands. Some analysts believe it severely damaged the negotiations and confirmed to the Japanese that Americans are barbarians.
- A soft drink was introduced into Arab countries with an attractive label that had stars on it—six-pointed stars. The Arabs interpreted this as pro-Israeli and refused to buy it. Another label was printed in ten languages, one of which was Hebrew—again the Arabs did not buy it.
- U.S. and British negotiators found themselves at a standstill when the American company proposed that they "table" particular key points. In the U.S. "Tabling

a motion" means to not discuss it, while the same phrase in Great Britain means to "bring it to the table for discussion."

In addition to interpersonal cross cultural gaffes, the translation of documents, brochures, advertisements and signs also offers us some comical cross cultural blunders:

- Kellogg had to rename its Bran Buds cereal in Sweden when it discovered that the name roughly translated to "burned farmer."
- When Pepsico advertised Pepsi in Taiwan with the ad "Come Alive With Pepsi" they had no idea that it would be translated into Chinese as "Pepsi brings your ancestors back from the dead."
- American medical containers were distributed in Great Britain and caused quite a stir. The instructions to "Take off top and push in bottom," innocuous to Americans, had very strong sexual connotations to the British.
- In Italy, a campaign for Schweppes Tonic Water translated the name into "Schweppes Toilet Water."
- In a Belgrade hotel elevator: To move the cabin, push the button for wishing floor. If the cabin should enter more persons, each one should press a number of wishing floor. Driving is then going alphabetically by national order.
- In a Yugoslavian hotel: The flattening of underwear with pleasure is the job of the chambermaid.
- In a Bangkok dry cleaner's: Drop your trousers here for best results.
- In an East African newspaper: A new swimming pool is rapidly taking shape since the contractors have thrown in the bulk of their workers.
- Detour sign in Kyushi, Japan: Stop—Drive sideways.
- At a Budapest zoo: Please do not feed the animals. If you have any suitable food, give it to the guard on duty.

In conclusion, poor cross cultural awareness has many consequences, some serious others comical. It is imperative that in the global economy cross cultural awareness is seen a necessary investment to avoid such blunders as we have seen above.

29.17. INTERCULTURAL ETIQUETTE—CROSS CULTURAL DINING ETIQUETTE

In today's inter-reliant, international and culturally diverse world economy, cross cultural differences can have an impact on business success. Both at an individual and organisational level understanding the values, etiquette and protocol of different cultures can positively influence your dealings in the worldwide marketplace.

A lack of cross cultural awareness can result in misinterpretations which may cause offense. Such outcomes may end in your reputation being tarnished and your business objectives impacted. Cross cultural understanding and appreciation of foreign etiquette is important for today's globe trotting business person to avoid such negative repercussions.

One area of importance in cross cultural awareness is the different dining etiquettes of the world. Understanding dining etiquette can help international business people polish their conduct and behaviour while dining or entertaining.

Cross cultural dining etiquette involves considering the following points:

Seating: Is there a protocol as to who sits where? Should one wait to be seated? Is it acceptable etiquette for men/women to sit next to one another?

Eating: What utensils, if any, are used? Is it a knife and fork, hands or chopsticks? Is there any etiquette around using them?

Body language: How should one sit? Is it bad etiquette to rest elbows on the table? If seated on the floor what is the correct position?

Conversation: Is the meal the proper place to engage in conversation? If so, is discussing business appropriate?

The Food: What foods are common to eat? Is it good etiquette to compliment the cook and how? Does one finish everything on the plate? Is it polite to ask for more.

Home/restaurant: What differences in etiquette or protocol would there be? Does one take a gift to the home? Who pays the bill at a restaurant?

By way of outlining some of the cross cultural differences in dining etiquette across the world, the following countries shall be used as examples:

29.17.1. Dining Etiquette in Germany

It is good etiquette to remain standing until shown where to sit.

Table manners are continental-fork in left hand and knife in right.

Do not begin eating until the host signals to do so.

It is bad etiquette to rest elbows on the table.

Try and cut food with the fork as it compliments the cook by showing it is tender.

Everything should be eaten on the plate.

Indicate you have finished by lying the fork and knife parallel across the right hand side of the plate.

29.17.2. Dining Etiquette in Japan

An honoured guest sits at the centre of the table furthest from the door and begins eating first.

Learn to use chopsticks - never point them, never pierce food with them, rest them on the chopstick rest when breaking for drink or chat.

It is good etiquette to try a bit of everything.

Conversation is subdued.

29.17.3. Dining Etiquette in Turkey

Meals are a social affair. Conversations are animate and loud.

The head of the family or honoured guest is served first. It is good etiquette to insist the most senior is served first instead of you.

Asking for more food is a compliment.

If taken to a restaurant, Turkish dining etiquette has strict rules that the one who extended the invitation must pay.

29.17.4. Dining Etiquette in the USA

The fork is held in the right hand and is used for eating.

To use the knife, the fork is switched to the left hand. To continue eating, the fork is switched back to the right hand.

If you are more comfortable eating in the Continental manner it will not offend anyone.

Foods or drinks can be refused without causing offense.

Many foods are eaten by hand.

29.17.5. Dining Etiquette in the Middle East

Guests are honoured with prime choice of meats - head, eyes, etc. Eaten with right hand only.

Meat is torn by holding down the piece against the dish and ripping off a desired amount with forefinger and thumb pressed together.

Rice is scooped up.

Do not be afraid of making a mess.

If you are finished leave food on your plate otherwise it will be filled immediately.

It is proper etiquette to compliment the host on the food and his hospitality.

The above are a very small number of examples of cross cultural differences in dining etiquette. It is prudent to try and ascertain some facts about the dining etiquette of any country you plan to visit on business. By doing so you present yourself to the best of your ability and maximise the potential of your business trip.

29.18. CRACKING CROSS-CULTURAL ETIQUETTE

As compared to a decade ago, the field of cross cultural communications is gaining more respect within the business community. The benefits brought by cross cultural communication training to the global marketplace are being recognised as an integral element in building successful cross cultural business relationships.

In addition to the recognition cross cultural training is receiving from the business community, the media are now following with interest the role cross cultural communication consultants are playing in bridging cross cultural gaps.

My recent consultancy work with the CNN Business Traveller Team has confirmed my belief that there is a real interest at the business, media and social levels in the positive impact cross cultural communication can bring to fostering better understanding between people of differing cultures, faiths and nationalities.

CNN, as an international media giant, are all too aware of the role cross cultural understanding has on building a solid, effective and co-operative workforce. Their recent programme on international negotiations, aired on CNN Europe on 10th October 2004, wisely decided to incorporate information on the impact cross cultural differences can have on the success or failure of negotiations abroad.

Below is an article written off the back of the program:

(CNN)—It may be *konnichiwa* in Japan, *Guten Tag* in Germany and *Merhaba* in Turkey—saying hello is easy—but understanding cultural nuances for international business is far more challenging.

Many people are familiar with business in the West, where there is little time for establishing relationships and getting straight down to business is not considered rude.

But in other parts of the world, achieving mutual success with an overseas partner involves a lot more than a few quick meetings and a signature on the dotted line.

"You could say that business is business in the West, and business is personal everywhere else," Neil Payne of Kwintessential, a culture specialist firm, told CNN.

"In other parts of the world being mindful of other cultures can give you the upper hand and help you clinch that deal."

For instance the consensual nature of Japanese society means that decision-making in a meeting can involve many members of a negotiating team.

"It is important to build a relationship not only with the director or the manager or the head of the team but all those involved," explains Payne.

One way of recognizing how the hierarchy works in a Tokyo boardroom is that the head of the team may normally sit in the middle of the table, furthest away from the door.

Payne suggests greeting the most senior person first—due to a respect for hierarchy—then greeting the rest of the team in descending order, in terms of rank.

In North Asia, handing out business cards with both hands in a respectful manner will also be noticed. For many in the West they are just bits of card, handed over as an after-thought, whereas in Asia they are tokens of value and esteem.

Speaking clearly and slowly, avoiding jargon and writing everything down can also help out in a meeting.

One common trait in Middle Eastern, Mediterranean, Asian and South American cultures is that many executives like to do business with people they know, trust and feel comfortable with.

"It is important to understand what these people may like, so if they are into sport it may be worth going to a match or having a round of golf," says Payne.

"It is more about putting yourself in a context where both parties can be relaxed and both parties can get to know each other as people—not just as business people."

It is best to remember that business will only continue once this relationship has been established. "(Many executives) will not enter into a relationship because they will not feel comfortable conducting business with someone that they do not feel 100 percent comfortable with," explains Payne.

A few words in the language of the country you are visiting as a sign of respect is always appreciated. And before you travel, contact your embassy to request briefing on business etiquette and cultural background.

"If you are going to give one specific pointer to everyone, which is applicable across the world, that would be—always maintain a sense of professionalism."

29.19. CROSS CULTURAL NEGOTIATION

Cross cultural negotiation is one of many specialized areas within the wider field of cross cultural communications. By taking cross cultural negotiation training, negotiators and sales personnel give themselves an advantage over competitors.

There is an argument that proposes that culture is inconsequential to cross cultural negotiation. It maintains that as long as a proposal is financially attractive it will succeed. However, this is a naïve way of approaching international business.

Let us look at a brief example of how cross cultural negotiation training can benefit the international business person:

There are two negotiators dealing with the same potential client in the Middle East. Both have identical proposals and packages. One ignores the importance of cross cultural negotiation training believing the proposal will speak for itself. The other undertakes some cross cultural training. He/she learns about the culture, values, beliefs, etiquette and approaches to business, meetings and negotiations. Nine times out of ten the latter will succeed over the rival. This is because (1) it is likely they would have endeared themselves more to the host negotiation team and (2) they would be able to tailor their approach to the negotiations in a way that maximises the potential of a positive outcome.

Cross cultural negotiations is about more than just how foreigners close deals. It involves looking at all factors that can influence the proceedings. By way of highlighting this, a few brief examples of topics covered in cross cultural negotiation training shall be offered.

Eye Contact: In the US, UK and much of northern Europe, strong, direct eye contact conveys confidence and sincerity. In South America it is a sign of trustworthiness. However, in some cultures such as the Japanese, prolonged eye contact is considered rude and is generally avoided.

Personal Space & Touch: In Europe and North America, business people will usually leave a certain amount of distance between themselves when interacting. Touching only takes place between friends. In South America or the Middle East, business people are tactile and like to get up close. In Japan or China, it is not uncommon for people to leave a gap of four feet when conversing. Touching only takes place between close friends and family members.

Time: Western societies are very 'clock conscious'. Time is money and punctuality is crucial. This is also the case in countries such as Japan or China where being late would be taken as an insult. However, in South America, southern Europe and the Middle East, being on time for a meeting does not carry the same sense of urgency.

Meeting & Greeting: Most international business people meet with a handshake. In some countries this is not appropriate between genders. Some may view a weak handshake as sign of weakness whereas others would perceive a firm handshake as aggressive. How should people be addressed? Is it by first name, surname or title? Is small talk part of the proceedings or not?

Gift-Giving: In Japan and China gift-giving is an integral part of business protocol however in the US or UK, it has negative connotations. Where gifts are exchanged should one give lavish gifts? Are they always reciprocated? Should they be wrapped? Are there numbers or colours that should be avoided?

All the above in one way or another will impact cross cultural negotiation and can only be learnt through cross cultural training. Doing or saying the wrong thing at the wrong time, poor communication and cross cultural misunderstandings can all have harmful consequences.

Cross cultural negotiation training builds its foundations upon understanding etiquettes and approaches to business abroad before focusing on cross cultural differences in negotiation styles and techniques.

There are three interconnected aspects that need to be considered before entering into cross cultural negotiation.

The Basis of the Relationship: In much of Europe and North America, business is contractual in nature. Personal relationships are seen as unhealthy as they can cloud objectivity and lead to complications. In South America and much of Asia, business is personal. Partnerships will only be made with those they know, trust and feel comfortable with. It is therefore necessary to invest in relationship building before conducting business.

Information at Negotiations: Western business culture places emphasis on clearly presented and rationally argued business proposals using statistics and facts. Other business cultures rely on similar information but with differences. For example, visual and oral communicators such as the South Americans may prefer information presented through speech or using maps, graphs and charts.

Negotiation Styles: The way in which we approach negotiation differs across cultures. For example, in the Middle East rather than approaching topics sequentially negotiators may discuss issues simultaneously. South Americans can become quite vocal and animated. The Japanese will negotiate in teams and decisions will be based upon consensual agreement. In Asia, decisions are usually made by the most senior figure or head of a family. In China, negotiators are highly trained in the art of gaining concessions. In Germany, decisions can take a long time due to the need to analyse information and statistics in great depth. In the UK, pressure tactics and imposing deadlines are ways of closing deals whilst in Greece this would backfire.

Clearly there are many factors that need to be considered when approaching cross cultural negotiation. Through cross cultural negotiation training, business personnel are given the appropriate knowledge that can help them prepare their presentations and sales pitches effectively. By tailoring your behaviour and the way you approach the negotiation you will succeed in maximising your potential.

29.20. INTERCULTURAL FACTORS WHEN MAKING INTERNATIONAL PRESENTATIONS

Making a presentation in front of international audiences is not for the fainthearted. People from different cultural backgrounds with varying language skills are definitely more challenging than a homogenous local audience. Are international audiences any different from local audiences? From a biological point of view, there are almost no differences as all humans behave similarly in response to basic stimuli like hunger and heat. The differences become crucial when one considers cultural conditioning.

Let us take the classical example quoted in many places. If the world were a village of 1,000 people, it would include: 584 Asians, 124 Africans, 95 Europeans, 84 Latin Americans, 52 North Americans, six Australians and New Zealanders, and 55 people from the former Soviet republics. They would speak more than 200 languages and reflect an astounding mix of different cultures. Fortunately, you would most likely never get such a mixed audience. Remember, what works in one culture doesn't always work in another. How can you make your presentation a success among people from different parts of the world?

Many factors influence audience behaviour *e.g.*, culture, profession, gender, age, reason for being in the audience, state of mind, time of day and year and general mood. In fact every audience is unique. An audience of insurance salesmen in Germany is very different from an audience of German chemical engineers. So whenever a typical behaviour is associated with certain nation states, you have to be extremely careful with these stereotypes.

The language barrier plays a very important role, both for the speaker and the listeners. Many people in your international audience actually have jumped over large chasms of language and cultural divides in order to be there in that very audience listening to you. "Can I understand everything that is spoken there as they are speaking in English and my English is very bad?" or "What if someone asks me a question and I can't answer it in French in this seminar held in France?" These are typical fears that many people have overcome before they turned up in the international gathering.

In mixed audiences the language used is bound to be a foreign tongue for someone, if not for the speaker. Deficient language skills might considerably limit their ability to grasp much of the presentation and they have no way of dealing with that frustration with themselves. The fear of losing face in front of other people is very common, more so in Asian cultures. Many people think in their mother tongue and speak with the help of simultaneous translation. Many ideas are very challenging to be put into another language. So the task of the presenter is to make sure that central ideas come across easily and even to people who are not natives to the language of presentation.

Culture influences how people in different countries prefer to receive information. How interactive a presentation is, depends much on the culture. Typically English speaking cultures like presentations to be lively and interactive. Paradoxically there are similarities among Far Eastern, Slavic and protestant cultures like Germany and Finland. There presentations are formal and there are few interruptions. Questions are answered either when the presentation ends or quickly as they arise.

Many Europeans, particularly Scandinavians and Germans prefer to receive information in detail, with lots of supporting documentation. They want their presenters to be systematic and build to a clear point within their presentation. The Japanese business audiences, where senior managers are more likely to hold technical or management degrees are very similar. American and Canadian audiences, on the other hand, like a faster pace. Many Asian and Latin cultures prefer presentations with emotional appeal.

Different cultures gather and process information differently, in a way that is unique to that culture. We assume that speaking Spanish is a safe option in all countries where Spanish is spoken, but Hispanic employees from different countries even have different words for the same thing, and this can create conflict. Sometimes logic or reason can evade us. For example, there is no concept of guilt in some Eastern cultures. There is no Heaven or Hell, but there may be karma and shame. The Chinese are very strict about Mianxi, not losing face. When a Chinese person doesn't understand something due to language problems, she still says, "Yes, yes it is clear." People from a western background often have difficulties understanding this.

Presenters use humour skilfully to relax the atmosphere. Another very powerful tool is telling personal anecdotes which reveal humaneness connecting the speaker with members of the audience. There must be a relevance to the topic or theme, as speakers who talk very much about themselves are often considered self-centred and even tiresome.

The response to humour varies greatly across different cultures. Humour based on making fun of someone else is not understood in many areas of the world and is considered disrespectful. In some cultures like Japan, laughing aloud is a sign of nervousness and is not appreciated.

How audiences respond to presentations varies across cultures. In Japan, for example, it's common to show concentration and attentiveness by nodding the head up and down slightly-and even closing the eyes occasionally. Don't think that they are falling asleep. In Germany and Austria, for example, listeners seated around a table may show their approval by knocking on the table instead of applauding. Applause is accepted as a form of approval in most areas of the world but in the U.S, you might even get a few whistles if you have really made a great impression. If you hear whistles in many parts of Europe, you had better run because someone might start throwing tomatoes and eggs next. If you were finishing a speaking engagement in a Latin American country like Argentina and you waved goodbye, the audience might all turn around and come back to sit down. For them the waving gesture means, "Come back! Don't go away."

Ways of handling questions are very different across cultures. Brits or Americans almost always ask challenging questions. In Finland or in some Asian cultures, audiences are more likely to greet a presentation with silence or just a few polite questions. This is not always indifference but a show of respect.

As a presenter, you should have a clear goal of what you want to accomplish and how you will accomplish it. The goal should be easy to understand - even to someone outside of your organization or industry. If you can't summarize your message, how can the listeners? When the audience is international, you'll need to step out of your own frame of reference and focus on making communication relevant for your target group. The aim is to "localize." By focussing on the audiences' own frames of reference, you acknowledge their importance and pave the way for them to come closer to you. If for example, you are using a metaphor about snow blizzards and sleet to sub-Saharan people, they might not get your point, as they have no experience of snow blizzards. The most vital thing to remember is that each and every member in your international audience is a fellow human being. If they feel treated well and get something for being there, they will appreciate your efforts. Good luck!

29.21. MULTI-CULTURAL MEETING

Of the many areas in international business where cultural differences manifest is in the corporate meeting room. International meetings are an area where differences in cultural values, etiquette, interpretations of professional conduct and corporate rules are at their most visible and challenging to control.

In international business meetings, cultural differences between professionals can and do clash. Although it can not always be avoided, the negative effects of cultural differences can be minimised with careful and effective planning, organisation and consideration prior to meetings.

Culture influences what we do, say, think and believe. Culture is different in different countries and contexts. In the context of international business it affects how people approach, perceive and contribute towards meetings. A few examples include:

29.21.1. Time

Not all cultures live by the clock. Time orientated cultures such as the British or Germans will have strict approaches to how meetings run. The start time, finishing time and all the different stages in between will be planned carefully. Other cultures will see the start time as an approximation, the finish time as non-fixed and all the different stages in between as flexible.

29.21.2. Hierarchy

The hierarchical nature of a culture can have a massive impact on the input given by participants in an international meeting. For those from hierarchical cultures speaking one's mind, criticising ideas, disagreeing openly, giving feedback and reporting problems in front of the boss or manager are all areas they would feel uncomfortable with. To offer a criticism of the manager's idea would be seen as a loss of face for both the manager and the criticiser.

29.21.3. The Purpose of Meetings

After a few pleasantries in the meeting room, the common term in the West is, 'let's get down to business'. Western meetings generally run to a tight schedule with an organised, pre-planned agenda. Meetings are for business. On the other hand, different cultures see the meeting as the arena for building personal relationships and strengthening bonds. Getting down to business comes further down the priority list.

When chairing an international business meeting it is always advisable to bear in mind the attendees' cultures and backgrounds. Is it a very varied group or do the majority of participants have cultural similarities? Think about their approaches to meetings. How have they acted in meetings before? Can you identify the cultural reason why?

Following are some guidelines that may assist you when approaching cultural diversity in your next international business meeting.

29.21.4. Meeting Etiquette and Mannerisms

In highly diverse international companies, one can find participants in a meeting from the four corners of the globe. Each will have their own cultural etiquettes, gestures, mannerisms and ways of expression. Shouting, throwing hands around and even storming out of meetings are all possibilities. In such a company it may be advisable to provide inter-cultural awareness training to staff to minimise misunderstandings. Where differences are not as acute it may be up to you as the chair to understand how certain etiquettes, gestures and general meeting room tactics may be perceived and how you can minimise any adverse impact.

Prior to the meeting make it clear what the purpose of the meeting will be. What is the goal of the meeting? Why are you asking each attendant? What do expect from them? Contact the participants and discuss the meeting and what you require of each person. If ready, send them the agenda. If it is a brainstorming meeting then maybe ask each participant to bring at least three suggestions with them. If it is a meeting bringing together different areas within a company, let each attendant know what people would like to hear about from them. Once a framework is in place people will know where they fit into the picture.

29.21.5. Take a Relaxed Approach to Meetings

Many people find business meetings daunting. This may be a combination of stage fright, sitting in front of the boss and feeling inferior to colleagues. This will lead to anxiety, tension, nervousness and general discomfort. Try introducing subtle differences to a meeting to put people at ease. Ice breakers offer a good tension release at the beginning of a meeting. Warm ups offer a similar benefit. Try using an alternative setting instead of the meeting room. Consider changes in the lighting or ambience.

29.21.6. Group Sizes in Meetings

In short, small groups will work more effectively in meetings. Smaller groups offer increased security and allow for greater participation. In international business meetings, using smaller groups can be used in two ways.

First, prior to a large international business meeting identify who will be coming and what they can contribute. Will the meeting cover different topics? Will it require input from different business areas? If you are organised enough you can initiate some smaller meetings where you group participants who are comfortable with one another or who share expertise in the same area. Ask the groups to take their conclusions to the next, larger, meeting. Participants there will now feel comfortable with their contributions and ideas.

Second, if the company culture allows, break your meeting up into smaller groups where feedback and open discussion may flow more easily. Then ask a delegated head of each group to summarise their findings. This may allow those who would not normally speak out in front of larger groups to get their views across.

A major mistake made when dealing with diverse cultures in one meeting room is to suggest that those of similar backgrounds work, group or be seated together. Rather than allow for greater fluency in the meeting this will have the opposite affect. Once cosy in their cultural groups, participants will slip into their cultural patterns. It is vital you mix up your meeting. The additional benefit to this approach is that it allows for cross cultural interpersonal relationships to develop, strengthening staff bonds.

29.21.7. Alternative Communication Methods in Meetings

Most international meetings take on a basic format and structure whereby an agenda is set and attendants contribute to the topic of discussion orally. If you have participants who potentially will be very quiet and non-participatory then consider some alternative methods of communication.

For example, prior to the meeting, e-mail members of staff some questions regarding the forthcoming topics. Give them open-ended questions as to their opinions. Ask them to e-mail back their replies which can then be used to instigate their contribution in the meeting.

If you know some participants are uncomfortable speaking, then why not let them write? Either use a white board or offer to take suggestions and opinions on paper?

29.21.8. Always Confirm Meanings in Meetings

Different cultural assumptions as to the meaning of a word, phrase, symbol, picture or agreement can cause confusion before and after a meeting. When approaching a topic or after consensus has been agreed upon a subject always confirm that the general meaning has been agreed upon and understood. Where potential problems may exist as to interpretation always simplify meanings. If the meeting will deal with complex language or concepts consider forming a consensus on the meaning all participants will be comfortable with, then circulating them in advance of the meeting for review.

At the end of a meeting, summarise and capture the main agreements and disagreements. Ensure everyone is happy with them.

International business meetings require great planning, organisation and consideration if they are to succeed in offering effective outcomes. Always consider the cultural variants you will be dealing with and think of ways to overcome potential problems. The above mentioned tips are merely basic pointers that will hopefully help you start to think about how culture impacts international meetings.

APPENDIX

1. AVERAGE CONFERENCE SIZE (NO OF DELEGATES)—MARKET SHARE OF SEGMENTS

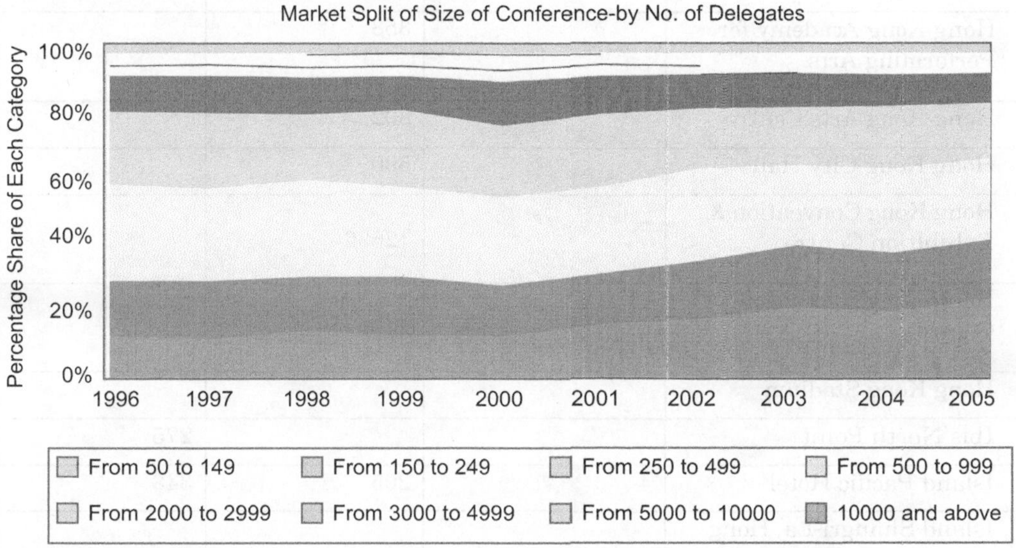

2. LIST OF HONG KONG HOTELS—CONFERENCE VENUES AND SPACE AVAILABILITY

Table 1: List of Hong Kong Hotels and their Capacities

Venue	Total number of function rooms	Largest function space (Sq. m)	Total no. of guest rooms
Bishop Lei International House		40	219
City Garden Hotel		242	598
Conrad Hong Kong		767	513
Cosmopolitan Hotel	4	189	454

Cyberport Conference & Exhibition Centre		4000	
Empire Hotel Hong Kong			360
Express by Holiday Inn Causeway Bay		43	269
Four Seasons Hotel Hong Kong		710	396
Grand Hyatt Hong Kong	26	680	549
Harbour Plaza North Point	3	140	940
Harbour View International House		88	320
Hong Kong Academy for Performing Arts		358	
Hong Kong Arts Centre		302	
Hong Kong City Hall		590	
Hong Kong Convention & Exhibition Centre		12636	
Hong Kong Exhibition Centre		2100	
Hong Kong Stadium			
Ibis North Point			275
Island Pacific Hotel	4	205	343
Island Shangri-La, Hong Kong		645	565
JW Marriott Hotel Hong Kong		736	602
L'hotel Causeway Bay Harbour View			275
Le Meridien Cyberport		370	173
Luk Kwok Hotel		145	196
Mandarin Oriental, Hong Kong		520	541
Metropark Hotel Causeway Bay (Formerly "Metropark Hotel")		42	266

Metropark Hotel Wanchai (Formerly "Hotel New Harbour")			173
Newton Hotel Hong Kong		61	362
Novotel Century Harbourview		133	274
Novotel Century Hong Kong		335	511
Plaza Conference Centre		48	
Queen Elizabeth Stadium		590	
Ramada Hong Kong Hotel		70	307
Regal Hong Kong Hotel		240	422
Renaissance Harbour View Hotel Hong Kong	8	561	860
Rosedale on the Park		55	274
South China Hotel			202
South Pacific Hotel		148	272
The Charterhouse		105	277
The Emperor (Happy Valley)			150
The Excelsior Hong Kong		363	884
The Park Lane Hong Kong	16	381	803
The Ritz - Carlton, Hong Kong		330	216
The University of Hong Kong		429	
The Wesley			251
Wharney Guang Dong Hotel Hong Kong	2	205	358

Source:http: / / www.discoverhongkong.com / eng / meetings / venue / ceb_venue

3. CASE STUDY: BUSINESS TOURISM IN UK

Business Tourism Leads the Way

A High Value Sector

Business tourism is worth over **£ 20 billion** in terms of its wider economic impact (through associated delegate expenditure on travel entertainment, shopping, pre-and post-conference tours, etc.). These figures take no account of the value of business transacted at trade events, estimated to generate in excess of **£100 billion** a year.

Business tourism includes:

- **Conferences and meetings:** £11.7 billion a year*
- **Exhibitions and trade fairs:** £1.69 billion annually* (this figure only takes account of large exhibitions. If smaller events are added together with the costs that venues charge organisers for tenancies, this figure could rise of £10 billion.
- **Incentive travel:** £165 million plus*
- **Corporate events:** £1 billion per annum*
- **Outdoor events:** £1 billion a year*

Latest available estimate

These individual segments are also referred to as **'discretionary business tourism'.**

- **Non-discretionary business tourism** (ie. individual business or corporate travel) is additional and is estimated to be worth well in excess of £7 billion per annum.

Over the past ten years, there has been a 53% growth in all business trips, exceeding the overall tourism growth rate. Over 7 million visits are made to the UK each year for business purposes, with international business visitors contributing a massive £3.5 billion to the British economy.

The sector generates 28% of all overseas visitor and 29% of inbound tourism earnings for the UK. Although business visitors have shorter visits than most other travellers, they spend more than twice as much per day, with conference delegates and visitors to trade shows and exhibitions spending even more.

Initial data on **investment in the sector,** captured by the British Association of Conference Destinations, reveals over £5 billion currently being spent on the infrastructure supporting business events by just 25 destinations.

4. HOTELS AND CONVENTION FACILITIES (10 KEY DESTINATIONS)

City	Hotel	Meeting Rooms	Capacity (Theatre Seating)			Total Capacity	Total Rooms & Suites
			Convention Hall 1	Convention Hall 2	Meeting Rooms		
New Delhi	Taj Palace Hotel	6	1100	800	400	2300	462
	The Taj Mahal Hotel	5	250		355	605	296
	Ashok Hotel	5	2000	300	400	2700	661
	Le Meridien	5	500		270	770	355
	Crowne Plaza Hotel	3	500		275	775	376
	Hyatt Regency	3	600		160	760	508
	Inter Continental The Grand New Delhi	4	500		375	875	0
	ITC Hotel Maurya Sheraton & Towers		250			250	484
	Welcom Hotel	1	300		70	370	220
	The Grand New Delhi	3	500		135	635	390
	The Oberoi	6	350		374	724	279
	The Park	2	250		100	350	220
	The Imperial	2	400		80	480	274
	The Leela Kempinski Gurgaon* (Upcoming)	1	800	450	180	1430	319
Mumbai	The Taj Mahal Palace & Tower	10	450	400	440	1290	567
	Taj Lands End	3	600		325	925	368
	Taj President	4	500		230	730	292

		Meeting Rooms	Seating			Capacity	& Suites
	ITC Hotel Grand Central Sheraton & Towers	1	430		200	630	242
	ITC Hotel Grand Maratha Sheraton & Towers	4	650		46	696	386
	The Oberoi	2			80	80	333
	Ramada Hotel Palm Grove		225			225	114
	Holiday Inn		200			200	192
	Grand Hyatt Mumbai	7	1100		350	1450	547
	Le Meridien	2	225	200	50	475	171
	Renaissance Mumbai Hotel & Convention Centre	6	1750	300	195	2245	286
	JW Marriott Hotel	3	700		240	940	358
	The Leela Kempinski	5	850		82	932	423
	Hyatt Regency Mumbai	3	550		85	635	295
Agra	Taj View Hotel	1	130		50	180	100
	Welcom Hotel Mughal Sheraton	2	750		245	995	285
	The Oberoi Amarvilas	2	150		40	190	63
	Jaypee Palace Hotel		1500			1500	350
	Holiday Inn	2	400		185	585	106
	Clarks Shiraz	1	500	250	100	850	237

		Meeting Rooms	**Seating**			**Capacity**	**& Suites**
	Hotel Howard Park Plaza International		300			300	83
	Atithi	1	200		40	240	44
Bangalore	The Taj West End	4	450		230	680	122
	Taj Residency	4	500		345	845	166
	Gateway Hotel	3	260		120	380	102
	ITC Hotel Windsor Sheraton & Towers	4	275		245	520	240
	The Oberoi	2	180		70	250	160
	Le Meridien	5	600		450	1050	195
	Leela Palace Kempinski	6	650	200	310	1160	256
Chennai	Taj Connemara	2	400	200	125	725	150
	Taj Coromandel	7	650		910	1560	205
	Chola Sheraton	1	225		60	285	92
	ITC Hotel Park Sheraton & Towers	6	200		320	520	283
	Le Royal Meridien	11	870		400	1270	240
Kochi	Taj Malabar		320			320	96
	Le Meridien Resort and Convention Centre	10	1600	600	1800	4000	223
Goa	Fort Aguada Beach Resort		225			225	130
	Taj Exotica	3	450		200	650	142
	Goa Marriott Resort	3	500		140	640	178
	The Leela Goa	2	400	200	48	648	152

		Meeting Rooms	Seating			Capacity	& Suites
	Park Hyatt Goa Resort and Spa	2	370		80	450	251
Hyderabad	Taj Banjara	2	250		70	320	118
	Taj Krishna		800			800	260
	ITC Hotel Kakatiya Sheraton & Towers	2	500		30	530	188
	Hyderabad Marriott Hotel	3	1400	220	280	1900	297
Jaipur	Jai Mahal Palace	2	187		94	281	100
	Le Meridien Jaipur	2	500		120	620	0
	Welcom Hotel Rajputana Palace Sheraton		500			500	216
Kolkata	Taj Bengal	3	450		135	585	229
	ITC Hotel Sonar Bangla Sheraton & Towers	4	450		139	589	238
	The Oberoi Grand	2	800		140	940	122
	The Park	5	250		400	650	166
	Hyatt Regency Kolkata	2	600		100	700	235

5. QUESTIONNAIRES USED DURING THE STUDY

Questionnaire for Consumer Survey

Questionnaire for Customer/Operator Survey

Survey among Convention Bureaus around the world

Survey among ICPB Members

Questionnaire for Case Studies

Questionnaire for Consumer Survey

Dear Respondent, this survey is conducted as a part of a research project to understand the needs of the International Conventions/Conferences Traveller, in order to develop services and amenities as well as look at Regulatory and Infrastructural aspects, which would adequately address these needs in the near future.

We would like to know you a little better, so please share a few details with us (all details provided here will be used **only for the current research and your identity as well as details will NOT be disclosed to anyone, or used for any commercial purposes).**

Name: ______________________ Nationality: ____________
Age: ________ years Arriving from (City): ____________________
Onward Travel to (City): __________________
Profession: Academic/Corporate/Independent Consultant/Other
(pls. Specify) ________________
Role at Current Convention/ Seminar: Delegate/Speaker/Organiser/Sponsor/
Other __________
Current Event Venue: ______________________________
Location: ________________
Reason for Travel: Academic/Business/Networking/Tourism/Others ____________
How often do you travel for Conferences/Conventions in a year? 1-2/3-5/more than 5

Q.1. In this section, we wish to understand your expectations regarding the convention venue, as far as amenities/facilities it should have:
Kindly Rank the following facilities according to their importance (High, Medium or Low)

Facility	Importance
Registration for Conference- Single Window facilitation:	↓ High ↓ Medium ↓ Low
Accommodation- Tie Up with Hotels (Range of Budgets)	↓ High ↓ Medium ↓ Low
Transportation (conference related)	↓ High ↓ Medium ↓ Low
Immigration Facilitation (VISA and other regulatory issues)	↓ High ↓ Medium ↓ Low
Access to Public Transport	↓ High ↓ Medium ↓ Low
Multimedia/ Equipment Support at Venue	↓ High ↓ Medium ↓ Low
Restaurant/ Catering Options	↓ High ↓ Medium ↓ Low
Travel Desk for Onward Travel	↓ High ↓ Medium ↓ Low
Recreational and hospitality Centres	↓ High ↓ Medium ↓ Low
Conference/ Convention Venue aspects: Aesthetics, Infrastructure, Ambience, Hygiene, Air Conditioning, etc.	↓ High ↓ Medium ↓ Low
Any other: Please specify____________________ ____________________	↓ High ↓ Medium ↓ Low

Q.2. Have you ever travelled to India earlier as a part of any delegation for a Conference/Convention?

☐ YES ☐ NO

Q.3. Who was the organiser for the previous conference that you last attended (Other than India)? Organiser: ____________________.
Location: ____________

Q.4. How would you rate INDIA as a conference destination on the following aspects as compared to your experience(s) abroad?

Registration Facilitation:	↓ Poor ↓ Need to Improve ↓ Satisfactory ↓ Excellent
Quality Accommodation-Range:	↓ Poor ↓ Need to Improve ↓ Satisfactory ↓ Excellent
Conference Related Transportation:	↓ Poor ↓ Need to Improve ↓ Satisfactory ↓ Excellent
Immigration Facilitation:	↓ Poor ↓ Need to Improve ↓ Satisfactory ↓ Excellent
Access to other Public Transport:	↓ Poor ↓ Need to Improve ↓ Satisfactory ↓ Excellent
Multimedia/ Equipment Support at the venue:	↓ Poor ↓ Need to Improve ↓ Satisfactory ↓ Excellent
Restaurant/ Catering Options	↓ Poor ↓ Need to Improve ↓ Satisfactory ↓ Excellent
Travel Desk for Onward Travel	↓ Poor ↓ Need to Improve ↓ Satisfactory ↓ Excellent
Recreational and hospitality Centres	↓ Poor ↓ Need to Improve ↓ Satisfactory ↓ Excellent
Venue- Aesthetics, Ambience, Facilities, Hygiene, etc.	↓ Poor ↓ Need to Improve ↓ Satisfactory ↓ Excellent
Any other: Please specify________________	↓ Poor ↓ Need to Improve ↓ Satisfactory ↓ Excellent

Q.5. How many days do you plan to stay in India? No of Days __________

Q.6. Out of these days how many do you plan to spend on the following activities?

- Conference/Convention: ______ Days
- Other Official Engagements: ______ Days
- Social Visits (Friends/Relatives) ______ Days
- Tourism: ______ Days
- Any other: ____________ ______ Days

Q.7. What was your primary reason for considering INDIA for this visit? (Please tick as applicable)

- Conference/Convention was important: (______)
- Other Official Engagements along with Conference: (______)
  - ➢ Can you please specify the nature of engagement? ________

- Visit to some place of particular interest: (______)
  - ➢ (Please mention name of place) ________________
- Any other- Please specify: ________________ (______)

Q.8. Please tell us in brief; how you would usually divide/split your expenditures at one of those Conferences/Conventions ABROAD (Other than INDIA) as compared to in INDIA?

Expense Head/ Description	Conference Abroad as Percentage or \$, £, € Amt	Conference in INDIA as Percentage or \$, £, € Amt
Conference Fee (NIL If Sponsored Delegate)		
Air Travel to and Fro		
Food & Beverage (other than Conference venue)		
Accommodation (Hotel during Conference)		
Tourism & Recreational Activities		
Local Transportation (AIR/ TRAIN/ ROAD)		
Gifts/ Souvenir		
Any other (please Specify): ________________		
Any other (please Specify):		

Q.9. What according to YOU should be the PRIORITY areas of improvement for INDIA, to emerge as a strong international Conventions/Conference destination? (Please TICK/Rank the items according to your perceived priority)

Facility/Aspect	Priority (High-Medium- Low)
Infrastructure at Conference/Convention Centres	↓ High ↓ Medium ↓ Low
Public transport facilities	↓ High ↓ Medium ↓ Low
Pre-Event Conference Management	↓ High ↓ Medium ↓ Low
Quality of Accommodation around Conference Venue	↓ High ↓ Medium ↓ Low
Recreational/Tourism Facilities	↓ High ↓ Medium ↓ Low
Food-court Quality/Ambience, Catering at Conference venue	↓ High ↓ Medium ↓ Low
Additional Services: Ticketing, FOREX, City Tours, etc	↓ High ↓ Medium ↓ Low
VISA/ Immigration formalities	↓ High ↓ Medium ↓ Low
Any Other:	↓ High ↓ Medium ↓ Low
Any Other:	↓ High ↓ Medium ↓ Low

Thank you very much for your time, wish you a very pleasant stay and onward journey!

Questionnaire for Customer/Operator Survey

Dear Respondent, this survey is conducted as a part of a research project to understand the needs of the International Conventions/Conferences Traveller, in order to develop services and amenities as well as look at Regulatory and Infrastructural aspects, which would adequately address these needs in the near future.

We would like to know you a little better, so please share a few details with us (all details provided here will be used only for the current research and your identity as well as details will NOT be disclosed to anyone, or used for any commercial purposes).

Name: ______________________ Designation: ______________

Organisation Name: ______________________

Headquartered at: __________

No. of years of Operation in Tourism/Convention or Conference Organisation: ____________

No of Events Organised each Year (Average): __________

Revenue (Approx in $ Mn): ______

Most Recent Convention/Conference/Seminar Organised:

Client: ______________________ Location: ______________

Q.1. What are the most important factors that you consider, when you organise an International Conference/Convention (please indicate the level of importance- High - Medium - Low)

Factor(s) for Consideration	Level of Importance
Availability of Infrastructure for Convention/ Conference	↓ High ↓ Medium ↓ Low
Political Stability	↓ High ↓ Medium ↓ Low
Relatively easy Connectivity by AIR	↓ High ↓ Medium ↓ Low
Availability of Qualified Manpower to handle event	↓ High ↓ Medium ↓ Low
Ease of Immigration Process	↓ High ↓ Medium ↓ Low
Availability of transport infrastructure in and around the venue	↓ High ↓ Medium ↓ Low
Tourism and Recreational Centres	↓ High ↓ Medium ↓ Low
Regulatory issues pertaining to hosting the Event	↓ High ↓ Medium ↓ Low
Quality of the Venue- infrastructure, reputation, ambience, etc.	↓ High ↓ Medium ↓ Low
Any other: ______________	↓ High ↓ Medium ↓ Low
Any other: ______________	↓ High ↓ Medium ↓ Low

Q.2. Have you ever organised an event in INDIA?

YES ☐ NO ☐

Q.2(a) If YES, then when? Date: ______________________

Venue/Location in India: ____________ Client: ____________

Q.2(b). If NO, then can you please tell us why? (Please mark on the options as applicable)

Reason(s) for **NOT ORGANISING** event in INDIA	Please mark as applicable
Lack of Availability of Convention/ Conference Infrastructure	
Political/ Economic Instability	
Infrequent/ Cumbersome Connectivity	
Availability of Qualified Manpower to handle event	
Immigration Process is too complicated	
Lack of adequate public transport around venue	
No Tourism and Recreational Centres	
Government Regulations	
Low Quality of the Venue- infrastructure, reputation, ambience, etc.	
Any other:______________________	
Any other:______________________	

Q.3. IN CASE YOU HAVE ORGANISED AN EVENT IN INDIA, how would you rate INDIA as a conference destination on the following aspects as compared to your experience(s) at other locations?

Factor(s) for Consideration	INDIA as a destination
Availability of Infrastructure for Convention/Conference	↓ Poor ↓ Need to Improve ↓ Satisfactory ↓ Excellent
Political Stability	↓ Poor ↓ Need to Improve ↓ Satisfactory ↓ Excellent
Relatively easy Connectivity by AIR	↓ Poor ↓ Need to Improve ↓ Satisfactory ↓ Excellent
Availability of Qualified Manpower to handle event	↓ Poor ↓ Need to Improve ↓ Satisfactory ↓ Excellent

Ease of Immigration Process	↓ Poor ↓ Need to Improve ↓ Satisfactory ↓ Excellent
Availability of transport infrastructure in and around the venue	↓ Poor ↓ Need to Improve ↓ Satisfactory ↓ Excellent
Tourism and Recreational Centres	↓ Poor ↓ Need to Improve ↓ Satisfactory ↓ Excellent
Regulatory issues pertaining to hosting the Event	↓ Poor ↓ Need to Improve ↓ Satisfactory ↓ Excellent
Quality of the Venue- infrastructure, reputation, ambience, etc.	↓ Poor ↓ Need to Improve ↓ Satisfactory ↓ Excellent
Any other:____________	↓ Poor ↓ Need to Improve ↓ Satisfactory ↓ Excellent
Any other:____________	↓ Poor ↓ Need to Improve ↓ Satisfactory ↓ Excellent

Thank you very much for your time, wish you a very pleasant stay and onward journey!

Survey among Convention Bureaus around the World. Questions asked were:

1. What are the most important attributes about your city/country, which makes it an important destination for conventions/conferences?
2. What kind of assistance do you receive from the local (city, regional) government as well as the central government for promoting your city/country?
3. What is the source of funds for running the bureau/ agency? Do you receive government funds or do you generate funds through other revenue sources, if so, kindly mention them. (Please note: All results will be kept confidential if you so desire, and no mention of specific cities will be made)
4. What are the different promotion tools you use to promote your city/country? (Advertising/Media coverage/Liaison with other agencies/Hotels/Tie-up with Associations/etc.)

Survey among India Convention Promotion Bureau (ICPB) Members.

Questions asked were:

1. What, in your opinion, will make INDIA a key international convention destination?
2. What kind of problems do you anticipate in promoting INDIA as an International Convention/ Conference destination?
3. What should be the role of India Convention Promotion Bureau (ICPB) in promoting Conventions/ Conferences in INDIA?
4. What should be the role of the Ministry of Tourism and that of the Central Government to promote INDIA as a convention/conference destination?
5. According to you, to what extent has ICPB been successful in promoting conventions in INDIA? What are your chief concerns?
6. Do you suggest any changes in the current mode of operation of ICPB as a facilitator?

7. What is YOUR vision for India Convention Promotion Bureau (ICPB) and its role in promoting INDIA?

Questionnaire for Case Studies (Administered to Conference Organisers)

1. What are the main benefits of holding {this conference} in India?
2. What was the procedure followed in bidding for this particular convention and what is generally the procedure adopted by associations in India when bidding for conventions. How does this compare with procedures followed by competing bidders?
3. What do you look for when selecting a country for the convention? In terms of infrastructure facilities (convention halls, hotels, transport, etc), regulatory issues (visas, taxes, etc), connectivity, prices, etc?
4. On which aspects India is competitive and where are we short of competitors?
5. The Ministry of Tourism had set up the India Convention Promotion Bureau (ICPB) to promote India as a favoured destination for conventions. Did you seek ICPB's support for the bid? Do you think ICPB can play any role in your future bids? If yes, please specify.
6. Will you be able to specify the impact of holding a convention like {this convention} in India? If possible, specify some details on various aspects like boost in tourist arrivals, business opportunities through networking, technology transfer, boosting the image of the organising association, members and country, etc.
7. Is it possible to specify the impact of participating in these events in promoting {related business}? Qualitative as well as quantitative aspects?
8. What role can industry associations like (your organisation) play in India to promote conventions in India? How do similar associations promote their countries for attracting conventions?
9. What support do they look for from the govt. (Ministry of Tourism)?
10. What factors give India an advantage while seeking to host conventions?
11. What are the constraints/inhibitors which prevent many conventions from being hosted in India?
12. Based on your experience, what role can the govt. and ICPB play in boosting India's capabilities for hosting conventions (Infrastructural, institutional, human resource, any others)?
13. Are there any other cases that we could follow up for success or failure?

6. CALCULATION OF DOMESTIC MARKET SIZE

Estimating Market Size for Business Events

Total Number of Events in India

Category	Optimistic	Normal	Pessimistic
	4500	4000	3000
Numbers	4500	4000	3000
	4500	4000	3000

Average Duration of Event

Category	Optimistic	Normal	Pessimistic
High End	2.5	2.5	2
Mid End	2	2.5	2
Low End	2	2.5	2

Percentage of Events

Category	Optimistic	Normal	Pessimistic
High End	0.30	0.40	0.30
Mid End	0.40	0.35	0.25
Low End	0.30	0.25	0.45

Number of Delegates

Category	Optimistic	Normal	Pessimistic
High End	500	450	400
Mid End	600	500	400
Low End	500	350	300

Delegate Fees

Category	Optimistic	Normal	Pessimistic
High End	6000	4500	4000
Mid End	3500	3000	2500
Low End	2500	1500	1000

Total Market Size (Billions of INR)

Category	Optimistic	Normal	Pessimistic
High End	22.61	20.34	7.56
Mid End	23.22	15.23	4.35
Low End	9.79	4.90	4.05
Total	55.62	40.47	15.96

Accomodation + Banquet Expenses

Category	Optimistic	Normal	Pessimistic
High End	11,000.00	9,500.00	8,500.00
Mid End	9,000.00	7,500.00	6,000.00
Low End	6,000.00	5,000.00	4,500.00

7. SCHEDULE OF LUXURY TAXES IN THE LEADING DESTINATIONS

Table 2: Luxury Tax at Top 10 Destinations

Sl. No.	States/Cities with Slabs)	Luxury Tax		
		Slab 1	Slab 2	Slab 3
1.	New Delhi (> ₹ 500)			12.50%
2.	Mumbai (₹ 200-1200, > ₹ 1200)	4.00%	10.00%	
3.	Kolkata	10.00%		
4.	Chennai* (₹ 200-500, 500-1000, > ₹1000)	5.00%	10.00%	12.50%
5.	Bengaluru	4.00%	8.00%	12.00%
6.	Hyderabad (₹ >300)	10.00%		
7.	Jaipur (>₹ 1000)	8.00%		
8.	Agra (>₹ 1000)	10.00%		
9.	Goa (₹ 200-1500, 1500-3000,>3000)	5.00%	8.00%	10.00%
10.	Kochi (<₹ 500, >₹ 500)	10.00%	15.00%	15.00%
	* Chennai has 12.5% tax on Published tariff, instead of Actual Tariff; therefore it can go upto 25-30% of Actual Room Tariff.			

8. VISA FEES AND SCHEDULES

Table 3: Visa Fees and Time Required at Various Locations

Country	Business	Tourism	Rupees	Business Visa time (Days)	Tourist Visa time (Days)
United States of America	$150.00	$150.00	6,900.00	5	5
United Kingdom	£30.00	£30.00	2,550.00	5	5
EU Region	€ 50.00	€ 50.00	3,000.00	5	5
Denmark	DKK 350.00	DKK 350.00	3,010.00	5	5
Argentina	ARS 138.00	ARS 138.00	2,000.00	5	5
Egypt	EGP 240.00	EGP 240.00	1,900.00	5	5
Singapore	SGD 260.00	SGD 260.00	7,280.00	5	5
Thailand	$ 65.00	$ 60.00	2,700.00	5	5
Sri Lanka	LKR 310.00	LKR 310.00	140.00	5	5
Australia	AUD 75.00	AUD 75.00	2,625.00	5	5
Canada	CAD 62.00	CAD 62.00	2,400.00	5	5

** Conference Visa has similar fee structures, however, the documentation required is more extensive in most cases.

In case of some countries, like Australia and Canada, the process can be expedited to 3 days.

9. AIR TRAFFIC ACROSS INDIAN CITIES (TOP 10 CONVENTION DESTINATIONS)

Table 4: Details of Air Traffic across Indian Cities in March 2006

Summary of Airport Statistics during March 2006									
Airport	No. of Destinations Served		Number of Air Carriers		Traffic (Aircraft)		Traffic (Passenger)	
	Domestic	Intern-ational	Domestic	Intern-ational	Domestic	Intern-ational	Domestic	Intern-ational
Mumbai	46	55		40	12,019	4,270	1,115,767	562,161
New Delhi	40	68	12	42	10,132	4,364	1,065,542	567,983
Chennai	25	20	10	19	5,028	1,951	451,557	216,376
Bengaluru	27	12	10	11	6,184	852	458,541	84,374
Kolkata	27	12	7	14	4,538	771	384,697	62,359
Hyderabad	24	20	11	9	4,162	878	321,946	81,599
Goa			7	5	1,350	350	134,956	65,848
Jaipur			3	7	652	118	41,249	3,868
Cochin			9	12	966	1,004	68,741	98,124
Agra			2	0				

Source: Airport Authority of India (AAI), www.airportsindia.org.in

10. CONVENTION FACILITIES IN PROMINENT WORLD DESTINATIONS

Table 5: Some Prominent Convention Destinations and Available Facilities

City/Convention Centre	Capacity (Theatre) of largest Hall	Meeting Rooms	Total capacity (theatre)	Hotel Rooms
Singapore				
Suntec Singapore International Convention and Exhibition Centre	12000	31	17424	5200
Conrad Centennial Singapore	500	4	1708	
Marina Mandarin Singapore	700	8	1690	
Swissotel The Stanford Singapore	3200	12	5540	
The Oriental Singapore	700		1210	
The Pan Pacific Singapore	800	10	1656	
Shanghai				
Shanghai International Convention Center/Oriental Riverside	3000	25	5000	260
International Conference and Exhibition City	3000	24	4200	
Kuala Lumpur				
Kuala Lumpur International Convention Center	3000	20	15700	5100
Malaysia International Exhibition and Convention Center	1000		10000	

	Capacity (Theatre) of largest Hall	Rooms	(Theatre)	Hotel Rooms
Putra World Trade Center	10000	17	13500	
Bangkok				
IMPACT Exhibition & Convention	2000	12	6020	
Bangkok Convention Centre	8500	8	16910	
Queen Sirikit National Convention Center	5500	4	7505	
Bangkok International Trade and Exhibition Center	20000	18	31480	
Hong Kong				
Hong Kong Convention & Exhibition Center	6100	52	7100	
Seoul				
Convention and Exhibition Center (COEX)	1800	16	5120	10000+
Jakarta				
Balai Sidang Jakarta Convention Center	5000	13	8500	
Vienna				
Reed Exhibitions Messe Wien Congress Centre	4000	19	8766	300+
Frankfurt				
Congress Center Messe Frankfurt GMbH	2207	3	5120	100
Paris				
Palais des Congrès de Versailles	1390		2680	10000
Barcelona				
Barcelona International Convention Center	3200	45	23921	7000
Geneva				
IATA Geneva Conference Center		15	400	
Geneva Palexpo	15000		25000	1500
Stockholm				
City Conference Centre		50	1400	181
Birmingham				
ICC	3000	10	9279	

	Capacity (Theatre) of largest Hall	Rooms	(Theatre)	Hotel Rooms
New York				
Jacob Javits Convention Centre	14702	40	31042	
San Francisco				
San Jose Conventional and Cultural Facilities	3060	30	8448	
Moscone Center	12150	48	27465	
Vancouver				
Vancouver Convention and Exhibition Centre	3500	20	10740	
Toronto				
Metro Toronto Convention Centre	2600	64	3930	10000
Sydney				
Sydney Convention and Exhibition Centre	3500	20	9345	
Melbourne				
Melbourne Exhibition and Convention Centre	2130	50	6892	
Dubai				
Dubai International Convention Centre	6000		11924	
Johannesburg				
Sandton Convention Centre	4100	13	15339	4300
Durban				
International Convention Centre	2600	23	8650	

REFERENCES

A.J. Schuler *'Tips for Successful Cross Cultural Communication, 2003'.*

Astroff, M. and Abbey, J. (1998).*Convention Sales and Services* (5th Ed.). N. J., Waterbury Press.

Berridge, Graham (2007). *Event Design and Experience*, Oxford: Butterworth- Heinemann

Bowdin, G. et al (2006). *Events Management 2nd Ed.*, Oxford: Butterworth-Heinemann.

Braun, Bradley (1992), *"The Economic Contribution of Conventions: The Case of Orlando, Florida,"* Journal of Travel Research, Winter, 32-36.

C. Burek *Post-Merger. Intercultural Communication in Multinational Companies: A linguistic analysis*. European university studies, 2004.

Carlsen, Jack (1999), *"A Review of MICE Industry Evaluation and Research in Asia and Australia 1988-1998,"* 1(4), 51-66.

Cheung, Catherine and Rob Law (2002), *"Virtual MICE Promotion: A Comparison of the Official Web Sites in Hong Kong and Singapore,"* Journal of Convention and Exhibition Management, 4(2), 37-51.

Crouch, G. I. and Ritchie, J. R. B. (1998). Convention site selection research: A review of conceptual model, and propositional framework. *Journal of Convention and Exhibition Management, 1*(1), 49-69.

Crouch, Geoffrey and Brent Ritchie (1998), *"Convention Site Selection Research: A Review, Conceptual Model and Propositional Framework,"* Journal of Convention and Exhibition Management, 1(1), 49-69.

Cultural Barriers to Effective Communication

D. Swallow. *Overcoming language barriers in communication 2009,*—URL http://www.diversitytrainingtoday.com

Darling, Arthur and Paulina Beato (2004), *"Should Public Budgets Finance Convention Centers?"* Inter-American Development Bank - Economic and Social Study Series.

Davidson, R. (2003). *Business Travel,* Pearson Education, London.

Davidson, R. and Rogers, T. (2006) *Marketing Destinations and Venues for Conferences, Conventions and Business Events*, Oxford: Butterworth-Heinemann.

Dotson, Penny C. (1995). *Introduction to Meeting Management,* 2nd Ed., Birmingham, AL: PCMA.

Fenich, George (1998), *"Convention Center Operating Characteristics,"* Journal of Convention and Exhibition Management, 1(2/3), 1-25. Weber, Karin and Adele Ladkin (2003), *"The Convention Industry in Australia and the United Kingdom: Key Issues and Competitive Forces,"* Journal of Travel Research, 42, 125-142. (141)

Fenich, George G. (1992). Convention centre development: Pros, cons and unanswered questions, *International Journal of Hospitality Management* 11 (3):183-196.

Fenich, George G. (2008). Meetings, Expositions, Events, Conventions: An Introduction to the Industry 2nd Ed., New Jersey: Pearson International Education.

G.RG. Clarke, R. Cull, M.S.M. Peria, S.M. Sanchez. *Foreign Bank Entry: Experience, Implications for Developing Countries, and Agenda for Further Research.* —Washington, 2003.

Getz, D. (2006). *Event Management and Event Tourism 2nd Ed.*, New York: Cognizant Communication Corp.

Go, Frank and Robert Govers (1999), *"The Asian Perspective: Which International Conference Destinations in Asia are the Most Competitive?"* Journal of Convention and Exhibition Management, 1(4), 37-50.

Goldblatt, J. (1997). *Special Events: Best Practices in Modern Event Management,* New York: Van Nostrand Reinhold.

Graham, S., Goldblatt, J., and Delpy, L. (1995).*The Ultimate Guide to Sport Event Management and Marketing*, Chicago: Irwin.

Hildreth, R.A. (1990). *The Essentials of Meeting Management*, Englewood Cliffs, NJ: Prentice Hall.

Intercultural Communication Tips.

Kim, Samuel, Kaye Chon and Kyu Chung (2003), *"Convention industry in South Korea: an economic impact analysis,"* Tourism Management, 24, 533-541.

Klopf, D.W. *Intercultural Encounters: The Fundamentals of Intercultural Communication.* 4th ed. —Englewood: Morton Pub. Co., 1998.

Lau, Chloe (2007). Hong Kong's position in MICE market challenged, *The Voice of TIC*, 3 (September): 2–6.

Lawson, F. (2000).*Congress, convention and exhibition facilities: Planning, design and management,* London: Architectural Press.

M.E. DuPraw & M. Axner. *Working on Common Cross-cultural Communication Challenges, 2007.*

McCabe, V. et al. (2000). *The business and management of conventions,* Milton, Queensland: Wiley and Sons.

McDonnell, I., Allen, J., and O'Toole, W., (1999).*Festival and Special Event Management,* Milton, Queensland: Jacaranda Wiley Ltd.

MPI (2006).*MPI's Planning Guide: A Source for Meetings and Conventions*, Texas: MPI Foundation.

Multicultural Communication Tips. American Management Association (AMA), 2005—URL http://www.amanet.org

Nelson, R. (2004) (Ed.) *Current Issues in Convention and Exhibition Facility Development*, New York: Haworth Hospitality Press.

Nelson, R. (2006) (Ed.) *Developing a Successful Infrastructure for Convention and Event Tourism*, New York: Haworth Hospitality Press.

Nelson, R. R. (1998). How a more competitive market is influencing public investments in convention centers, *Journal of Convention and Exhibition Management, 1*(2/3), 27-37.

Oppermann, Martin (1996a). Convention cities - Images and changing fortunes, *Journal of Tourism Studies* 7 (1):10-19.

Oppermann, Martin (1996b). Convention destination images: Analysis of association meeting planners' perceptions. *Tourism Management* 17 (3):175-182.

Oppermann, Martin, and Kye-Sung Chon (1997). Convention participation decision-making process, *Annals of Tourism Research*, 24 (1):178-191.

Pais, Jesim (2006), *"Tourism Employment: An Analysis of Foreign Tourism in India,"* Working Paper, 2006/04, ISID, June, 1-30.

PCMA (2006).*Professional Meeting Management: Comprehensive Strategies for Meetings, Conventions and Events 5th Ed.*, Iowa: Kendall/Hunt.

Petersen, D.C. (2001). *Developing Sports, Convention and Performing ArtsCenters. 3rd Ed.*, Washington, DC: Urban Land Institute.

Price, C. H. 1999. *The Complete Guide to Professional Meeting and Event Coordination*. Washington, D.C.: George Washington University.

Rogers, T. (1998).*Conferences: A twenty-first century industry,* Harlow, Essex: Addison Wesley Longman.

Rogers, Tony (2008). *Conferences and Conventions: A Global Industry 2nd Ed.*, Oxford: Elsevier Ltd.

Tay, Linda (2006), *"Strategic Facilities Management of SUNTEC Singapore International Convention and Exhibition Centre,"* Facilities, 24 (3/4), 120-131. Baloglu, Seyhmus and Curtis Love (2001), *"Association Meeting Planners' Perceptions of Five Major*

Convention Cities: Results of the Pre-Test," Journal of Convention and Exhibition Management, 3(1), 21-30.

Tum, J., Norton, P., and Wright, J. N. (2006). *Management of Event Operations*, Oxford: Butterworth-Heinemann.

Upchurch, Randall S., Gang-hoan Jeong, Christine Clements, and Inhoan Jung.(1999). Meeting planners' perceptions of site selection characteristics: The case of Seoul, Korea. *Journal of Convention and Exhibition Management,* 2 (1):15–35.

V.H. Milhouse, M.K. Asante, P.O. Nwosu. *Transcultural Realities Interdisciplinary Perspectives on Cross-Cultural Relations. —SCI, 2001.*

Weber, K. and Chon, K. (2002).*Convention Tourism: International Researchand Industry Perspectives (Ed.)*, New York: Haworth Hospitality Press.

Wiseman R.L. *Intercultural Communication Competence, Handbook of Intercultural and International communication,* Newbury Park: Sage Publications, 2001.

Wu, Ann and Karin Weber (2005), *"Convention Center Facilities, Attributes and Services: The Delegates' Perspective,"* Asia Pacific Journal of Tourism Research, 10(4), 399-410.

INDEX

L

M

N

O

P

Q

R